SPREADING THE WORD

SPREADING THE WORD

The Bible Business in Nineteenth-Century America

PETER J. WOSH

CORNELL UNIVERSITY PRESS

ITHACA AND LONDON

First published 1994 by Cornell University Press.

Library of Congress Cataloging-in-Publication Data
Wosh, Peter J.
   Spreading the word : the Bible business in nineteenth-century
America / Peter J. Wosh.
      p.   cm.
   Includes bibliographical references and index.
   ISBN 0-8014-2928-5 (alk. paper)
   1. American Bible Society—History—19th century. 2. Bible—
Publication and distribution—United States. 3. United States—
Social conditions. 4. United States—Economic conditions.
   I. Title.
BV2370.A7W674   1994
267'.13'0973—dc20   93-43880

Printed in the United States of America

For my wife, Pat Schall,

my mother, Josephine Wosh,

and in memory of my father, Frank J. Wosh

C O N T E N T S

ILLUSTRATIONS

4

ACKNOWLEDGMENTS

Institutions are important, but people really matter. This book owes much to the patience, good humor, tolerance, and reality therapy provided by a wide range of friends, colleagues, and significant others over the years. Many were not aware that I was working on this project, but all helped shape my view of the way things work. I owe a special debt to Thomas Bender, my adviser at New York University, for help, encouragement, and extraordinary insights. Carl Prince and Paul Mattingly also worked through several drafts and helped me understand what the nineteenth century was all about. David Reimers, as always, offered excellent comments.

Colleagues at the American Bible Society provided considerable support at key stages. I am especially grateful to Mary Ellen Gleason, S.C., a good friend and a fine archivist. Maria Martinez offered the gift of time at an important moment. Eugene Habecker proved supportive of this decidedly "unofficial" version of ABS history, and I benefited from discussions with Alice Ball, Boyd Daniels, Laton Holmgren, Martin Quigley, and Harold Scanlin. Special thanks are due to Dorothea Colligan, Mary Cordato, Anca Giurescu, Liana Lupas, Alexander Plaza, Antoine Rivette, Alexandra Saddler, C. Denise Stuempfle, and Serge Taluy for keeping the ship afloat.

Some institutions chipped in as well. The American Bible Society allowed some leave time; New York University funded a working-class graduate student through its University Tuition Fellowship program; and the Institute for the Study of American Evangelicals at Wheaton College supported my revisions through a research grant.

I have always relied on the kindness of archivists, and professionals at the following understaffed repositories were helpful indeed: American Baptist Historical Society; Cumberland Presbyterian Historical Society; General Commission on Archives and History of the United Methodist Church at Drew University; New Jersey Historical Society; New-York Historical Society; New York Public Library; New York University; Presbyterian Historical Society; Reformed Church in America Archives; Rutgers University Department of Special Collections; South Street Seaport Museum; and Williams College Archives.

Brief portions of Chapters 1 and 7 appeared in an article, "Bibles, Benevolence, and Bureaucracy: The Changing Nature of Nineteenth Century Religious Records," *American Archivist* (Spring 1989), copyright © 1989 Society of American Archivists.

Cornell University Press has the dual virtue of being highly professional and fun to work with. I have especially enjoyed my brief associations with Peter Agree, Teresa Jesionowski, and the editorial pen of Trudie Calvert.

Some friends discussed the book with me, and others helped me take my mind off it. The following especially deserve mention: Dave Bennett, John Celardo, Lorraine Coons, Robert Cvornyek, Maureen Duffy, Anthony E. Lee, Leroy Lyons, and Margaret McGuinness. Pat Schall appears on the dedication page, but her support permeates every page. My parents stressed education, and the process continues. The family cats provided heavy purring; basketball offered an emotional rescue; and the New York Mets, as always, proved a major disappointment.

P. J. W.

SPREADING THE WORD

INTRODUCTION

American historians have devoted considerable attention to the founding of various philanthropies and benevolent organizations. Yet, although scholars have studied the establishment and early years of these agencies with great care, we know little about how these institutions evolved. Specifically, few historians have examined the manner in which organizations founded for one purpose assume, out of their own need for survival as much as in response to objective needs and opportunities, new forms and structures. It is especially important to understand this process, for such transformed institutions often exert a greater influence on American life than the pristine original organizations.

This book will explore the history of one such philanthropy—the American Bible Society—to illuminate a fundamental change that characterized many nineteenth-century institutions: the transformation from missionary moral reform agency to national nonprofit corporate bureaucracy. Within the Bible movement, this shift occurred gradually, provoked considerable institutional debate and tension, and eventually generated a series of internal schisms. The historical actors confronted some of the most complex issues plaguing nineteenth-century American society: the relationship between Protestantism and American capitalism; the conflict between large national institutions dominated by an emerging business elite and smaller institutions accountable to local pressures and interests; the redefinition of public culture and the consequent breakdown of a civic humanitarian vision; the removal of the notion of community from its traditional local context and its redefinition within larger institutional and professional structures; and the limits of religion and reform in a market society. The people involved wrestled with these problems within the urban context of New York City, and that metropolis's role as the geographic center of Protestant religious reform (as well as much else) is another important component of this story.

The American Bible Society provides a useful window through which to view these changes for several reasons. Established in 1816, it constituted a principal element in the "benevolent empire" of interdenominational Protestant urban reform movements founded in early nineteenth-century America. Throughout the nineteenth century, the Bible Society remained an extraordinarily innovative, flexible, and adaptable organization. Its officers helped create new forms of corporate organization, readily implemented technological innovations in printing, developed new techniques for disseminating information to a mass audience, and built a solid financial base through the use of novel fund-raising methods. The Society remained vital throughout the nineteenth century by shifting its institutional priorities, redefining its audience, and transforming its operations in response to external socioeconomic changes.

The American Bible Society has not suffered from a paucity of published histories. It has greeted virtually every anniversary and significant milestone in its past by commissioning a celebratory chronicle.[1] Encyclopedic in scope, these institutional histories reflect the characteristic strengths and weaknesses of the genre. They present an uncritical story of growth, accomplishment, consensus, and unswerving fidelity to an unchanging mission. Although rich in detail, these compilations offer little perspective on the Society's larger role in American history. They do, however, provide a longitudinal view of institutional development often absent from other historical works.

Beginning in the late 1950s and early 1960s, professional denominational, intellectual, and social historians turned their attention to Jacksonian America's religious voluntary associations. In most cases, their research frameworks handicapped the usefulness of their works. A myopic concentration on the antebellum period often produced a linear and suspiciously neat logic of historical change. Organizations like the American Bible Society "rose" dur-

---

1. Internal histories include William P. Strickland, *History of the American Bible Society, from Its Organization to the Present Time* (New York: Harper & Brothers, 1849); Henry Otis Dwight, *The Centennial History of the American Bible Society* (New York: Macmillan, 1916); and Creighton Lacy, *The Word-Carrying Giant: The Growth of the American Bible Society (1816–1966)* (South Pasadena: William Carey Library, 1977).

ing a period of theological ferment based on new notions of human perfectibility and flourished during an era of millennial optimism associated with the Second Great Awakening. They "declined" during an age of increasing secularization and Social Darwinism. A general social transformation from "religious" to "secular" reform occurred over the course of the nineteenth century, and the Protestant philanthropies appeared reactive and largely irrelevant by the late Victorian period.

Historians expended considerable energy debating the religious reformers' motivations. Some praised their efforts to release Christians from the harsh Calvinist doctrines of a predestinarian past and viewed their institutions as precursors of more liberal antebellum reforms. Others damned their elitism, their notions of cultural superiority, and their inability to accommodate themselves to Jacksonian America's diverse, pluralist, democratic character. By ignoring the changing administrative structures, personnel shifts, and internal institutional dynamics of the organizations constituting the "benevolent empire," such interpretations slighted the complexities of historical change. American history itself assumed an essentially disconnected character as institutions floated in and out of the story, "rising" and "declining" in response to vaguely defined "broader" socioeconomic developments.[2]

2. Timothy L. Smith, *Revivalism and Social Reform: American Protestantism on the Eve of the Civil War* (Baltimore: Johns Hopkins University Press, 1980), originally published in 1957, remains a pathbreaking study. Smith linked the theology of antebellum evangelicalism, based on a belief in human perfectibility and a millennial reformist vision, with such crusades as temperance, antislavery, and urban social welfare. John L. Thomas, "Romantic Reform in America, 1815–1865," *American Quarterly* (Winter 1965), 656–681, viewed the Bible, tract, Sunday school, missionary, and other societies as conservative manifestations of a larger romantic reformist vision. In his view, the evangelical institutions largely spent their energies by 1830, after which time waves of "humanitarian" and "communitarian" reformers moved to the forefront. Thomas posited that an intellectual counterrevolution, produced by the Civil War, ended the period of "romantic reform" and produced a variety of more efficient and "professional" bureaucratic institutions in late nineteenth-century America.

Reformers' sinister motivations and a somewhat mechanistic "rise" and "decline" framework inform two especially influential and standard treatments of the "benevolent empire": Clifford S. Griffin, *Their Brothers' Keepers: Moral Stewardship in the United States, 1800–1865* (New Brunswick: Rutgers University Press, 1960), and Charles I. Foster, *An Errand of Mercy: The Evangelical United Front, 1790–1837* (Chapel Hill: University of North Carolina Press, 1960). In addition, I believe these notions can be seen in the more recent literature concerning American reform, such as Paul Boyer, *Urban Masses and Moral Order in America* (Cambridge: Harvard Uni-

An essentially static conception of institutional development further handicapped many of these studies. In such accounts, organizations constituting the "benevolent empire" remained committed to an unchanging set of traditional values and goals. Internal institutional debate never seriously shaped, altered, or affected official organizational ideology. Boards of managers, middle-level administrators, and functionaries shared the same well-defined goals. Official ideology determined actual performance; public statements adequately described the institution's real functions. People appeared particularly lifeless and interchangeable, and local contexts seemed irrelevant. Stable administrative structures appeared at the outset: a general commitment to system, order, formality, and bureaucratic organization always existed and merely intensified over time. Such claims resulted in a lack of historical specificity.

Institutions usually develop in far more complex ways than such interpretations suggest. Recently, historians have paid greater attention to institutionalization as a *process* and have charted the development and evolution of large organizations in nineteenth-century America.[3] Several important insights from this new literature provide a theoretical base for studying the American Bible Society. First, the new institutional historians stress the importance of linking social sectors. Specific institutions did not constitute isolated arenas of specialized activity, but rather shared their structures and personnel with other social institutions. Thus, for example, an analysis of the American Bible Society must explain why the first generation of managers brought the savings bank movement to America, promoted the Erie Canal and a wide range

---

versity Press, 1978); and Ronald G. Walters, *American Reformers, 1815–1860* (New York: Hill and Wang, 1978).

3. See the discussion in Thomas Bender, Peter D. Hall, Thomas L. Haskell, and Paul H. Mattingly, "Institutionalization and Education in the Nineteenth and Twentieth Centuries," *History of Education Quarterly* (Winter 1980), 449–472, for an elaboration of many of these points. Examples of recent histories that I would place in this new institutional historiographic framework include Peter Dobkin Hall, *The Organization of American Culture, 1700–1900: Private Institutions, Elites, and the Origins of American Nationality* (New York: New York University Press, 1982); Alfred D. Chandler, *The Visible Hand: The Managerial Revolution in American Business* (Cambridge: Harvard University Press, 1977); David F. Allmendinger, *Paupers and Scholars: The Transformation of Student Life in Nineteenth-Century New England* (New York: St. Martin's Press, 1975); and Gregory Singleton, "Protestant Voluntary Organizations and the Shaping of Victorian America," in Daniel Walker Howe, ed., *Victorian America* (Philadelphia: University of Pennsylvania Press, 1976), pp. 47–58.

of civic improvements, linked their personal fortunes with the economic rise of New York City, and transacted commercial business within the social context of the family firm. One cannot understand the innovations that a subsequent generation of managers brought to Bible Society work without considering the rise of managerial capitalism, the creation of the railroad, the growth of the life insurance company, the economic pressures forcing New England farm youths to seek new lives in the city, the founding of small antebellum colleges emphasizing a particular notion of character training, the changing social composition of the Protestant ministry, and New York's dynamic urban milieu. Linking, rather than merely listing, such sectors constitutes one burden for the institutional historian.

Second, recent institutional histories underscore the importance of dissecting internal, as well as external, relationships. Organizations rarely move forward in a linear, unified manner. Internal conflicts develop and intensify as administrative hierarchies emerge within an institution. Further, as organizations revise their goals and policies in the face of internal and external pressures, such conflicts help elucidate general historical shifts and the emergence of new attitudes within the institution. Finally, conflicts between different administrative levels reveal the presence of competing social groups and different goals within the institution. The early nineteenth-century ABS managers, for example, sat on the governing boards of a wide range of institutions and often promoted policies that fostered cooperation with other philanthropies; career-oriented administrators and agents, on the other hand, depended upon individual institutions for their salaries and positions, tended to view the great benevolences as competitors, and often implemented policies with one eye cast on the marketplace. Remaining sensitive to the levels and complexities of internal conflict and juxtaposing the reality of an organization's operations against the rhetoric of its stated goals and public pronouncements thus constitutes a second task for the institutional historian.

Finally, sensitivity to the process of institutionalization means examining the ways in which organizations transform themselves to persist and remain vital. Historians must study the way institutions interpret their successes and failures, redefine their audience and clientele, and respond to conflict with external groups representing different social orientations. The American Bible Society, for example, narrowed its role from reforming the nation and restoring a consensual vision to republican life to providing a series of support services for America's network of Protestant agencies. By concentrating large amounts of capital in one organization, creating a worldwide network of auxiliaries and Bible agents, accumulating vast quantities of information concerning the Bible, and modernizing its production and distribution techniques, the Society effectively performed valuable services for reform organizations and denominational efforts by the mid-nineteenth century. This redefinition arose in part out of a series of unsuccessful reform efforts and a grudging recognition of the hopelessly pluralistic character of American life. It also reflected external criticism of the Society by Jacksonian Democrats, predestinarian Calvinists, immediate abolitionists, and competing elites within various denominations. Institutional survival was the immediate issue, but the Society successfully effected the transition because of its willingness and ability to adapt to changing socioeconomic forces in American life.

These three analytical themes—an effort to link the development of the American Bible Society with developments in other sectors of social action, an attempt to dissect the internal relationships within the institution to discern specific historical shifts, and a sensitivity to the ways the organization transformed itself in order to survive—remain central to the story. Explaining institutional persistence and examining the process of institutionalization over the course of the nineteenth century, rather than presenting a comprehensive narrative history of the American Bible Society, is my central goal.

This particular story ends in Constantinople in 1890. The process of institutionalization, of course, did not end there. New socioeconomic pressures, new generations of managers and administrators, new external challenges, new internal tensions, and important continuities with the past would continue to alter, adapt, and reshape the American Bible Society through the twentieth century. By 1890, however, a "great transformation" had taken place in the history of the Society, as well as in the history of American society generally. The story of this transformation begins in the city.

1

A Bible House in the City

New York City, boasted a popular mid-nineteenth-century guide-book, "is the great commercial centre of the United States." The compiler of *Phelps' New York City Guide* described the urban metropolis's "vast marts of commerce, fleets of merchant-ships, magnificent public buildings, palacelike dwellings, and gorgeous shops and streets, thronged with a gay, busy, and enterprising population." Written primarily for middle-class travelers and visiting businessmen, this guidebook conveniently ignored other equally telling signs of New York's commercial rise: the increasingly unequal distribution of wealth, dilapidated tenements and transient boardinghouses, problems of disease and crime, and the notorious Five Points slum. Still, the author accurately chronicled the institutions of the wealthy and powerful. A stranger forming an impression of New York from this 1854 pocket directory would imagine a city of seemingly limitless capital resources, elegant and opulent life-styles, boundless energy and enthusiasm, constant growth, and perpetual motion.[1]

1. *Phelps' New York City Guide; Being a Pocket Directory for Strangers and Citizens to the Prominent Objects of Interest in the Great Commercial Metropolis, and Conductor to Its Environs, with Engravings of Public Buildings* (New York: Ensign, Bridgman, & Fanning, 1854), p. 19. On guidebook literature, see Allan Stanley Horlick, *Country Boys and Merchant Princes: The Social Control of Young Men in New York* (Lewisburg: Bucknell University Press, 1975), pp. 48–64.

Bible House on Astor Place, 1853. *Courtesy of the American Bible Society Archives.*

But New York, according to *Phelps' Guide,* also offered "something far more attractive to the eye of humanity, far more suggestive of the true greatness of the people" than the sights and sounds of Wall and South streets. The real measure of municipal progress, this urban chronicler asserted, lay in the numerous "beneficent institutions," which appeared "scattered like green oases, in the midst of a desert of selfishness incident to the progress of a great city." Educational institutions, health care facilities, orphanages, asylums, libraries, penitentiaries, and the great religious philanthropies offered testimony that "the divine principles of Christianity" still guided New York's growth and provided the essential underpinning of "righteousness for a great city." Manhattan contained its temples to Mammon, but it was also the headquarters of an enormous benevolent empire dedicated to advancing an evangelical conception of social order.[2]

Benevolence and business, the sacred and the secular, religious reform and the culture of commerce—all coexisted comfortably between the covers of *Phelps' New York City Guide,* illuminating both the spiritual components and the tangible material accomplishments of an aggressively capitalist American city. Urban

2. *Phelps' New York City Guide,* pp. 19–20.

guidebooks provide useful snapshots at specific moments in time, but they convey little sense of the complex social and institutional relationships that develop over longer periods and characterize modern city life. Phelps considered religion and business the hand-maidens of progress and presented them side by side as static and separate symbols of urban greatness. In fact, evangelicalism and capitalism shared a dynamic, complex, intimate, and constantly changing relationship over the course of the nineteenth century. In New York City, a single building captured and articulated this relationship more satisfactorily than even the most carefully crafted guidebook.

In May 1853, the members of the board of managers of the American Bible Society opened the double iron doors of their new Bible House on Astor Place for the first time. Costing over $300,000 to build and occupying a full city block, the six-story brick struc-ture was an imposing and important addition to New York's city-scape. The building committee responsible for planning the Bible House, which included some of New York's wealthiest citizens, de-scribed it as "a monument of the goodness of God, and a testimony to the liberality of its native city!" In guiding the architect, they self-consciously sought to create "an atmosphere congenial to all who love the Bible" and considered the building "a beautiful develop-ment of that Christian civilization and 'good will to men,' which is the glorious offspring of that very cause under whose encircling influence they have found a home."[3]

Contemporaries immediately recognized that Bible House made a significant and powerful statement. Guidebooks featured it as an essential stop for tourists. The religious and secular press offered extensive coverage of the cornerstone laying and formal opening. J. F. Richmond's study *New York and Its Institutions* in 1872 noted that "the Bible House is visited annually by thousands of strangers, and can scarcely cease to be an object of profoundest interest." Even Mark Twain toured the Society's facilities in 1867, finding "that I enjoyed the time more than I could possibly have done in any circus." The Society's brick-and-mortar accomplishment amused some Gilded Age observers and amazed others. The board of man-agers had undeniably placed their enterprise squarely in the public

3. "Report of Building Committee," American Bible Society, *Thirty-eighth An-nual Report* (New York: American Bible Society, 1854), pp. 297–304, hereafter cited as ABS, [number] *Annual Report* (year); Minutes of Meeting of the ABS Board of Managers, February 2, 1854, ABS Archives, New York, N.Y.

eye. Their success signaled the transformation of the American Bible Society from a missionary moral reform organization to something very new and very different: a national nonprofit corporate bureaucracy. Indeed, both the antebellum New Yorker and the twentieth-century historian might learn much more about the business of religion by visiting this Bible House than its planners ever intended.[4]

The wealthy and respectable Christians who established the American Bible Society in 1816 perceived no need for an elaborate, expensive physical facility. They did not plan to employ a full-time paid administrative staff. Guaranteeing "a wider circulation of the Scriptures without note or comment" required making arrangements for printing and binding, but the managers merely subcontracted these tasks to appropriately pious master workmen. Bringing such mundane mechanical operations under their own roof appeared wasteful and counterproductive. The board, after all, hoped to reform the world, not superintend a manufacturing concern.

Most of the American Bible Society's founders were born into mid-eighteenth-century colonial society and reached maturity around the time of the American Revolution. These socially conservative patricians grew up believing themselves eminently qualified—by birth, talent, and virtue—to guide America's social, political, and economic fortunes. Courtroom and countinghouse affairs occupied much of their youthful business lives, but they always dutifully accepted the "burdens" and responsibilities of public office. Dedicated to preserving the traditional, deferential, and hierarchical values they treasured, the founders drew no distinctions

4. Guidebook descriptions can be found in *Phelps' New York City Guide*, p. 40; Henry Levy, *The New-York Hand Book and Merchants' Guide, Written, Arranged and Compiled from Authentic Sources* (New York: Henry Levy, 1859), p. 18; *Miller's New York as It Is; Or Stranger's Guide-Book to the Cities of New York, Brooklyn, and Adjacent Places* (New York: James Miller, 1860), p. 51; and Townsend Percy, comp., *Appleton's Dictionary of New York and Vicinity* (New York: D. Appleton, 1879), p. 33.

Accounts of the cornerstone laying and opening include *New York Weekly Tribune*, April 2, 1853; *New York Observer*, July 1, 1852; *New York Evening Post*, June 24, 25, 1852; and three articles in the *Bible Society Record:* "Laying the Corner Stone of the New Bible House," July 1852; "Why Has the Bible House Been Made So Large?" June 1853; "Completion of the Bible House," February 1854.

J. F. Richmond, *New York and Its Institutions, 1609–1872* (New York: E. B. Treat, 1872), p. 122; Samuel L. Clemens, *Mark Twain's Travels with Mr. Brown* (New York: Knopf, 1940), p. 202.

between their public and private pursuits. By the time they coalesced to establish the American Bible Society, however, these
men were increasingly finding their claims to undisputed social,
political, and cultural authority under siege.[5]

A series of political events, beginning with the controversy
surrounding American reaction to the French Revolution in the
1790s, undermined traditional civil and ecclesiastical authority,
fragmented cultural coherence, and threatened elite hegemony.
Thomas Jefferson's Revolution of 1800 legitimized political dissent
and ruptured the notion of a unified consensual society. The men
who established the American Bible Society understood the implications and lamented the consequences. Elias Boudinot (1740–
1821), the first president and symbolic leader of the ABS, learned
the lessons of Jeffersonianism from bitter personal experience. A
prominent New Jersey Presbyterian layman and chief congres-
sional advocate of Alexander Hamilton's economic program in the
early 1790s, Boudinot became the object of intense political attacks
by the middle of that decade. For a genteel patrician who, in the
words of one admiring biographer, "never sought office, but had
office thrust upon him," the source and substance of such public
partisan warfare proved intolerable. Within one month of Hamilton's resignation as secretary of the treasury in January 1795, the
former president of the Continental Congress resigned his own seat
in the House of Representatives. By 1796, Boudinot worried that
"open & professed Deists" like Jefferson and Aaron Burr aggressively sought and nearly captured the highest public office in the
Christian republic. He interpreted Jefferson's later electoral success as "evidence of our degenerating from the zeal of our forefa-
thers."[6]

5. Chapter 2 presents a more detailed analysis of the managers. On this patri-
cian generation of New Yorkers generally, see Thomas Bender, *New York Intellect: A
History of Intellectual Life in New York City, 1750 to the Beginnings of Our Own Time*
(New York: Knopf, 1987), esp. pp. 46–88; M. J. Heale, "From City Fathers to Social
Critics: Humanitarianism and Government in New York, 1790–1860," *Journal of
American History* (June 1976), 21–41; Michael Wallace, "Changing Concepts of
Party in the United States: New York, 1815–1828," *American Historical Review* (De-
cember 1968), 453–491. For an important account of the lack of distinction between
public and private, see John S. Whitehead, *The Separation of College and State:
Columbia, Dartmouth, Harvard, and Yale, 1776–1876* (New Haven: Yale University
Press, 1973).

6. Peter Dobkin Hall, *The Organization of American Culture, 1700–1900: Private
Institutions, Elites, and the Origins of American Nationality* (New York: New York

In 1801, this disgruntled pious Federalist published his answer to both Thomas Paine and Thomas Jefferson in *The Age of Revelation,* appropriately subtitled *The Age of Reason Shewn to Be an Age of Infidelity.* Expressing concern that "children, servants, and the lowest people" purchased Paine's inexpensive volume and uncritically accepted its theories, Boudinot hoped to stem the nation's moral and political decline by crafting an orthodox response. *The Age of Revelation,* however, proved little more than an obscure theological treatise, largely ignored and without significant influence. The public's apathetic response confirmed Boudinot's worst fears. His final years in public life were especially acrimonious and unfulfilling. As director of the United States Mint between 1795 and 1805, Boudinot was subjected to a long and tiresome barrage of partisan criticism, politically motivated investigations of his conduct, and public ridicule. When he finally retired from public service to his private estate in 1805, Boudinot harbored great fears concerning the future course of American politics.[7]

Boudinot's colleagues on the ABS board of managers shared his pessimism concerning the impact of Jeffersonian dissent on American social and religious values. They described recent political events in their first "Address to the People of the United States" as "a period of philosophy, falsely so-called ... under the imposing names of reason and liberality," which sought "to seduce mankind from all which can bless the life that is, or shed a cheering radiance on the life that is to come." Some Federalists adapted the rhetoric of popular sovereignty to their own uses and participated in the new style of politics. After the War of 1812, such partisan

---

University Press, 1982), pp. 79–94, discusses these issues. Paul H. Mattingly, *The Classless Profession: American Schoolmen in the Nineteenth Century* (New York: New York University Press, 1975), treats the central problem of character in nineteenth-century culture. Gary B. Nash, "The American Clergy and the French Revolution," *William and Mary Quarterly* (July 1965), 392–412, notes the centrality of that event to American debates in the 1790s. The Whiskey Rebellion, Jay's Treaty, and Hamilton's economic program were other key political issues. See also the discussion in Harry Ammon, *The Genet Mission* (New York: Norton, 1973).

For the most scholarly treatment of Boudinot, see George Adams Boyd, *Elias Boudinot: Patriot and Statesman, 1740–1821* (Princeton: Princeton University Press, 1952). The quotes are on pp. 221 and 230.

7. Elias Boudinot, *The Age of Revelation, or The Age of Reason Shewn to Be an Age of Infidelity* (Philadelphia: Asbury Dickins, 1801), p. xx. On Boudinot's problems as director of the mint, and especially his quarrels with Dr. Benjamin Rush, see Boyd, *Elias Boudinot,* pp. 224–250.

tactics no longer seemed a viable strategy. Others realized that restoring the unity of economic, cultural, and political power could occur only by effecting a reformation of the national character. If traditional elites no longer controlled political life, they might still use other, equally powerful tools to mold a virtuous republic. They had, after all, established a wide range of humanitarian, educational, literary, scientific, and civic institutions.[8]

By the second decade of the nineteenth century, these organizations formed the core elements in a massive counteroffensive directed against Jeffersonian values. The American Bible Society occupied a central role in this effort. Placing the Good Book in every household, in the minds of many, might lay the foundation for a common Christian social consensus. Certainly, the managers intended their new institution to be all-inclusive: "All our voices, all our affections, all our hands, should be joined in the grand design," and "local feelings, party prejudices, sectarian jealousies are excluded" by the very nature of the institution. Perhaps the seemingly unambiguous Word of God could socially cement the forces dividing Americans into contentious factions.[9]

Commercial greatness, civic improvement, and cultural achievement were linked in the founders' minds. They conceived their enterprise as a profoundly civic endeavor, and early arrangements underscored their efforts to link the Bible movement with the rise of New York City. John Pintard, the society's first recording secretary, articulated this concept in an 1817 letter to ABS president Elias Boudinot: "A spirit is aroused that will soon make us the seat of intellectual as we are of commercial wealth & enterprize. The Grand Canal, our Colleges, Academies—Theological, Biblical & Scientific Institutions will proudly elevate the city of N. York to that rank which her geographical situation & advantages entitle her to hold." An expansive commercial capitalism would provide

8. On the Federalists see James M. Banner, Jr., *To the Hartford Convention: The Federalists and the Origins of Party Politics in Massachusetts, 1789–1815* (New York: Knopf, 1970); David H. Fischer, *The Revolution of American Conservatism: The Federalist Party in the Era of Jeffersonian Democracy* (New York: Harper & Row, 1965); Linda K. Kerber, *Federalists in Dissent: Imagery and Ideology in Jeffersonian America* (Ithaca: Cornell University Press, 1970); and Carl E. Prince, *The Federalists and the Origins of the U.S. Civil Service* (New York: New York University Press, 1977). American Bible Society Board of Managers, *Address to the People of the United States,* May 1816, ABS Archives.

9. American Bible Society Board of Managers, *Address to the People of the United States,* May 1816, ABS Archives.

the economic prosperity necessary for a rich, unified public culture. The founders of the American Bible Society missed no opportunity to thrust their enterprise into the center of this public culture. A constitutional provision mandated that two-thirds of the managers reside in Manhattan. The Society's inaugural meeting was held in New York's City Hall. The board regularly convened in such places as the New-York Historical Society and New York Hospital. In 1817, the Society was granted some space in the New York Institution of Learned and Scientific Establishments. Thomas Bender has argued that the New York Institution constituted an effort "to consolidate and concentrate the existing elements of the city's intellectual culture in the interest of invigorating it and giving it more social force." The Bible Society, in its founders' eyes, offered the moral imperative and established the Christian base upon which to build a broad and patrician-directed intellectual culture.[10]

The ABS's institutional growth soon prompted the Society's leaders to secure a more permanent home. When they decided to construct their own quarters in 1822, the managers engaged a particularly appropriate architect for the task. John McComb (1763–1853) had designed some of the most important civic structures and ecclesiastical edifices in New York: New York City Hall, the Society of Mechanics and Tradesmen Building on Park Place, Castle Garden, the New York Free School House, St. John's Chapel on Varick Street, Bleecker Street Presbyterian Church, and Cedar Street Presbyterian Church. A man of refined taste and excellent family background, McComb moved easily in the patrician society of early Federal New York. The American Bible Society, a professedly public and aggressively civic institution, had selected an architect whose work, in the words of one biographer, illustrated "the persistence of American Colonial tradition, with strong British influence, into the nineteenth century." The board planned to assert traditional moral values in its modest structure on Nassau

10. John Pintard to Elias Boudinot, May 20, 1817, Recording Secretary's Papers, ABS Archives. Minutes of Meetings of the Board of Managers, 1816–1818, ABS Archives, give the meeting places. *The Constitution, Charter, and By-Laws of the American Bible Society* (New York: American Bible Society's Press, 1853), p. 3, states the residential requirements for managers. For an account of the initial meeting, see *Proceedings of a Meeting of the Citizens of New-York and Others, Convened in the City Hall on the 13th of May, 1816* (New York: J. Seymour, 1816). Bender, *New York Intellect*, p. 65.

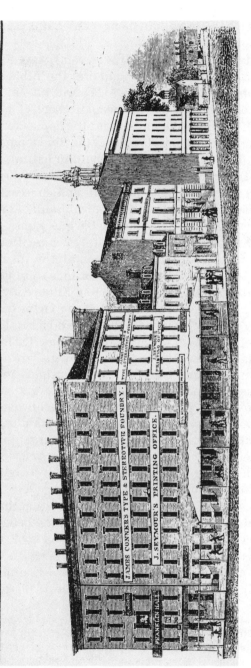

THE NEW-YORK MIRROR:

A REPOSITORY OF POLITE LITERATURE AND THE ARTS.

VOLUME VIII.   NEW-YORK, SATURDAY, SEPTEMBER 4, 1830.   **NUMBER 9.**

Ann and Nassau Streets, 1830. The American Bible Society's stately and subdued three-story home is the second major structure from the right, between the three residences and an empty lot. J. Seymour, whose office is on the corner, briefly served as the ABS's printer during the early years. Charles Starr, the Society's binder, occupied an office in Franklin Hall, on the extreme left. *Courtesy of the American Bible Society Archives.*

Street in the hope of building a new city culture and restructuring American life.[11]

The career of John McComb contrasts markedly with the architectural firm responsible for building the Bible House on Astor Place. Thomas Thomas (1787–1871) and his son Griffith (1820–1879) owed their success to the patronage of banks, insurance companies, and department stores. T. Thomas & Son constructed many of the new cast-iron buildings that lined upper Broadway, announcing the centralization and institutionalization of the American capital market in New York City. A partial list of their clients includes some of the most powerful and successful forces in the mid-nineteenth-century city: Chemical Bank (1850–1851), Broadway Bank (1852–1853), Greenwich Savings Bank (1854), New York Bank for Savings (1854–1856), Fifth Avenue Hotel (1856–1858), Lord & Taylor (1858–1859), Continental Life Insurance Company (1862–1863), and New York Life Insurance Company (1868–1870). Their buildings, crafted in the Second Empire style and featuring extensive cast-iron work, celebrated the virtues of privatism and achieved great popularity with the city's business elites. When they applied their talents to residential dwellings, T. Thomas & Son successfully fashioned many of the uptown brownstones and row houses that sheltered New York's increasingly prosperous upper middle classes. They sought no return to the colonial past, but rather enjoyed the company of bankers and brokers. Thomas and Griffith Thomas pioneered the use of iron framing techniques and are remembered primarily for their structural innovations.[12]

The choice of an architect hints that the American Bible Society had redefined its mission and brought some structural innovations of its own to the work of organized religion. When the Society began its operations, the managers assumed that their philanthropy could be administered along traditional lines. Prominent local clergymen and benevolently disposed laymen took time from their regular business activities to manage the Society's affairs on a part-time basis. Richard Varick (1753–1831), for example, served as the Society's first treasurer between 1816 and 1819. A former mayor of

11. For a brief history of the Society's real estate arrangements, consult Minutes of Meeting of the Board of Managers, December 4, 1851, ABS Archives. On McComb, see Talbot Faulkner Hamlin, "John McComb," in *Dictionary of American Biography*, 20 vols., 8 supplements (New York: Charles Scribner's Sons, 1927–36), 6:599–600.

12. "Thomas Thomas and Griffith Thomas," in Adolf Placzek, ed., *Macmillan Encyclopedia of Architects* (New York: Free Press, 1982), 4:204.

the city, speaker of the state assembly, and New York attorney general, he viewed the position as part of his public charge and maintained the Society's books when not involved in other activities. The first few corresponding secretaries and treasurers drew no salary for their efforts, and the board regulated every detail of the operation through its committees.[13]

By 1818, however, the work of purchasing paper, inspecting printed volumes, ensuring quality control over binding, caring for the depository, and maintaining the eight sets of stereotype plates owned by the ABS convinced the managers to hire a full-time salaried agent to superintend operations. Gradually, the Society moved toward creating and redefining other administrative positions and subdividing work among them: corresponding secretary (1826), general agent and accountant (1827), recording secretary and accountant (1832), general agent and assistant treasurer (1832), editor and librarian (1836), treasurer (1838), assistant agent (1840), financial secretary (1840), general agent (1853). Administrative work had become a full-time occupation. Fixed monetary compensation and contractual obligations increasingly governed terms of employment, and an internal hierarchy developed among the Society's employees. Richard Varick relinquished his post as treasurer in 1819 but remained active on the board and eventually served a term as president. When he resigned as assistant treasurer after seventeen years in 1886, Andrew L. Taylor accepted a position as secretary of Dr. Jaeger's Sanitary Woollen System Company on Broadway. His association with the Society terminated with his final payroll check. Increasingly, full-time administrators seeking bureaucratic rewards and career opportunities, rather than part-time philanthropists hoping to dispense benevolence, managed internal affairs.[14]

The new administrators introduced a commitment to efficiency, an emphasis on productivity, and a more systematic approach to benevolence. Bible House enshrined these values and constituted as well a monument to industrial technology. It was, first of all, a place of production, and its "many improvements and facilities for the convenient dispatch of work" received the most comment in

13. "Richard Varick," *Dictionary of American Biography,* 10:226–227.

14. On the initial decision to hire a paid employee, see Minutes of Meeting of the Board of Managers, January 22, 1818, ABS Archives. Andrew L. Taylor's subsequent place of employment has been reconstructed from New York City directories at the New-York Historical Society.

newspapers and guidebooks. T. Thomas & Son designed the facility so that "the process of manufacture commences in the upper part of the building, and the books descend by a progressive movement from one department to another" until they arrived at the first-floor depository. Stereotyping took place on the sixth floor, which also included a recreational area "in which the women employed in the building can take air and exercise at their leisure." The fifth floor was occupied by compositors, pressmen, and employees engaged in wetting paper, drying sheets, and washing rollers. Fourteen Adams presses, the most technologically advanced labor-saving machines available, were in use during working hours. From the fifth floor, printed sheets descended to the fourth floor bindery, where approximately 250 women did the folding, gathering, and sewing tasks. In its public statements, the Society carefully included a note that "the tables and seats have been arranged with a view to the comfort and health, as far as possible, of those employed" and that "there are cloakrooms on this floor for the use of each ten of the young ladies." Unbound books then moved to the third floor, where the rounders, backers, forwarders, gilders, and finishers applied their hands to the labor. Finally, the completed volumes "arrive at the trunk through which they descend to the depository."[15]

Observers marveled at the system and order of the enterprise, the logical progression of the work, and the staggering production statistics. The ABS had begun to centralize production in the 1840s, and Bible House represented the culmination of a long campaign to eliminate independent contractors and bring all Bible work in-house. The ABS had created its own printing department (1845), established a bindery (1848), made its own stereotype plates (1851), and manufactured its own electrotyping equipment (1853) before Bible House opened its doors. Extraordinary growth in production resulted, as annual issues from the depository increased from 228,000 in 1842 to 841,500 a decade later. Bible House provided a physical form that articulated an already existing commitment toward systematization and centralization; to understand the origins of these trends, it is necessary to examine briefly developments in the printing and publishing business.[16]

Large periodical and book plants, using the latest technology

15. *New York Weekly Tribune,* April 2, 1853.
16. Margaret T. Hills, "Production and Supply of Scriptures, 1831–1860," ABS Historical Essay 18, pt. III (1964), pp. 8–36, ABS Archives.

and employing hundreds of workers, dominated New York's printing trades at midcentury, reflecting the city's emergence as the nation's information capital. New York dispensed up-to-date market information, fresh foreign intelligence, and the latest in literature to a national audience through its penny press, specialized weeklies, and monthly journals. The great book publishers—Harper & Brothers, Charles Scribner, D. Appleton & Company, and John Wiley—also concentrated in Manhattan, and by 1856 New York produced 38 percent of the $16 million worth of books manufactured in the United States. Religion dominated the antebellum book market. The leading historian of American book publishing has observed that "no trade publisher could even approach" the volume of receipts amassed by the American Bible Society in 1855, and evangelical houses remained industry leaders and innovators.[17]

This concentration of large, highly capitalized, technologically sophisticated firms in the metropolis generated intense local competition. The Society traditionally specialized in cheap pocket Testaments and relatively uniform, plainly bound Bibles. Such Bibles sufficed for charity distribution and circulation by the auxiliaries, but an increasingly prosperous middle class demanded more attractive, lavish products. By 1848, the managers complained of competition from "the influx of a large amount of English books of very showy appearance, calculated favorably to strike the eye of the superficial observer." The greatest threat, however, did not originate in Europe but came from a family of pious Methodists located at 82 Cliff Street.[18]

In 1846, the Harper Brothers published their revolutionary *Illuminated and New Pictorial Bible*. Described by one bookseller as "the great publishing event of the period," this lavishly illustrated, morocco-bound, hand-tooled, gold-embossed, and gilt-edged volume earned its publisher one-half million dollars in retail receipts

17. Edward K. Spann, *The New Metropolis: New York City, 1840–1857* (New York: Columbia University Press, 1981), pp. 406–410; Sean Wilentz, *Chants Democratic: New York City and the Rise of the American Working Class, 1788–1850* (New York: Oxford University Press, 1984), pp. 129–132; John Tebbel, *A History of Book Publishing in the United States* (New York: Bowker, 1972), 1:229, 279, 588; Alfred D. Chandler, Jr., *The Visible Hand: The Managerial Revolution in American Business* (Cambridge: Harvard University Press, 1977), pp. 71–73; Allan Pred, *Urban Growth and the Circulation of Information: The United States System of Cities, 1790–1840* (Cambridge: Harvard University Press, 1973). Pred dates New York's domination of the national informational market to the 1820s (p. 28).

18. ABS, *Thirty-third Annual Report* (1849), p. 24.

in its first twelve years. The Harpers had engaged a prominent engraver to handle the woodcuts, contracted with artist John G. Chapman to supply the designs, and mounted an extraordinary publicity campaign to excite the public's attention. They established the Bible as an article of mass consumption, an attractive centerpiece for the proper Victorian bookshelf. The medium rather than the message assumed center stage as mere possession of the volume conferred cultural status on, and testified to the good taste of, the purchaser. Everyone, Christian or heathen, could appreciate the attractive design, as well as the unique and occasionally provocative illustrations. Perhaps most significant, production depended on a technological miracle that allowed the firm to price the extraordinarily beautiful item at an unbelievably low cost: the Harpers issued their Bible in fifty-four installments over three years at twenty-five cents per installment.[19]

Ostentatious religious display was an important expression of wealth in the Jacksonian city. By the late 1840s, a new aristocratic style developed among fashionable urbanites. Wealthy New Yorkers drove elaborate equipages, vacationed at such resort spas as Newport and Saratoga, hosted formal dinner parties and balls, employed a battery of servants, and lived in luxurious uptown mansions. Attending a socially proper church and supporting fashionable charitable endeavors also conferred social standing upon status-seeking New Yorkers. Rising middle-class Victorians, anxious to acquire the symbols and emulate the life-styles of the rich, developed their own variations of these social trends. Sentimentally displaying one's religiosity, whether on family tombstones, in public parlors, or through the prominent presence of large and sometimes gaudy family Bibles, served an important cultural function for such aspiring aristocrats.[20]

19. For the story of the *Illuminated Bible,* see Eugene Exman, *The Brothers Harper* (New York: Harper & Row, 1965), pp. 163–165, 172, 190, 244. The Harpers announced their intention to publish the Bible in 1843. Margaret T. Hills, *The English Bible in America: A Bibliography of Editions of the Bible and the New Testament Published in America, 1777–1957* (New York: American Bible Society and New York Public Library, 1962), p. 172.

20. Douglas T. Miller, *Jacksonian Aristocracy: Class and Democracy in New York, 1830–1860* (New York: Oxford University Press, 1967), pp. 155–184, provides an excellent overview of the new aristocratic style. See also the discussion in William G. McLoughlin, *The Meaning of Henry Ward Beecher: An Essay on the Shifting Values of Mid-Victorian America, 1840–1870* (New York: Knopf, 1970), esp. pp. 98–118.

THE

OLD TESTAMENT.

THE FIRST BOOK OF MOSES, CALLED

GENESIS.

CHAPTER I.

1 The creation of heaven and earth, 3 of the light, 6 of the firmament, 9 of the earth separated from the waters, 11 and made fruitful, 14 of the sun, moon, and stars, 20 of fish and fowl, 24 of beasts and cattle, 26 of man in the image of God. 29 Also the appointment of food.

N the ªbeginning ᵇGod created the heaven and the earth.

2 And the earth was without form, and void; and darkness *was* upon the face of the deep: ᶜand the Spirit of God moved upon the face of the waters.

3 ᵈAnd God said, ᵉLet there be light: and there was light.

4 And God saw the light, that *it was* good: and God divided †the light from the darkness.

5 And God called the light ᶠDay, and the darkness he called Night: †and the evening and the morning were the first day.

6 ¶ And God said, ᵍLet there be a †firmament in the midst of the waters: and let it divide the waters from the waters.

7 And God made the firmament, ʰand divided the waters which *were* under the firmament from the waters which *were* ⁱabove the firmament: and it was so.

8 And God called the firmament Heaven:

the gathering together of the waters called he ·Seas: and God saw that *it was* good.

11 And God said, Let the earth ˡbring forth †grass, the herb yielding seed, *and* the fruit-tree yielding ᵐfruit after his kind, whose

Before CHRIST 4004.

a John 1, 1, 2. Heb. 1, 10.
b Ps. 8, 3, & 33, 6, & 89, 11, 12, & 102, 25, & 136, 5, & 148, 5. Isai. 44, 24. Jer. 10, 12, & 51, 15. Zech. 12, 1. Acts 14, 15, & 17, 24. Col. 1, 16, 17. Heb. 11, 3. Rev. 4, 11, & 10, 6.
c Ps. 33, 6. Isai. 40, 13, 14.
d Ps. 33, 9.
e 2 Cor. 4, 6.
† Heb. *between the light and between the darkness.*
f Ps. 74, 16, & 104, 20.
† Heb. *And the evening was, and the morning was.*
g Job 37, 18. Ps. 136, 5. Jer. 10, 12, & 51, 15.
† Heb. *expansion.*

B.C. 4004.
h Prov. 8, 28.
i Ps. 148, 4.
k Job 26, 10, & 38.

Harper's *Illuminated and New Pictorial Bible,* 1846. This depiction of the Garden of Eden captures the character of the beautiful and somewhat provocative illustrations that helped revolutionize the nature of the Bible consumer market in nineteenth-century America. *Courtesy of the American Bible Society Library.*

The American Bible Society resisted direct competition with the Harpers but revised its policies to accommodate emerging Victorian trends and tastes. In 1841, the Society printed English Bibles in seven formats and thirty bindings and Testaments in four formats and eleven bindings. Nine years later, the managers listed twelve Bible formats in forty-five bindings and five Testament formats in twenty-three bindings. Volumes were now bound in morocco, calf, and roan, and Scriptures with highly ornamented gilt covers, embossed with names or initials, were available. If ABS products no longer carried the stigma of being designed exclusively for the poorer classes, a new pattern of invidious distinctions developed. A prosperous citizen of the great democracy could visit the ABS depository and find a volume sufficiently attractive for home display. Producing a broad range of books to satisfy the new consumer tastes necessitated technological innovation. By 1845, the managers recognized that they must remain on the publishing frontier to flourish, even at the cost of sacrificing long-established procedures, technologies, and relationships.[21]

Daniel Fanshaw had been the Bible Society's printer from 1817 through 1844, except for a brief period in the mid-1820s, when a competitor underbid him. Born in New York City in 1789, Fanshaw reflected in his career the opportunities and perils facing master tradesmen in a rapidly industrializing metropolis. He apprenticed with David and George Bruce, the two brothers who introduced the stereotyping process to America in 1814. Stereotyping, whereby a metal plate is cast from a solid mold of a page of movable type, dramatically increased the speed of press runs and reduced the amount of skill necessary in the composing room. It was the first step in a technological revolution that would transform the printing trades by midcentury. Fanshaw took advantage of his opportunities in the Bruce firm, eventually bought part of their printing office, and carved out an independence that earned him a mention in Moses Y. Beach's *Biography of the Wealthy Citizens of New York City* in 1845. Devoutly religious and somewhat eccentric, Fanshaw specialized in the increasingly lucrative religious book market. His exclusive contracts with the American Bible Society and American Tract Society assured a tremendous volume of annual business, and this rising entrepreneur invested his capital in new technologies. Although many printers refused to use Daniel Treadwell's

21. Hills, "Production and Supply of Scriptures," p. 42.

new power presses and hostile hand pressmen protested that their craft was being bastardized, Fanshaw installed the first steam presses ever used in a New York book office. By 1831, his establishment boasted eight Treadwell presses and twenty hand presses. Daniel Fanshaw had risen above his fellow printers and accumulated sufficient resources to remain competitive in an increasingly capital-intensive industry. His good fortune placed him outside the ruthless, competitive world of the small jobbers, and his willingness to innovate helped accelerate the mechanization of his craft. Beach commented in 1845 that, in contrast to many wealthy merchants who relied on handsome inheritances, Fanshaw had "made his money," a feat beyond the reach of most journeyman printers by that date.[22]

In 1844, the managers decided to review their printing operation. A working group within the publications and finance committee was formed, and their sobering conclusions dismayed the full board. "Unless we speedily take measures to improve the quality of our books, and reduce their price," this subcommittee warned, "the community will do it for us." To underscore the point, they emphasized that "with our present mode of printing we shall not be able much longer to compete with private printing establishments throughout the country." Competition already threatened their traditional market, and commercial publishers appeared ready to make greater inroads. *Harper's Illuminated Bible*, "which is confessedly as handsome Press work, as this Country has ever produced," owed its success to superior equipment. And it had been produced at a price the ABS could never match. The managers placed the blame for this dilemma squarely on the shoulders of Daniel Fanshaw.[23]

The Harpers even bid to undertake all of the Society's business "at one half the present prices," guaranteeing better workmanship and a more attractive final product. The managers did not wish to

22. "Daniel Fanshaw," *American Dictionary of Printing and Bookmaking, Containing a History of These Arts in Europe and America, with Definitions of Technical Terms and Biographical Sketches* (New York: Howard Lockwood, 1894); Wilentz, *Chants Democratic*, pp. 129–132; Moses Y. Beach, *Wealth and Biography of the Wealthy Citizens of New York City* (New York: The Sun, 1845), p. 12; "Daniel Treadwell," in Luther J. Ringwalt, ed., *American Encyclopedia of Printing* (Philadelphia: Menamin and Ringwalt, 1871), p. 360.

23. Minutes of Meeting of the Committee on Publications and Finance, January 30, 1844, ABS Archives.

forfeit their autonomy and control over Bible work, however, and decided to pursue another course. After touring the Harpers' plant, interviewing machinists and "Practical Printers," and discussing the matter with Fanshaw, the subcommittee criticized his seventeen-year-old Treadwell presses: "While it might have been better than any thing in use in 1827 it is now quite behind the times." The new Adams presses, introduced in the 1830s and manufactured by R. Hoe & Company, required only one attendant operative and printed in double, as well as single, media. Fanshaw, now fifty-five years old and seemingly set in his ways, refused to invest in the new presses. The subcommittee found him "very much wedded to old customs and to his old presses, and unwilling to admit, that any presses have been introduced superior or even equal to his." Fanshaw built his early fortune on mechanization, the division of labor, and the dilution of skills affecting journeymen after 1815. In 1845, the managers charged him with failing to keep up with the times. He demanded older perquisites of the trade such as the traditional two outside quires of paper in each ream, which cost-conscious manufacturers no longer provided. Ultimately, he became a victim of the technological revolution he helped foster. Fanshaw lost the American Bible Society contract in 1844 and the American Tract Society business shortly thereafter. His printing concern, according to one chronicler of the trade, dwindled "to very small proportions," and he lived off his real estate investments until his death in 1860.[24]

When they initially engaged Fanshaw, the managers described him as "a worthy, conscientious man, and a good mechanic." Such virtues no longer guaranteed success in the printing trades. Samuel L. Tuttle, a Bible House secretary, described the virtues of the new system shortly after Bible House opened: "In order to publish the entire number of Bibles and Testaments issued by the Society last year, by means of the facilities formerly possessed, it would require nearly a hundred presses, and about two hundred men and boys; whereas the work was actually accomplished by means of eleven presses under the direction of eleven young women and five men!" ABS contributors could rest assured that the Society had

---

24. Ibid.; "Daniel Fanshaw," p. 183.

wisely invested their funds and had, therefore, remained competitive with the commercial houses.[25]

If the internal arrangements at Bible House reflected an increased emphasis on system, order, rationality, and efficiency, the Society's physical relocation to Astor Place underscored an even more fundamental change in its institutional focus. The evangelicals who pioneered the Bible, tract, city mission, and Sunday school movements in the second and third decades of the nineteenth century hoped to bring religion into the homes of the urban poor and unchurched. They criticized the existing pew rent systems that effectively excluded poorer parishioners and established "free" churches like Bowery Presbyterian to attract a nontraditional clientele. City missionaries divided New York into wards and systematically visited the homes of the poor, distributing tracts and preaching salvation. Members of the New York Female Moral Reform Society stationed themselves outside brothels and bawdy houses, proselytizing among prostitutes and hoping to shame their patrons. Personal participation in the battle against sin involved penetrating alien spheres of existence and physically confronting the objects of reform.[26]

Ward Stafford (1788–1856), an early nineteenth-century missionary in New York, exemplified this approach. His 1817 report to the Female Missionary Society for the Poor of the City of New York was based on his "exploring sections of the city, for the purpose of obtaining further information" concerning the poor. Stafford's shocking findings revealed "a great mass of people almost entirely beyond the restraints of religion, among whom are interspersed thousands who are grossly vicious." Drunkenness, idleness, interracial mixing, widespread Sabbath-breaking, and heathen superstition permeated the great metropolis. The city contained evil subcultures, and urban living destroyed the traditional communal restraints that discouraged such vice. Stafford believed that immo-

---

25. Minutes of Meeting of the Board of Managers, August 5, 1819, ABS Archives; Samuel L. Tuttle, "Progress of Printing at the American Bible Society's House," August 8, 1853, Samuel L. Tuttle Papers, ABS Archives.

26. Paul Boyer, *Urban Masses and Moral Order in America, 1820–1920* (Cambridge: Harvard University Press, 1978), pp. 8–64; Carroll Smith-Rosenberg, *Religion and the Rise of the American City: The New York City Mission Movement, 1812–1870* (Ithaca: Cornell University Press, 1971), esp. pp. 1–124; S. D. Alexander, *The Presbytery of New York, 1738–1888* (New York: Anson D. F. Randolph, 1887).

rality could be eliminated only if wealthier, morally upright citizens accepted Christ's command "to go out into the highways and ledges" and preach the Gospel: "We must enter their dwellings— we must preach from house to house." He prescribed a detailed program of formal education, Sunday schools, Scripture distribution, Gospel preaching, and neighborhood houses of worship. Each step required the responsible Christian to enter the poor household, personally confront the Sabbath-breaker, and aggressively preach the Word of the Lord. True Christian philanthropy, in Stafford's view, involved more than merely contributing money to the cause or donating land for a new church. Only personal exertion could bridge the growing gap between pious and immoral New Yorkers that his explorations had uncovered.[27]

New York at the time of Stafford's observations was a physically compact, relatively integrated walking city. All activity—business, social, and recreational—revolved around the waterfront, and the area north of Fourteenth Street remained sparsely populated with a few farms and country residences. The built-up portion of the city extended only two miles from Manhattan's southern tip, and most New Yorkers lived above or near their places of work. Immigrants were primarily arrivals from England and Scotland, and Protestants dominated local religious life. Neighborhoods, in the sense of clearly defined and relatively homogeneous residential districts, did not exist. New York's spatially compact setting assured a jumble of commercial, mixed-use, and residential dwellings. Specific blocks, streets, and alleyways possessed distinguishable characteristics, but this did not imply extensive residential segregation. Yet, as Stafford's report illustrates, the city's wealthier classes knew remarkably little about the lives and thoughts of their less fortunate neighbors. Rich and poor moved in separate spheres, and New York's city fathers did not possess the undisputed, integrated cultural authority enjoyed by elites in smaller towns.[28]

27. Ward Stafford, *New Missionary Field: Report to the Female Missionary Society for the Poor of the City of New York and Its Vicinity, at Their Quarterly Prayer Meeting, March, 1817* (New York: Clayton & Kingsland, 1817), pp. 16, 26. For a biographical sketch of Stafford, see Franklin Bowditch Dexter, *Biographical Sketches of the Graduates of Yale College with Annals of the College History* (New Haven: Yale University Press, 1912), 6:496–499.

28. Horlick, *Country Boys and Merchant Princes*, pp. 25–44, and Jay P. Dolan, *The Immigrant Church: New York's Irish and German Catholics, 1815–1865* (Baltimore: Johns Hopkins University Press, 1975), pp. 11–19, discuss early nineteenth-

Early urban missionaries hoped to apply techniques of moral oversight effective in smaller, less complex environments to the problems of a growing metropolis. Stafford, a native of Washington, New Hampshire, believed that Christians could transform New York City into a pious, respectable community. Placing tremendous faith in moral suasion, education, and personal salvation, he believed that intimate and direct contact with the poor would hasten their conversion. From the vantage point of 1817, Stafford's vision may have appeared plausible. New York was an overcrowded town, and few citizens looked upon its social divisions as permanent or particularly menacing. Events in the next thirty years, however, would change the face of the city and stimulate Christians to redefine the nature of benevolence.[29]

Robert G. Albion has argued that the ten years between 1815 and 1825 "had done more for the port of New York than the whole two centuries which had gone before" and that the forty-five years following the Treaty of Ghent constituted "the most significant period of the port's development." Many historians have chronicled the familiar story of New York's economic rise: the beginnings of packet service between New York and Liverpool; the opening of the Erie Canal; the city's role as America's major entrepôt for European goods and its domination of the southern cotton trade; its emergence as the most productive manufacturing city in the republic; the concentration of banking, credit, and capital resources on Wall Street. Economic growth generated unprecedented concentrations of wealth and sharp inequality, stimulated immigration from rural New England and overseas, created new social divisions within the city's artisan classes, and molded a new city remarkable for its diversity and defying simple classification.[30]

century New York City. See also Ira P. Rosenwaike, *The Population History of New York City* (Syracuse: Syracuse University Press, 1972).

29. Boyer, *Urban Masses and Moral Order*, pp. 8–64.

30. Robert G. Albion, *The Rise of New York Port, 1815–1860* (New York: Charles Scribner's Sons, 1939), pp. 1, 15. The following works describe the growth of New York City during the antebellum period: Wilentz, *Chants Democratic;* Pred, *Urban Growth;* Robert Ernst, *Immigrant Life in New York City, 1825–1863* (Port Washington: Ira J. Friedman, 1949); James F. Richardson, *The New York Police: Colonial Times to 1901* (New York: Oxford University Press, 1970); Carl F. Kaestle, *The Evolution of an Urban School System: New York City, 1750–1850* (Cambridge: Harvard University Press, 1973); Spann, *New Metropolis;* Amy Bridges, *A City in the Republic: Antebellum New York and the Origins of Machine Politics* (Ithaca: Cornell University Press, 1987); John Barkley Jentz, "Artisans, Evangelicals and the City: A Social His-

The metropolis underwent a profound physical transformation. After 1820, population grew at an average rate of nearly 60 percent per decade, and the city numbered over five hundred thousand residents by 1850. Business spread northward, and the waterfront no longer constituted the focal point of urban life. By the late 1840s, separate commercial and residential neighborhoods had been established. Business and fashion concentrated along lower Broadway, while the wealthy moved uptown to residential enclaves north of Fourteenth Street. Horse-drawn rail cars on the New York and Harlem Railroad began carrying uptown commuters to downtown workplaces in the 1830s, and an elaborate street railway system existed by the 1850s. Separate residential districts resulted. Class-segregated neighborhoods, ethnic enclaves, the separation of work and residence, and the concentration of the poor in overcrowded tenements near the shipyards redefined the nature of urban life. Names like "Washington Square," "Gramercy Park," "Fifth Avenue," "Five Points," and "The Bowery" implied a social geography in which certain neighborhoods and areas had become off-limits for particular classes of citizens. A city divided by ethnic origin, political party, social class, and neighborhood had no center. Ward Stafford's conception of a unified Christian civic culture appeared lost in the complexity of the midcentury metropolis.[31]

As they moved uptown, wealthy and middling New Yorkers carried their social institutions with them. Beginning in the 1830s and accelerating in the next two decades, downtown churches abandoned their older chapels and constructed elaborate edifices uptown to serve the migrating upper middle classes. An extraordinary number of congregations dedicated new and elaborate houses of worship in the late 1840s and early 1850s. In 1846 the First Presbyterian Church relocated from Wall Street to Fifth Avenue between Eleventh and Twelfth streets. Grace Church, designed by

tory of Abolition and Labor Reform in Jacksonian New York" (Ph.D. dissertation, City University of New York, 1977); Edward Pessen, *Riches, Class, and Power before the Civil War* (Lexington, Mass.: D. C. Heath, 1973); Howard B. Rock, *Artisans of the New Republic: The Tradesmen of New York in the Age of Jefferson* (New York: New York University Press, 1979). For an excellent account of a later period, see David C. Hammack, *Power and Society: Greater New York at the Turn of the Century* (New York: Russell Sage Foundation, 1982).

31. Spann, *New Metropolis*, pp. 94–116; Dolan, *Immigrant Church*, pp. 12–19; Smith-Rosenberg, *Religion and the Rise of the American City*, pp. 15–43; Horlick, *Country Boys and Merchant Princes*, pp. 25–44; Ernst, *Immigrant Life in New York City*, pp. 37–44.

James Renwick, opened its doors at Tenth Street and Broadway in December 1848. That same year, St. George's Episcopal Church moved into new quarters on Rutherford Place and Sixteenth Street, on land donated by Bible Society manager Peter G. Stuyvesant. South Reformed Dutch Church sold its downtown Murray Street facility and relocated on Fifth Avenue and Twenty-first Street in 1849. Duane Street Church, the parish where former Bible Society secretary for domestic correspondence John B. Romeyn preached between 1808 and 1825, erected a new building at the southeast corner of Fifth Avenue and Nineteenth Street in 1853, changing its name to Fifth Avenue Presbyterian Church. Fifth Avenue Baptist Church laid its cornerstone on Fifth Avenue and Thirty-fourth Street the following year. By 1858, prestigious Brick Presbyterian Church found Beekman Street "no longer a fit place for religious worship . . . no longer a place of repose either for the preacher or the hearers" and moved to fashionable Murray Hill.[32]

All of this movement generated a serious social and moral crisis for New York's religious leadership. Baptists, proud of their popular parishioner base and ability to attract the poorer classes, publicly excoriated the city's Presbyterian and Episcopal clergy as early as 1842. Observing that "it is the fashion, it seems, for the wealthy to have their residences in the upper part of Broadway, and in the streets intersecting it in which magnificent mansions have been erected," the *New York Baptist Register* criticized the urban clergy for erecting "chapels of correspondent taste and splendor" to "accommodate Dr. Phelps and his people." Meanwhile, "a great body of the people, many families poor, many young clerks and other persons connected with stores, many large hotels and boarding houses filled with strangers" in lower Manhattan suffered for want of religion. Baptists blamed "a secular spirit, much allied with the

32. I. N. P. Stokes, *The Iconography of Manhattan Island, 1498–1909*, 6 vols. (1915–1928; rpt. New York: Arno Press, 1967), 5:1795, 1821, 1846, 1859, 6:344; Gardiner Spring quoted in *Brick Church Memorial Containing the Discourses Delivered by Dr. Spring on the Closing of the Old Church in Beekman St., and the Opening of the New Church on Murray Hill* (New York: M. W. Dodd, 1861), pp. 7, 38.

On the uptown movement and the churches, see Seymour J. Mandelbaum, *Boss Tweed's New York* (New York: Wiley, 1965), pp. 29–31. Interestingly, even the parishioners of the Roman Catholic church located closest to the new Bible House—Saint Ann's, opened in 1852 at Eighth Street near Astor Place—catered "to the upper strata of society that lived in the fine homes of the Washington Square district." The first two pastors of this church had been Episcopal converts. See Dolan, *Immigrant Church*, p. 20.

pomp and show of Papacy" for this neglect of the city's southern section because ministers refused "to occupy places where there is to be any abridgement of their rich income." Indeed, although New York's most prominent mid-nineteenth-century clergymen served on the boards of the great benevolent societies and discoursed on disinterested benevolence, few preached to the urban poor directly from their pulpits. The direct and personal Christian commitment preached by Ward Stafford a generation earlier no longer appeared relevant to clergymen engaged in massive building programs and the administrative challenges of urban parish life.[33]

Soul-searching and introspection occurred within all the major denominations. In the first six months of 1853, the very Old School Presbyterian *New York Observer* published a series of articles with the following headlines: "Churches Moving Up-Town," "Something Must Be Done for the Destitute in the Lower Wards," "Religious Destitution in New York City," "Proposed Removal of Brick Church." The *Observer* recited a familiar problem but proposed a novel solution. The number of Christian churches in the five lower wards of New York, according to the editors, had declined from thirty-five in 1838 to sixteen in 1853. The latter figure included several Roman Catholic congregations which, in the eyes of most evangelicals, exacerbated the problem of religious destitution. Some claimed that population had drifted uptown, but the editors noted that the number of inhabitants of the lower wards actually had increased over the last several years. A new population had moved in, "demanding much more [religious instruction] than the original inhabitants." The *Observer* estimated that only six thousand of the estimated ninety thousand New Yorkers living south of Canal Street regularly attended services. This, warned the newspaper, should shame "Christians, many of whom are daily attending to their business and amassing wealth in the very midst of this destitute population." Labeling it "a crying reproach, a grievous sin . . . if Christians should come into this quarter six days in the week, and carry on their secular business, and leave it on the Sabbath without the Gospel and its institutions," the editors called on the laity to resolve the problem.[34]

The *New York Observer* did not expect its readers to preach the

33. *New York Baptist Register* (Utica, N.Y.), June 3, 1842, p. 66.

34. "Religious Destitution of New York City," *New York Observer,* June 23, 1853. Other *Observer* articles concerning this theme appeared in issues dated March 3 and April 14, 1853.

Gospel to the denizens of lower Manhattan, nor did it expect the wealthy to move back downtown. Rather, the editors urged philanthropic readers to step up their contributions to denominational causes. Protestants might then erect new chapels specifically for the poor. The editors even suggested placing the words "The poor have the Gospel preached unto them" on downtown church doors. Accepting class segregation as a reality, wealthy evangelicals in 1850 exhibited little interest in personally stirring revivals and visiting the homes of the poor. Such social work might better be left to professional reformers or ministers specializing in that field. Philanthropic responsibilities ended with underwriting expenses, and the urban rich contributed unprecedented sums to evangelical causes in the 1850s. Converting the poor remained a goal, but maintaining a physical distance from the dangerous classes seemed equally important. The consensual Christian republic appeared to be in ruins.[35]

The American Bible Society built its new house in the neighborhood of the wealthy and powerful in 1853. Its building committee gave much thought to "the whole question of location" and decided that an uptown site best suited the needs. Nassau Street, complained the committee, had developed into "so great a thoroughfare & place of business" that street noise frequently disrupted transactions "in the Managers Room & front offices." The committee sought a place "where the streets are wider and less crowded and noisy" and to which the 163 operatives living north of Canal Street might more conveniently commute. If the Society's employees had vacated the lower wards, most working people, heavily immigrant and increasingly Roman Catholic, had not. In 1845, the foreign-born percentage of residents in Manhattan's four southernmost wards stood at 49, 39, 36, and 52. Ten years later, following heavy postfamine Irish immigration, the percentages increased to 68, 61, 48, and 70. The American Bible Society, like the Protestant churches, had conceded the lower city to the poor, the immigrants, the working classes, and the Roman Catholic church.[36]

---

35. On the growing tendency to hire professional, salaried social workers to deal with the problems of poverty and the tendency of pious New Yorkers to limit their contributions to pecuniary aid, see Smith-Rosenberg, *Religion and the Rise of the American City*, p. 191.

36. Minutes of Meeting of the Board of Managers, December 4, 1851, ABS Archives. The statistics were compiled from tables in Ernst, *Immigrant Life in New York City*, p. 193.

The building committee carefully surveyed New York and found "important improvements in the upper part of the city." Above Chambers Street, on Broadway and Union Place, they observed "nine Hotels of the largest class" with "far more extensive accommodations than can be found" below that area. Further, "establishments extensively engaged in selling goods to the country, are now found on Broadway above Chambers St., and there can be little doubt that this branch of business will continue to extend in the same direction for many years to come." An uptown location would place the Society in the center of commercial activity and would also prove "convenient of access for those engaged in the general management of the Societies affairs" and close to services essential for "those calling to transact business either from the city or country." Grand hotels, elegant restaurants, spectacular department stores, and the attractions of Broadway offered a business atmosphere superior in style to the sights, sounds, and smells of the immigrant city downtown.[37]

Ultimately, the building committee selected a triangular block on Astor Place, bounded by Eighth and Ninth streets and Third and Fourth avenues, to house the enterprise. Contemporaries described the area as New York's "Athenian Quarter," and a listing of the institutions located nearby in the mid-1850s conveys a somewhat deceptive image of philanthropy, wealth, and consolidated cultural power: the New-York Historical Society on Second Avenue, the Astor Library, the Mercantile Library, Cooper Union for the Advancement of Science and Art, University of the City of New York, the Century Club, the National Academy of Design, and the Academy of Music. The physical concentration of these elite institutions in a single area, however, seems less remarkable than their relative isolation and withdrawal from public and civic life. The New-York Historical Society increasingly pursued an antiquarian course and narrowed its original claims as "an association for the purposes of general knowledge." The University of the City of New York quickly abandoned its original commitment to inclusive urbanity and functioned as a marginal and traditional elite training institution. The National Academy of Design had become a professional interest group, seeking to divorce art from the cultural life of a democratic

---

37. Minutes of Meeting of the Board of Managers, December 4, 1851, ABS Archives.

society, and the Century Club has been described as little more than "the headquarters for a clubbish, genteel culture."[38]

Movement uptown and residential segregation indicated that the wealthy and powerful could no longer hope to forge a common civic consensus in a complex, pluralist metropolis. The proliferation of enormous institutional cultural edifices, each claiming its special prerogative and staking out its limited sphere, prevented the elite from speaking with a single voice. The Astor family located its substantial Romanesque library half a block south of the American Bible Society. It boasted a copy of the first printed Bible among its most valuable holdings. William B. Astor donated some money to build the new Bible House, but no family member ever served on the board of managers or exerted any influence over Bible Society affairs. Peter Cooper's Union for the Advancement of Science and Art adhered to a strictly nonsectarian admissions policy, yet he described his "great object" as opening "the volume of nature by the light of truth—so unveiling the laws and methods of Deity, that the young may see the beauties of creation, enjoy its blessings, and learn to love the Being 'from whom cometh every good and perfect gift.'" He built his Union across the street from Bible House in 1857, but Cooper's unorthodox brand of Unitarianism precluded any connection with the Bible Society. Each building in the Athenian Quarter stood alone, an impressive monument to private philanthropy. No institution possessed sufficient breadth or support to recreate a unified public culture or redefine civic discourse.[39]

How, then, did the American Bible Society redefine itself? Social change had compromised its centrality to city life and urban reform. Elite divisions limited its representativeness as a patrician cultural center. Still, the Society found a new role for itself, and to discover it one need look no further than the first floor of Bible House. Entering the office rooms from Fourth Avenue, a visitor would find not only the ABS depository and administrative staff but a series of rooms used by other benevolent organizations. The Society had decided to rent space to other groups sympathetic to its missionary goals, and a list of tenants in 1853 included the Ameri-

38. Spann, *New Metropolis*, pp. 220, 425. See Bender, *New York Intellect*, pp. 72–77, 88–116, 127–129, 139.

39. On the Astor Library, see *Appleton's Dictionary*, p. 19. Cooper quoted in *Charter, Trust Deed, and By-Laws of the Cooper Union for the Advancement of Science and Art with the Letter of Peter Cooper, Accompanying the Trust Deed* (New York: Wm. C. Bryant & Co., 1859), p. 26.

can Board of Commissioners for Foreign Missions, American Home Missionary Society, Protestant Episcopal Church Foreign and Domestic committees, Protestant Episcopal Society for the Promotion of Christian Knowledge, New York State Colonization Society, Society for the Amelioration of the Condition of the Jews, New York House of Refuge, Children's Aid Society, Evangelical Knowledge Society, New York Association for Improving the Condition of the Poor, New York Home for the Friendless, and the New York Society Library.[40]

Just as New York City evolved into a great metropolis, providing important financial and informational services for the nation as a whole, the American Bible Society redefined its mission as providing similar support services for the nation's network of Protestant reform agencies. By concentrating large amounts of capital in one organization, creating a worldwide network of auxiliaries and Bible agents, accumulating vast quantities of information concerning the Scriptures, and possessing specialized knowledge of linguistics and translations issues, the Society could perform valuable services for broadly based reform organizations and more narrow denominational efforts. At the same time, by defining itself as a service agency for institutions and never directly confronting the individuals and groups that were the targets of reformers, it could remain insulated from the failures of specific reform efforts and its existence did not hinge on the outcomes. Bible House remained in the city, but the organizations it served constituted a translocal evangelical elite, with tenuous connections to the urban metropolis.

The American Bible Society, like many other flourishing mid-century institutions, survived by narrowing its functions, withdrawing from public life, and cultivating a specific and limited constituency. "That this Society stands at the head of all benevolent institutions and is in fact the foundation on which all others rest, must be universally conceded," argued the managers in 1851. No longer claiming to stand at the head of all *social* institutions or *public* institutions, the Society had evolved into a very efficient and successful private philanthropy in the service of other very efficient and successful private philanthropies.[41]

40. Minutes of Meeting of the Building Committee, August 1853, ABS Archives; *New York Weekly Tribune,* April 2, 1853.
41. Minutes of Meeting of the Board of Managers, December 4, 1851, ABS Archives.

2

From Civic Humanitarianism
to Corporate Benevolence:
The Changing Nature of the Board
of Managers

National interdenominational benevolent organizations such as the American Bible Society, American Tract Society, American Education Society, and American Sunday School Union vested their corporate authority in lay boards of managers, who met monthly to shape and direct institutional policies. Wealthy businessmen and urban professionals made the critical decisions and dominated these philanthropic governing boards over the course of the nineteenth century, while clergymen remained in the background, lending their support in less visible and more informal ways. Indeed, the men who founded the organizations associated with Christian America's benevolent empire institutionalized the concept of lay control. William Jay (1789–1858), whose 1816 *Memoir on the Subject of a General Bible Society of the United States of America* essentially outlined the administrative framework adopted by the ABS, presented a strong argument for lay governance. His proposed Article VIII of the Bible Society's constitution stipulated that "a large majority" of the Society's board of managers "shall be laymen," and he vigorously defended this point. Jay's argument centered on one key observation: laymen were "more conversant with the details of business" and thus "better qualified" to manage a national Bible Society than were clergymen.[1]

William Jay had been born into a late eighteenth-century pre-industrial capitalist culture in which the "details of business" carried a very specific commercial meaning. General merchants dominated the economic life of the coastal port towns, and the small partnership was the principal form of business organization. Individual entrepreneurs imported and exported goods, provided credit to farmers and artisans, engaged in wholesale and retail trades, and played key public roles in their communities. Familial and social connections largely determined commercial success, and personal ties linked the Anglo-American trading world. The family remained the basic business unit, and small-scale production characterized both northern agriculture and southern manufacturing.[2]

At the time Jay was drafting his proposed Bible Society constitution, however, men who paid attention to "the details of business" had begun behaving in new ways. As James Henretta has observed, American merchant capitalism in 1815 was undergoing an important transformation in which "the once indivisible functions of trading, insuring, financing, and banking would be performed by separate institutions." Distinctions grew between importers and exporters. Merchants began specializing in specific goods and carrying on trade with distant regions of the world. Incorporated joint stock companies began replacing partnerships as larger amounts of capital became concentrated in fewer individual firms. Commercial banks, insurance companies, brokerage houses, and transportation enterprises eased the flow of goods through the economy, and salaried managers began administering the daily transactions of these relatively complex enterprises.[3]

By the time of Jay's death in 1858, the well-ordered, family-

1. A Citizen of New York [William Jay], A Memoir on the Subject of a General Bible Society for the United States of America (N.p.: N.p., 1816), p. 12; William Jay to Elias Boudinot, April 23, 1816, Elias Boudinot Papers, ABS Archives.

2. See Stuart Bruchey, The Roots of American Economic Growth, 1607–1861: An Essay in Social Causation (New York: Harper & Row, 1968), pp. 48–54; and Alfred D. Chandler, The Visible Hand: The Managerial Revolution in American Business (Cambridge: Harvard University Press, 1977), pp. 15–19.

3. James Henretta, The Evolution of American Society, 1700–1815: An Interdisciplinary Analysis (Lexington, Mass.: D.C. Heath, 1973), p. 83. See also Thomas C. Cochran, "The Business Revolution," American Historical Review (December 1974), 1449–1466.

oriented business world of the late eighteenth-century merchant had given way, in Alfred Chandler's words, to "the specialized impersonalized world of the jobber, importer, factor, broker, and the commission agent of the river and port towns." New York City's merchants, financiers, and lawyers dominated the nation's commerce by the 1850s. Large-scale corporate concerns, financed by New York City capitalists, developed in the transportation and communications industries. The nation's first specialized investment banking firms coalesced in the city, the New York Stock Exchange began trading hundreds of thousands of shares weekly, and men such as Jay Gould, Jim Fiske, and Daniel Drew began earning national reputations for their shady speculative dealings in railroad securities.[4]

William Jay, born near the end of an age characterized by the merchant-capitalist, the small artisanal producer, and the independent yeoman farmer, died near the beginning of a period dominated by large-scale capital investment, new forms of mass production and distribution, and the emergence of managerial corporate capitalism. One of his enduring institutional legacies was the American Bible Society. Jay's constitution ensured that the ABS would always be governed by men "conversant with the details of business," but the nature of these details changed dramatically during the framer's lifetime. As different generations of managers, representing very different social experiences, occupied seats in the boardroom, they altered the nature, purpose, and scope of the Society's activities. Before examining the institutional revolution they wrought, it is instructive to inquire into the managers' changing lives, thoughts, and career patterns over the course of the early nineteenth century.

From its founding in 1816 through the early 1830s, the Bible Society steered a steady course and remained remarkably faithful to its founders' precepts. The managers created relatively few full-time administrative positions, met at least once a month, and maintained a tight grip over every detail of Bible work. They relied on outside contractors to coordinate the production and distribution of Scriptures and conducted Bible business on Nassau Street, near the docks and wharves of the commercial city. No serious schism disrupted the Society's work, and a sense of optimism and harmony permeated the annual reports and board minutes. The managers

4. Chandler, *Visible Hand*, p. 27 and the discussion which follows.

faithfully adhered to the spirit and letter of Jay's original by-laws, and the Society remained voluntary in all its essentials. Fifty-seven pious laymen actively served on the board between 1816 and 1835. They differed somewhat in age, place of birth, and career patterns, but considered together their stories provide an interesting entrée into the complex intellectual and institutional currents that directed elite life in early republican New York City.[5]

5. The subsequent analysis is based on the life histories of members of the ABS's board of managers (including both the board members and the vice–presidents) who attended at least half of the board meetings in any single year between 1816 and 1835. My purpose in limiting the sample is to define and analyze the life careers of managers who influenced and actively participated in board deliberations. Thus I have excluded men who filled honorary seats. Henry Rutgers (1745–1830), for example, was one of the wealthiest Christian philanthropists in federal New York; his name is connected with virtually every benevolent association organized in the nineteenth-century city. The American Bible Society elected him to its board in 1816, and he remained on the board until his death. The attendance roster, however, reveals that he attended only nine meetings in fourteen years and only one between 1817 and 1830. His continued presence on the roster illustrates something about the types of men the managers sought to have associated publicly with their enterprise so as to confer legitimacy on its activities. It reveals little about actual power relationships and influence on the board.

Accordingly, I have compiled attendance figures and accumulated the following list of managers who attended 50 percent or more of the meetings in any year between 1816 and 1835: Matthew Clarkson (1758–1825), Richard Varick (1753–1821), John Aspinwall (1774–1847), John Bingham (n.d.–1833), Leonard Bleecker (1755–1844), Samuel Boyd (1768–1839), Thomas Carpenter (1757–1825), John E. Caldwell (1763–1822), Thomas Eddy (1758–1827), Cornelius Heyer (1773–1843), John Richardson Bayard Rodgers (1757–1833), Thomas Stokes (1765–1832), John Watts (1786–1831), Peter Wilson (1746–1825), Divie Bethune (1771–1824), Thomas Collins (1779–1859), George Griffen (1778–1860), Henry Rogers (dates unknown), Zechariah Lewis (1773–1840), Benjamin Clark (dates unknown), Theodore Dwight, Jr. (1796–1866), John Adams (1772–1863), Peter William Radcliff (1774–1840), George Suckley (1756–1846), Francis Bayard Winthrop (1787–1841), William Walton Woolsey (1766–1839), John D. Keese (dates unknown), John Pintard (1759–1844), Isaac Collins (dates unknown), Hubert Van Wagenen (1785–1852), Benjamin Woolsey Rogers (1775–1860), Edward Delafield (1794–1875), Timothy Hedges (1780–1860), Francis Hall (1785–1866), Anson Greene Phelps, Sr. (1781–1853), Robert Troup (1757–1832), George Gallagher (dates unknown), Eleazer Lord (1788–1871), James L. Phelps (1785–1869), Isaac Carow (1778–1850), Benjamin L. Swan (1787–1866), Arthur Tappan (1786–1865), Najah Taylor (1770–1860), John Varick Freligh (dates unknown), Garrat Noel Bleecker (1767–1833), Thomas Darling (1785–1843), James William Dominick, Sr. (n.d.–1852), John Bolton (1774–1838), William Bedlow Crosby (1786–1865), Pelatiah Webster Perit (1785–1864), Peter Gerard Stuyvesant (1778–1847), Timothy R. Green (n.d.–1840), Britton L. Woolley

The laymen who directed the Society's affairs during its first twenty years were born and bred in the same late eighteenth-century business culture that produced William Jay. Nearly two-thirds of the forty-seven managers whose birth dates are known began life during the 1770s and 1780s. An additional 30 percent were born before 1770; only 6 percent belonged to the post-1790 generation. Their occupations reflected the relatively straightforward and orderly eighteenth-century urban economy: 71 percent functioned as merchants, lawyers, or doctors. Fewer than 10 percent made their money in the more specialized and rapidly changing disciplines of insurance, banking, and transportation. Their birthplaces reflected the fluid nature of New York City's late eighteenth-century population. Only one-quarter of the forty managers whose origins can be documented grew up in New York City. Eighteen percent arrived in the urban metropolis from foreign ports, 30 percent hailed from New England farming villages, and 15 percent made their way to the city after spending their early lives in rural upstate locales. All took advantage of the growing port's booming mercantile economy to amass sizable fortunes.

Several common social and ideological threads bound the managers and wove a coherence through Bible Society affairs. First, and perhaps foremost, a broad cosmopolitan outlook and extensive

---

(1787–1849), Thomas Cock (1782–1869), William Colgate (1783–1857), and William Forrest (1791–1865).

A wide range of sources were consulted to reconstruct biographies for these individuals. Among the most useful were Allen Johnson and Dumas Malone, eds., *The Dictionary of American Biography*, 20 vols., 8 supplements (New York: Charles Scribner's Sons, 1927–36); *The National Cyclopaedia of American Biography* (New York: James T. White, 1897); James Grant Wilson and John Fiske, eds., *Appleton's Cyclopedia of American Biography*, 12 vols. (New York: D. Appleton, 1898–1931); Moses Y. Beach, *Wealth and Biography of the Wealthy Citizens of New York City* (New York: The Sun, 1845); Franklin Bowditch Dexter, *Biographical Sketches of the Graduates of Yale College, with Annals of the College History* (New Haven: Yale University Press, 1912); Lyman Horace Weeks, *Prominent Families of New York* (New York: Historical Company, 1898); Joseph A. Scoville [Walter Barrett], *The Old Merchants of New York City* (New York: Carleton, 1863); *Leslie's History of the Greater New York (Volume III): Encyclopaedia of New York Biography and Genealogy* (New York: Arkell Publishing Company, 1899); and Margaret R. Townsend, "Biographical Data on the Managers of the American Bible Society, 1816–1966," 3 vols., ABS Historical Essay 102-C (1966). Obituaries in the *New York Times, New York Herald,* and other city dailies also yielded useful information, as did city directories, and Biographical Files in the American Bible Society's Archives.

participation in a transatlantic, Anglo-American world of business, benevolence, and intellectual life characterized the founders and the early managers. William Jay's *Memoir* consistently cited British practice to justify every aspect of the ABS's constitution, and developments in Great Britain directly influenced the course of the Bible movement in America. The British and Foreign Bible Society (BFBS) had been established in 1804, and this London-based organization shipped Bibles, Testaments, and stereotype plates to local societies throughout the United States during the next decade. Subsidies continued, even during the War of 1812, and supporters of the Bible cause in America maintained close contact with the merchants and ministers who directed BFBS affairs.[6]

British precedent permeated every aspect of ABS work. When Elias Boudinot questioned one article in the Society's proposed constitution, William Jay effectively ended the debate by observing that it "is the prominent feature of the Constitution of the British Society, & the success of that wonderful institution is the highest eulogium on the wisdom of its constitution." The ABS's annual reports devoted considerable space to BFBS activities on the Continent, and the secretaries for foreign correspondence wrote regular, if somewhat stiff and formal, letters to their British counterparts. Proposed policy initiatives such as the auxiliary system, the employment of paid agents, and entry into the foreign field all required research into BFBS practices. Upon deciding to publish a monthly informational periodical, the board announced its intention to follow "in the steps of the British and Foreign Bible Society, and hope to realize benefits similar to those which have resulted ... in Great Britain and on the continent of Europe."[7]

The private lives and activities of the managers who served the ABS between 1816 and 1835 underscore this orientation toward the commercial and intellectual capitals of London, Edinburgh, and the British Empire. Seven of the forty managers whose birthplaces are known had been born and educated in England and Scotland. Others possessed extensive familial connections in Great Britain, and many spent several years traveling and studying abroad. Three

---

6. Charles I. Foster, *An Errand of Mercy: The Evangelical United Front, 1790–1837* (Chapel Hill: University of North Carolina Press, 1960), pp. 82–107, demonstrates the links between antebellum America's benevolent empire and developments in Great Britain. [Jay], *Memoir*, pp. 3–4, 6–7, 9–10.

7. William Jay to Elias Boudinot, April 23, 1816, Elias Boudinot Papers, ABS Archives; Minutes of Meeting of the Board of Managers, July 2, 1818, ABS Archives.

South Street near Dover Street, 1829, drawn by A. J. Davis and engraved by J. Yeager. Masts and sails dominated lower Manhattan during the early years of the American Bible Society, and the first generation of ABS managers played critical roles in propelling New York port to commercial prominence. *Courtesy of the South Street Seaport Museum.*

of the five medical men on the board, for example, received their advanced professional training in London and Edinburgh, and each played an important role in the movement for incorporated medical societies, professional collegiate training, and medical licensing. British sources of capital and credit proved especially critical for the merchants, who constituted over half the active members of the board during the 1816–1835 period. John Aspinwall (1774–1847) built his substantial fortune on consignments from foreign ports, conducting over $100,000 worth of business per year with one large house in St. Petersburg alone. Thomas Stokes (1765–1832) made his money initially through woolen imports, selling uniform cloth to the British army. Divie Bethune (1771–1824) lived in Tobago before arriving in New York, and his West Indian contacts procured substantial sums for his firm, which included fellow Bible Society manager Robert Ralston. Pelatiah Perit (1785–1864), in the words of his biographer, remained "interested in the commercial progress of every country and led to the maintenance of a wide personal acquaintance in different parts of the globe."[8]

Perhaps the Anglo-American nature of business and benevolence is summarized best in the life of ABS manager Thomas Eddy (1758–1827), a Quaker philanthropist active in virtually every early nineteenth-century New York City reform crusade. In his early mercantile career Eddy handled consignments on goods from England and Ireland, but his British orientation was not limited to the relatively trifling boundaries of commercial affairs. As the architect of New York's penitentiary system, his enthusiastic en-

8. The seven managers born overseas were John E. Cauldwell, in Birmingham, England; Thomas Stokes, in London, England; Peter Wilson, in Ordequhill, Scotland; Divie Bethune, in Rosshire, Scotland; Francis Hall, in Taunton, England; Isaac Carow, in St. Croix, West Indies; and William Colgate, in Kent, England. The three physicians trained abroad were John Richardson Bayard Rodgers, John Watts, and Edward Delafield. Concerning the importance of British models for American physicians, see Joseph Kett, *The Formation of the American Medical Profession: The Role of Institutions, 1780–1860* (New Haven: Yale University Press, 1968), pp. 9–13, 30–34; and Daniel Calhoun, *Professional Lives in America: Structure and Aspiration, 1750–1850* (Cambridge: Harvard University Press, 1965), esp. pp. 28–29. On the significance of Edinburgh for New York's patrician Federalists, see Thomas Bender, *New York Intellect: A History of Intellectual Life in New York City, 1750 to the Beginnings of Our Own Time* (New York: Knopf, 1987), p. xiv. Robert G. Albion, *The Rise of New York Port, 1815–1860* (New York: Charles Scribner's Sons, 1939), contains excellent information on the merchants' overseas commercial contacts. The Perit quote is from *National Cyclopaedia of American Biography*, 1:499.

dorsement of solitary confinement was based on penal reform experiments in England. When he turned his attention to lunatic asylums, the young Quaker diligently studied precedents in England and Wales, corresponding with leading reformers overseas. He influenced the New York Free School Society to conduct its classrooms according to the system advocated by Joseph Lancaster in England. Eventually, contemporaries dubbed Eddy "the Howard of America," thus acknowledging his cosmopolitanism and recognizing his intellectual debt to British philanthropist John Howard. Upon Eddy's death, the *New York Daily Advertiser* accurately observed that "an extensive correspondence with persons of distinction in Europe, and particularly in Great Britain, rendered his name and his character familiar to many of the great philanthropists of the age." In sum, Eddy and his fellow ABS managers were characterized by an aggressive Anglo-American consciousness, and they self-consciously modeled their institutions on established British precedents.[9]

Anglo-American reform currents steered early nineteenth-century benevolent institutions. Family ties bound these organizations into tightly knit, coherent units. Genealogical connections linked many of the ABS's early managers, but a single example can illustrate how familial bonds permeated the city's economic, social, and civic institutions. William Walton Woolsey (1766–1839), who helped found the American Bible Society and served as its treasurer between 1819 and 1827, was born to a prominent Long Island family. One of his sisters married Moses Rogers, a successful Queen Street merchant, and another married the noted painter and playwright William Dunlap. Woolsey eventually went into business with Rogers and the latter's son, Benjamin Woolsey Rogers (1775–1860). When Moses Rogers died in 1798, Woolsey and his nephew continued the partnership for six years, until William had amassed

9. Samuel L. Knapp, *The Life of Thomas Eddy, Comprising an Extensive Correspondence with Many of the Most Distinguished Philosophers and Philanthropists of This and Other Countries* (London: Edmund Fry and Son, 1836), pp. 42–43, 57–58, 137–243, 260. Eddy's efforts to introduce Lancasterian pedagogical techniques into New York City's schools are chronicled in Carl Kaestle, *The Evolution of an Urban School System: New York City, 1750–1850* (Cambridge: Harvard University Press, 1973), pp. 80–84. On solitary confinement, which Eddy and his philanthropic colleagues viewed as a humanitarian practice that would remove prisoners from vice and allow them to contemplate their situation, see David J. Rothman, *The Discovery of the Asylum: Social Order and Disorder in the New Republic* (Boston: Little, Brown, 1971), pp. 92–93, 96–101.

a substantial fortune in the hardware trade and decided to pursue other financial interests. Benjamin Rogers maintained the import business but devoted an increasing amount of energy to benevolent activity. He served as vestryman of Trinity Church between 1821 and 1828 and joined his uncle on the ABS board of managers in 1824.[10]

Meanwhile, Benjamin's brother Henry Rogers had established his own firm—Rogers and Lyle—in 1784, which carried on "an immense iron import business on Pearl Street," according to merchant-biographer Joseph A. Scoville. When Henry Rogers's partner started his own business in 1807, Rogers and Lyle reorganized as Rogers, Son and Company. Henry Rogers, like his uncle and brother, participated on the ABS board of managers between 1817 and 1828. Francis Bayard Winthrop (1787–1841) entered this complicated familial situation in 1807. Born in Boston, he had moved to New York in 1804 to pursue a mercantile career, and he wisely married Julia Ann Rogers, sister of Henry Rogers, in 1808. Shortly thereafter, Winthrop joined the firm of Rogers, Son and Company. In 1819, he became an active board member of the American Bible Society.

When Julia Rogers Winthrop died suddenly in 1814, Winthrop quickly remarried, choosing as his bride Elizabeth Woolsey, the daughter of Rogers's uncle William Walton Woolsey and his wife, Elizabeth Dwight. Pursuing the Dwight connection further, one finds that Woolsey's brother-in-law Theodore Dwight, Jr. (1796–1866), served as an ABS manager between 1818 and 1835. The significant point appears clear. Family mattered in federal New York as firms and philanthropies often assumed distinct genealogical characters. Merchants seeking reliable partners frequently turned to family connections. Furthermore, board membership in a benevolent institution or a religious concern conferred the virtues of orthodoxy and reliability on men making their fortune in the city. For such men, the American Bible Society served a distinctly social as well as philanthropic purpose.[11]

One theme that consistently recurs and in fact dominates the biographical tributes prepared for early nineteenth-century members of the ABS board of managers is the concept of public service. Some

10. Scoville, *Old Merchants*, 2:317–321; Weeks, *Prominent Families*, p. 280.

11. Scoville, *Old Merchants*, 2:308; "Francis Bayard Winthrop," in Dexter, *Biographical Sketches*, 5:730–731; "Dwight, Theodore," in *Dictionary of American Biography*, 3:570–571.

managers participated directly in public life: Richard Varick (1753–1831) served as mayor of New York from 1790 to 1801, Matthew Clarkson (1758–1825) held a variety of elected and appointed state offices, John Bingham (n.d.–1833) earned a place on the Common Council, Thomas Carpenter (1757–1825) worked diligently as an alderman, and Peter Wilson (1746–1825) represented Bergen County in the New Jersey legislature and helped revise and codify that state's laws following independence. Others shied away from the rough-and-tumble of elective politics but served the public in other ways. Pelatiah Perit found that "civil life was not congenial to his tastes," yet he earned the business community's approbation as president of the New York Chamber of Commerce from 1853 to 1863. Leonard Bleecker (1755–1844) played an important role in establishing such ventures as the New York Exchange, Public School Society, Society for the Relief of Distressed Prisoners, and New York Samaritan Society. His memorialist described him as "esteemed and respected by the community in which he lived," a coveted epitaph among his fellow board members of the American Bible Society.[12]

For the men who dominated New York's civic institutions during the first quarter of the nineteenth century, the concepts of public service, civic advancement, and republican genius coalesced in one important technological achievement. The Erie Canal, completed in 1825, symbolized the grand potential of a unified city, asserting its commercial supremacy over the nation and harmoniously advancing toward its urban destiny. Truly a public work on an unprecedented scale, the canal illustrated how a patrician-directed government could advance common social interests by aiding, regulating, and intervening in the economy. The canal offered the illusory promise of social harmony and public commitment to common social goals. In its construction, patrician interests and public interests appeared as one.[13]

12. On Perit, see New York Times, March 10, 1864, p. 5; National Cyclopaedia of American Biography, 1:500. Bleecker's characterization is in Jerome B. Helgade, American Genealogy; Being a History of Some of the Early Settlers of North America and Their Descendants (Albany: Joel Munsell, 1848), p. 89.

13. Nathan Miller, The Enterprise of a Free People: Aspects of Economic Development in New York State during the Canal Period, 1792–1838 (Ithaca: Cornell University Press, 1962), esp. pp. xi–xii, 11–19. Ronald Shaw, Erie's Waters West: A History of the Erie Canal, 1792–1854 (Lexington: University of Kentucky Press, 1966), also examines the canal. Sean Wilentz, Chants Democratic: New York City and the Rise of the American Working Class, 1788–1850 (New York: Oxford University Press, 1984),

Not surprisingly, several key figures in the early history of the American Bible Society played important roles in making "Clinton's ditch" a reality. As early as 1790, Thomas Eddy toured the Mohawk River with Philip Schuyler, and he encouraged the general to draw up the articles of incorporation for the Western and Northern Inland Lock Navigation companies. When these private concerns proved incapable of building the canal, Eddy vigorously lobbied the New York State legislature to assume responsibility for the project. In 1810, the state appointed Eddy to a six-man board of canal commissioners, which ultimately guided the undertaking. Six years later, Eddy proved influential in organizing a public meeting and petition drive, rallying New York City's leading citizens to the canal cause and pressuring the state to appropriate additional funds. The American Bible Society's links with the Erie project did not end with Eddy. Future ABS managers Stephen Van Rensselaer and De Witt Clinton also served on the 1810 board of commissioners, and prominent private investors in the canal included ABS managers and land speculators Robert Troup and William Bayard.[14]

The Erie Canal symbolized the way federal New York's elite patricians linked civic advancement, private profit, and public commitment. Another institutional invention of the second decade of the nineteenth century brought together many of these themes and demonstrated the way New York's leading men simultaneously promoted good business and active benevolence. On March 26, 1819, the Bank for Savings in the City of New York received its incorporation. Like so many of the American urban experiments established during this period, the savings bank movement began in late eighteenth-century England as a means for managing paupers. In fact, 465 such institutions existed throughout the British Isles by 1818. John Pintard, the ABS recording secretary whose philanthropic memberships rivaled Thomas Eddy's, began advocating a New York savings institution in 1809, and Eddy became interested in 1816. Nine of the original twenty-eight trustees affiliated with the bank also served on the ABS's board of managers.[15]

---

considers the 1825 celebration upon the canal's completion an important symbol of cultural unity (pp. 87–97).

14. Knapp, *Life of Thomas Eddy*, pp. 117–123, discusses Eddy's role in promoting the canal. See also Miller, *Enterprise of a Free People*, pp. 23–43, 88–89.

15. Alan L. Olmstead, *New York City Mutual Savings Banks, 1819–1861* (Chapel Hill: University of North Carolina Press, 1976), pp. 5–13. See also Raymond A. Mohl,

Pintard articulated the purpose of the institution in a letter to his daughter dated December 5, 1816. "You will see by the Herald," he remarked, "the plan of a Savings Bank for laying up the earnings of domestics & the labouring community. . . . It will remove one of the causes of mendicity & thereby lessen the burthens on the more favoured class of citizens in supporting paupers, by exciting thrift, frugality, a pride of character & independence which will be productive of moral & religious habits." The savings bank would link the interests of rich and poor, providing the latter with a small stake in the economic system and an incentive to moral uplift, while simultaneously pooling resources for reinvestment. The bank became the principal investor in Erie Canal stock, providing much-needed capital at a time when wealthy investors were reluctant to risk their funds.[16]

A recent study of New York's antebellum savings institutions has concluded that the Bank for Savings remained remarkably faithful to its philanthropic origins, at least through the 1840s. Trustees continued to take a personal interest in bank affairs, supported few salaried officers and a minimal professional staff, accumulated relatively large surpluses to minimize risks for small investors, regularly turned away deposits from large investors and philanthropists, and purchased stock primarily in such public concerns as the Croton Aqueduct. The city's upper and middle classes accounted for the majority of depositors, but approximately one-quarter were unskilled laborers. The savings bank promoted New York's interests in other important ways as well. It helped establish the state's credit, encouraged and financed the great transportation projects that ensured the city's commercial supremacy, and even loaned money to New York's Public School Society. It remained essentially a philanthropy, directed by the city's self-proclaimed

---

Poverty in New York, 1783–1825 (New York: Oxford University Press, 1971), pp. 250–251. *Charter and By-Laws of the Bank for Savings in the City of New York* (New York: J. Seymour, 1819) lists the original trustees. The bank actually grew out of the work of the Society for the Prevention of Pauperism. Savings bank trustees who also served on the American Bible Society board included John Pintard, Thomas Eddy, Najah Taylor, Peter A. Jay, Zechariah Lewis, William Bayard, John Murray, Jr., George Arcularius, and Duncan P. Campbell.

16. Dorothy C. Barck, ed., *Letters from John Pintard to His Daughter Eliza Noel Pintard Davidson* (New York: New-York Historical Society, 1940), 1:38; Miller, *Enterprise of a Free People*, pp. 88–89.

"best men" and always responsible to their perception of the "public good."[17]

Shortly after the Bank for Savings opened in 1819, John Pintard provided the appropriate symbolic touch. He instructed a New York sign maker to have his favorite biblical verses "printed in letters of Gold, framed & glazed & suspended in the Savings Bank," where, he hoped, the words might "remain when I am dead & gone, & produce the same happy influence on my successor that I have myself experienced." Pintard's inspirational message to depositors and cashiers consisted of the words of the Forty-first Psalm, and they effectively articulated the impulses that drove Christian capitalists to create a network of philanthropic organizations, savings banks, Bible societies, and other specialized institutions in Jeffersonian New York: "Blessed is he that considereth the poor & needy; the Lord will deliver him in the time of trouble. The Lord preserve him & keep him alive, that he may be blessed upon earth; and deliver not Thou him into the will of his enemies. The Lord comfort him when he lieth sick upon his bed; make Thou all his bed in his sickness. Amen."[18]

The mid-1830s marked an important divide in the history of the American Bible Society. The board suffered its first serious schisms when abolitionist sympathizers (1834) and Baptists (1836) resigned because they disagreed with institutional policies. New men filled the vacancies and began directing the Society's affairs. The thirty-six-member board experienced a 69 percent turnover in the decade following 1835, which was uncharacteristically high. By 1845, only four managers could trace their ABS service to 1825. As new men gradually replaced the earlier managers, they shifted institutional practices and priorities, revolutionizing the Society's operations: the managers secured incorporation from the New York legislature (1841), overhauled the Society's by-laws (1845), began a lengthy campaign to centralize all production and distribution activities under their direct supervision, and expanded the full-time, paid administrative staff to manage daily operations. These men conceived and constructed the grand Bible House on Astor Place and altered the image, as well as the work, of the Society. Voluntarism remained a relic of the ABS's Jeffersonian past as cen-

17. Olmstead, *New York City Mutual Savings Banks,* pp. 3–5, 13, 27, 46, 52–53, 71–73.

18. Barck, ed., *Letters from John Pintard to His Daughter,* 2:219.

tralization, efficiency, and a more businesslike structure assumed greater importance.[19]

The year 1837 was a critical one in the history of New York City and nineteenth-century America generally. An unprecedented panic, financial collapse, and protracted depression caused enormous suffering and had important long-term implications for the city's manufacturing and philanthropic sectors. By the time full-scale recovery and an economic boom occurred in the mid-1840s, New York had become an increasingly Irish and German immigrant city with large-scale industries crowding the waterfront and outskirts, a real estate crisis in the lower wards, and a fragmented artisanal labor system. Anxiety, despair, and uncertainty prevailed in the short term. Sean Wilentz has observed that the depression years produced "the greatest plebian Protestant revival in the city's history," with prophets of doom and street preachers roaming the working-class streets to evangelize new Christians and offer millennial hope. The city's upper classes, their faith in the market temporarily challenged, went about the task of restructuring the banking system, reinventing their institutional lives, and recapitalizing their enterprises to buttress themselves against future disaster.[20]

The managers who began sitting on the ABS board during this time of controversy, uncertainty, and change looked and acted very different from the elite patricians who shepherded the institution through its first twenty years. First, they represented a new generation. Only 11 percent of the thirty-five board members who began active service between 1837 and 1865 had been born by 1790; 61 percent were born between 1795 and 1810. Whereas the earlier managers financed the Erie Canal and created the great public works that fueled antebellum capitalist enterprise, these new men came of age during a period of unprecedented prosperity, fluidity, and economic opportunity. Second, their hometowns reveal a pronounced representation of New Englanders, upstate New Yorkers, and mobile men from rural New Jersey (62 percent compared with

19. On the abolitionist and Baptist schisms, see Chapter 5. Turnover was 44 percent between 1816 and 1825 and 61 percent between 1825 and 1835. Chapters 4, 5, and 6 trace the events of the 1830s in detail and provide background for considering the middle of this decade as a key divide in the Society's history.

20. Richard B. Stott, *Workers in the Metropolis: Class, Ethnicity, and Youth in Antebellum New York City* (Ithaca: Cornell University Press, 1990), pp. 12–24; Wilentz, *Chants Democratic*, pp. 299–301.

50 percent for the 1816–1835 managers). The typical manager began life in a small town, migrated to the big city in his late teens, and took advantage of the burgeoning urban economy to maximize his opportunities and make his fortune.[21]

The men who began regularly attending board meetings between 1837 and 1865 present intriguing difficulties for historians. Thomas Eddy, John Pintard, Richard Varick, William Woolsey, and the other Christian gentlemen who established the American Bible Society provided excellent subjects for pious nineteenth-century biographers. They played important public roles in their communities. Fellow patricians presented their lives and careers as exemplary models for Christian youths. The historical societies that they founded eagerly sought and collected their papers, and great men discoursed on their contributions to preserving social order. Few biographies, however, celebrate the lives and accomplishments of mid-nineteenth-century brokers, insurance men, and investment bankers. One must examine the monotonously constructed corporate histories, the privately printed family pamphlets, the memorial proceedings of boards of trustees, and the occasional newspaper obituaries to reconstruct their existence. The very privatization of their lives and deaths contains one important lesson; occasionally, such sources reveal much more.

Business occupied much of the new managers' time and energy, and their commercial careers present a sharp contrast with those of the pre-1835 board. Approximately half of the earlier managers

21. This analysis is based on the life histories of managers who attended 50 percent or more of the board meetings in any year between 1837 and 1865. Criteria for limiting the sample, as well as the basic sources used to compile biographical data, are discussed in note 5 above. The managers are Frederick S. Winston (1806–1885), Thomas Lowery Servoss (1786–1866), Norman White (1805–1883), Cornelius Du Bois, Jr. (1810–1882), Edward Richardson (1789–1876), Isaac Wood (1793–1868), Nathaniel Richards (n.d.–1855), Samuel A. Foot (1790–1878), Archibald Russell (1811–1871), Alexander Robertson Walsh (1809–1884), John Slosson (1806–1872), James Donaldson (1802–1872), Horace Holden (1793–1862), Frederick T. Peet (1799–1867), Theodore Frelinghuysen (1787–1862), Luther Bradish (1783–1863), Daniel Fanshaw (1789–1865), Abijah P. Cumings (1803–1871), George D. Phelps (1803–1872), James Suydam (1797–1872), Charles E. Tracy (1810–1885), Charles N. Talbot (1802–1874), James W. Dominick, Jr. (1816–1880), Alfred Edwards (1803–1882), Frederick H. Wolcott (1808–1883), Charles Starr (dates unknown), Anson G. Phelps, Jr. (1818–1858), Washington R. Vermilye (1810–1876), Alexander Van Rensselaer (1815–1878), John D. Wolfe (1792–1872), Marshall S. Bidwell (1799–1872), Schureman Halstead (1805–1868), Chandler Starr (1791–1876), Nathan Bishop (1808–1880), and William H. Crosby (1808–1892).

functioned as merchants; only one-third of 1837–1865 board pursued mercantile occupations. A negligible 7 percent of the first group occupied significant positions in insurance, banking, financial, and transportation companies. The percentage jumps to 40 for the newer board members. Qualitatively, their business experiences also differed. These new managers worked longer and harder at their private business concerns than their patrician predecessors had. The mid-nineteenth-century businessman internalized a strong sense of Christian duty, but he typically exhibited his commitments by narrowly and faithfully serving a particular firm rather than broadly attending to the public interest. Benevolent affiliations still conferred status and respectability on businessmen. Philanthropic connections mattered in both a personal and a business sense. Devotion to specific corporate concerns, however, emerges as the most noticeable virtue in the new managers' obituaries.

The lawyers provide a good case study. Barristers composed a higher percentage of the new board (23) than the old (14), but the nature of their legal work was very different from the gentleman-lawyer career pursued by William Jay and his contemporaries. Charles Edward Tracy (1810–1885) for example, served as senior partner in the Wall Street law firm of Tracy, Olmsted and Tracy. Early in his career, Tracy operated a general practice in Utica, New York, but by 1849 he had moved to the metropolis and developed a lucrative legal specialty. His "success and reputation," according to one obituary, derived from his talent for "protecting large corporate interests." Major clients included the Rock Island and Pacific Railroad and the Union Pacific Railroad. Similarly, Samuel Alfred Foot (1790–1878) spent much of his legal career attending to the interests of the New York and Erie Railroad. Cornelius Du Bois (1810–1882) eventually abandoned his law practice to pursue a partnership with a tobacco commission merchant, and Marshall Bidwell (1799–1872) largely confined his legal business to trusts and wills. Specialization, extensive work with a corporate clientele, and participation in the new capitalist economy characterized their careers.[22]

Specialization and devotion to a single enterprise or industry

22. On Tracy, see *National Cyclopaedia of American Biography*, 12:140–141, and *New York Times*, March 15, 1885, p. 2. Foot's career is described in the *National Cyclopaedia of American Biography*, 7:236.

also typified the new merchants. General merchants belonged to the past; commercial entrepreneurs who affiliated with the ABS now traded in more limited types of goods and carried on highly focused enterprises. Thomas Lowery Servoss (1786–1866), John Pintard's son-in-law, dealt primarily in cotton and developed a line of sailing packets that plied the waters almost exclusively between New York and New Orleans. Alexander Robertson Walsh (1809–1884) traded only in hardware, and George Dwight Phelps (1803–1872) concentrated on the expanding drug market. Alfred Edwards (1803–1882), a great-grandson of Jonathan Edwards, nephew of ABS manager Arthur Tappan, and son-in-law of ABS manager Zechariah Lewis (1773–1840), gained fame as "the first merchant in New-York who ventured to carry a stock of silk to the exclusion of other goods." His innovation made him one of the wealthiest merchant-princes in the city.[23]

One newspaper also credited Edwards with creating "the agitation which eventually led to the 'up-town' movement" by relocating his silk store from Pearl Street to Park Place, just west of Broadway, in 1852. Indeed, the mid-nineteenth-century managers experienced a fundamentally new relationship with the city. They exhibited far less interest in reforming, residing in, and supporting the interests of the traditional commercial city than their predecessors had. More than half the new managers died outside Manhattan. Wealthy enclaves like Staten Island and comfortable, fashionable suburbs such as Englewood, New Jersey, seemed more hospitable to their tastes than the disorderly immigrant industrial city New York had become. Many of those who stayed, like Edwards, moved their businesses up Broadway and their residences to Murray Hill.[24]

In the earlier years, the board counted New York City's comptroller, a former mayor, the governor of the state, and several councilmen among its members. By midcentury, few managers held public office, and none exhibited much interest in municipal politics. Abijah P. Cumings (1803–1871), a newspaperman and associ-

23. On Servoss, see *Dictionary of American Biography,* 8:593; on Walsh, see *In Memoriam. A. Robertson Walsh* (Stamford, Conn.: Privately printed, 1884), and entries under his name in New York City directories, 1832–1881; on Phelps, see *Appleton's Cyclopaedia of American Biography,* 25:259; on Edwards, see *New York Times,* September 10, 1882, p. 7.

24. *New York Times,* September 10, 1882, p. 7. On the uptown movement and elite suburbanization, see Edward K. Spann, *The New Metropolis: New York City, 1840–1857* (New York: Columbia University Press, 1981), pp. 101–114, 181–204.

ate of Samuel F. B. Morse, had been "solicited" as a legislative candidate "in days when honest men were more sought for than now," observed an 1871 obituary, but like most Bible men, "he had no taste for a political career." Norman White (1805–1883), a manufacturer and bank director, "took but little public part in the political movements of his day," according to family members. When the managers sought public office, they usually did so in the hopes of advancing specific private interests. Luther Bradish (1783–1863) represented Franklin County in the state legislature for several years, hoping to develop interior navigation, introduce railroads, and incorporate insurance companies, "his object being to bring into market the lands in the town of Moira, in which he had a large interest." Such men sought a favorable political climate for business, but their "public charge" ended there. Municipal politics increasingly revolved around ethnic rivalries, working-class issues, and the saloon. Many wealthy urbanites elected to withdraw from the local democratic fray and concentrate their energies elsewhere. New York City was now first and foremost a place to conduct business.[25]

The new managers' hegemony and the institutional revolution they effected at the ABS did not go unchallenged. Caleb T. Rowe's complaints provide one clue to the magnitude and significance of the changes that had occurred. Rowe (1822–1898) served as the Society's general agent from 1854 until his death forty-four years later. Upon his decease, colleagues at the Bible Society observed that "there was nothing in his life or character so striking as to arrest the attention of the passing world." He seemed a model employee, and his life "moved on its quiet steady course" from youth through old age with few disruptions or controversies. Rowe compiled a remarkable attendance record, and his quiet demeanor impressed fellow administrators, who found him "courteous to all." A lifelong bachelor, the general agent left little outward mark on society, and his memorialist recalled "the neatness of his person and dress, and the orderly distribution of the letters upon his desk and the books upon his table" as the defining characteristics of his tenure. It would appear unlikely that a stable, steady, loyal Victorian employee like Rowe would threaten to resign his office over a pol-

25. On Cumings, see *New York Times,* November 30, 1871, p. 3; on White, see Erskine Norman White, *Norman White: His Ancestors and Descendants* (New York: Printed for Private Distribution, 1905), p. 55; and on Bradish, see *National Cyclopaedia of American Biography,* 3:463, and *New York Times,* September 2, 1863, p. 2.

icy dispute. Yet the mild-mannered general agent contemplated leaving the ABS in 1885.[26]

For several years, Rowe had grown disgruntled with the business methods employed by the managers. A devoted evangelical, he felt uncomfortable with some of the career administrators headquartered at Bible House and with the increasing pressure to produce surpluses and make Bible work profitable. By 1885, seeking a sympathetic ear, he voiced his frustrations to an overseas Bible agent. The ABS needed, in his view, "if possible [to] get back what we have lost—a general interest in the Society's work as a benevolent Society *and that only.*" The Society had steered off course. "Business and bookselling," Rowe believed, must recede to the background and become "merely incidental" to the philanthropic aspect of the Society's work. Fortunately, the general agent believed that a "singular providence" had intervened that might return the American Bible Society to its original purpose. This Divine blessing consisted of the death of one of the Society's longest-lived managers. Frederick S. Winston had been the man whom the career administrators "depended upon to put their plans through" and had emerged as "the Society's leader, having occupied that place for several years." With the death of Winston and the nearly simultaneous demise of corporate attorney Charles Tracy, "who stood next to him & was on the same side," Rowe decided to remain with the Society in the hope that benevolence might once again take precedence over business. Winston had begun his active association with the board in 1838. A detailed examination of his career reveals the distance the ABS had traveled since John Pintard hung his Forty-first Psalm over the doorway of the Bank for Savings in 1819.[27]

Like most of the new managers, Winston spent his early life in a small town. Born at Ballston Spa, near Saratoga Springs, New York, in 1806, he lived his childhood on the family farm. As a child of the early nineteenth century, Winston was educated in a more formal fashion than were earlier generations. Ballston boasted a common school system, and Winston progressed through the lower grades. The family apparently possessed sufficient means to send the promising youngster to an academy in Utica, where he completed his formal training. Farm life in a marginal agricultural region of-

26. "In Memoriam. Caleb T. Rowe," *Bible Society Record,* December 1898, and "The Late Caleb T. Rowe," *Bible Society Record,* January 1899.

27. Caleb T. Rowe to Isaac P. Bliss, April 24, 1885, Isaac P. Bliss Papers, Levant Collection, ABS Archives.

fered few incentives for Winston, and at age fifteen he decided to explore the urban attractions of the nation's most dynamic commercial metropolis.[28]

After arriving in New York in 1821, Winston obtained a clerkship in the dry goods store of Halsted, Haines, and Company. Richard Townley Haines (1795–1870), the firm's founder, also served on the American Bible Society's board of managers, founded the American Tract Society and chaired its financial committee for forty years, and was elected the first president of the board of trustees of Union Theological Seminary in 1837. Winston learned the lessons of business and benevolence at the firm, and apparently thrived in the Christian capitalist environment. He quickly received a series of promotions and eventually became a partner.[29]

Ambitious young businessmen in antebellum cities ultimately hoped to establish their own firms, and before long F. S. Winston and Company, with offices on Pearl Street, appeared in New York City directories. It soon became one of the largest dry goods firms in the metropolis, and by the time of Winston's election to the Bible Society's board, he was one of New York's most respectable businessmen. Membership on the ABS board indicated acceptance by the established Christian business community. In 1846, Winston received another honor. That year, he joined other successful capitalists on the board of directors of the Mutual Life Insurance Company of New York. Although most businessmen viewed such a position as an opportunity to receive some additional dividends and as subordinate to their principal concerns, association with Mutual Life proved to be Winston's economic salvation. Early in the 1850s, unbeknownst to his colleagues, Winston's firm suffered a series of reverses, and his dry goods business nearly failed. Winston responded by orchestrating a coup on the Mutual Life board. Capitalizing on some dissatisfaction with the profitability of the firm, he successfully used proxy voting to fire Mutual Life's president and install himself in this highly paid position. Shortly after Winston gained control over Mutual Life in 1853, F. S. Winston and Com-

28. Biographical details on Winston can be found in "Winston, Frederick Seymour," *National Cyclopaedia of American Biography*, 12:123; *Proceedings of the Board of Trustees of the Mutual Life Insurance Company of New York, in Memory of Frederick S. Winston President of the Company* (New York: Mutual Life Insurance Company, 1885); and *New York Times*, March 29, 1885, p. 3.

29. On Haines, see "Haines, Richard Townley," *Appleton's Cyclopaedia of American Biography*, 3:28.

pany declared bankruptcy. He would spend the remainder of his life attending to the insurance company's corporate interests.[30]

The savings institution, with its promise of moral uplift and dedication to the values of sobriety and thrift, characterized the urban reforms promulgated by New York's patrician Federalists; the life insurance company remains an appropriate legacy for the more mature capitalist society of the mid-nineteenth century. Specialized life insurance companies, in their modern form, did not exist in 1840. By 1853, twelve major companies wrote life policies for thousands of Americans annually. The value of insurance covering the nation's citizenry rose from less than $10 million in 1840 to nearly $164 million twenty years later. The Panic of 1837 taught middle-class Americans some harsh economic lessons. Genteel background, sentimental religion, sobriety, and thrift did not ensure survival in a competitive, individuated economy. Only capital counted, and only substantial accumulations of capital could protect families from seemingly random and impersonal economic forces. Craft knowledge appeared less relevant to a society in which labor constituted the principal commodity; elusive and perplexing virtues such as administrative skill and investment knowledge seemed the only guarantors of middle-class comfort. Perpetuating a family's class status across generational lines and guaranteeing security for one's children required new forms of protection. Life insurance offered Americans a seductive and seemingly safe investment opportunity. When Mutual Life opened its doors at 44 Wall Street in 1843, it proclaimed the dawn of a new age in American capitalist development.[31]

The years spanning Winston's election to the board of Mutual Life in 1846 and his death in 1885 witnessed the birth of the basic principles governing modern life insurance. Mutual developed the concept of the "American Experience Table," or actuarial table, to predict individual mortality and adjust premiums according to "scientifically" compiled statistics. Medical examinations by com-

30. Shepard B. Clough, *A Century of American Life Insurance: A History of the Mutual Life Insurance Company of New York, 1843–1943* (New York: Columbia University Press, 1946), pp. 112–114.

31. Morton Keller, *The Life Insurance Enterprise, 1885–1910: A Study in the Limits of Corporate Power* (Cambridge: Harvard University Press, 1963), pp. 3–11, provides an overview of the development of the life insurance industry in the nineteenth century. Keller portrays Winston as "a cold, overbearing, often arrogant executive." See also Clough, *Century of American Life Insurance*, pp. 8–39.

pany-employed doctors, designed to weed out the aged, the weak, and the infirm; to exact greater premiums from policyholders in hazardous occupations; and to verify that the insured practiced sound living habits became standard procedure. Insurance bureaucrats designed standardized policy applications for hopeful clients and hired a large, specialized headquarters staff consisting of actuaries, premium ticklers, policy examiners, cashiers, bond and mortgage clerks, and policy clerks. Sophisticated and aggressive marketing techniques characterized the industry as full-time traveling "insurance agents" contracted with the home office to peddle life policies in the urban centers.[32]

Winston not only witnessed these developments, but he helped shape Mutual Life into a far-flung national concern. His active implementation of the reforms described above "gave the Mutual a recognition previously unknown among insurance companies," according to one biographer. The president "worshipped size," recalled Mutual Life's corporate historian, and his annual messages to the trustees emphasized territorial expansion and growing cash reserves. He enjoyed pointing out that the company's assets doubled within five years of his assuming the corporate helm. One year before his death, Winston happily announced that "the accumulations of the Company had reached the sum of One Hundred Millions of Dollars," a figure "never before, to our knowledge, attained by any moneyed institution here or elsewhere." He added, almost as an afterthought, "It is a clean pile—large as it is." In his final years, Winston devoted considerable energy to articulating Mutual Life's economic expansion in architectural terms. His final project involved planning and personally supervising every construction detail for a grand, new, powerful Mutual Life Building on the site of the old Murray Street Reformed Church. He died shortly after its completion while in Florida on company business.[33]

How did Winston's corporate colleagues choose to remember their fallen comrade? Richard A. McCurdy, vice-president of Mutual Life at the time of Winston's death, praised the late president by observing that "his life was essentially in and for this Company . . . his heart was here, he reached his official desk with enjoyment

32. Clough, *Century of American Life Insurance*, pp. 13, 40, 109–110.

33. "Winston, Frederick Seymour," *National Cyclopaedia of American Biography*, 12:123; Clough, *Century of American Life Insurance*, p. 197; Frederick S. Winston, *An Address to the Trustees of the Mutual Life Insurance Company of New York* (New York: Mutual Life Insurance Company, 1884), pp. 3–4.

and he left it with regret." Fellow trustee Samuel D. Babcock agreed that "this great Corporation['s] . . . interests so permeated the very tissues of his being, that he found neither opportunity nor inclination to comply with frequent invitations to become identified with the management of other secular organizations." One tribute to Winston noted that he gave "his undivided care to the insurance company of which he was the president." This same memorial conveniently misread his earlier career, concluding that "in his younger days he never allowed any interests to take his attention from the dry goods business." A newspaper obituary reported that, for thirty-two years, Winston daily arrived in the office before 8 A.M. and stayed until well after 4 P.M. The story of Winston's life, observed the *New York Times,* "is practically the history of the Mutual Life Insurance Company."[34]

If participation in public life no longer appeared necessary for the city's "best men," the public role of the corporate concern had become redefined in a peculiar new way. George S. Coe, another Mutual Life trustee, began his tribute to Winston by praising the president's quantitative achievements. The company's capital accumulations, he proudly revealed, "stand to-day equal in amount to the surplus and the combined capital of all the National Banks in this city" and rivaled "the capital of the Bank of England and the Bank of France together." But Coe moved beyond the balance sheet and claimed much more. Mutual Life's influence, he declared, "extends throughout this whole country." One hundred thousand policyholders depended on the company's solvency, and each client was responsible for several dependents. Coe could not even begin to calculate "the actual number dependent upon this Company, whose lives have been interwoven with" that of the late president. Winston "gathered up the small sums received from each of these persons" and successfully brought "comfort and happiness to those who would otherwise have been left destitute." Further, Winston heroically "protected the interests of corporations and municipalities" and, through his sound fiscal policies, "aided in matters of grave importance to this great country."[35]

His corporate colleagues depicted Winston not as the calculating capitalist who methodically seized power at Mutual Life when bad

34. *Proceedings of the Board of Trustees,* pp. 4, 8, 13; *New York Times,* March 29, 1885, p. 3; "Unidentified Newspaper Clipping," in *Proceedings of the Board of Trustees,* p. 15.

35. *Proceedings of the Board of Trustees,* p. 20.

debts nearly forced his own bankruptcy but as a caring, human figure whose devotion to private business constituted the ultimate act of selfless benevolence. Even though standardized applications and medical examinations resulted in the ruthless rejection of those who did not deserve life insurance, Winston's associates claimed that he loved "to personally examine the applications for insurance which were flowing into the office in large numbers." Presiding over the Mutual Life Insurance Company with a firm yet paternalistic hand, Winston was remembered as a great public servant who took an intense personal interest in the objects of his benevolence. According to the corporation's purposeful mythology, all of his business associates "received encouragement from his genial smile, and from the cordial grasp of his hand." As the insurance business grew more routine and impersonal, Winston gave Mutual Life a friendly and neighborly image by mastering the increasingly important corporate managerial techniques of the knowing nod and the hearty handclasp.[36]

One of the men who helped lay Winston's body to rest at Calvary Protestant Episcopal Church on March 28, 1885, was a fifty-seven-year-old insurance executive and Bible Society manager named Henry Augustus Oakley. *Herringshaw's City Blue Book of Biography* in 1917 described this vice-president of the Howard Fire Insurance Company as an "author and biographer," and Oakley had contributed such unmemorable works as "A Christmas Reverie and Other Sketches" to the city's literary press. A historian wishing to make sense of the complex relationship between business and benevolence in the Gilded Age might well ignore Oakley's fiction and turn attention instead to his *Addresses as President of the National Board of Fire Underwriters of the United States,* compiled between 1871 and 1876.[37]

Oakley's reports constituted essentially a diatribe against any public regulation of the insurance industry, repetitive assertions that taxation directed against insurance was "a tax upon the providence of the people," and praise for the National Board of Underwriters. The NBU, under Oakley's leadership, established uniform

36. Ibid., pp. 11, 15.
37. "Oakley, Henry Augustus," *Appleton's Cyclopaedia of American Biography,* 4:548; Mae Felts Herringshaw, ed., *Herringshaw's City Blue Book of Biography: New Yorkers of 1917* (Chicago: Clark J. Herringshaw, 1917); *Addresses as President of the National Board of Fire Underwriters of the United States, on Several Occasions, by Henry A. Oakley* (New York: National Board of Fire Underwriters, 1876).

national rates, examined the books of local agents who attempted to promote "unwholesome competition," and served as an important communications forum for the industry. Oakley took credit for raising the fire insurance "profession at once to a position of dignity" and for helping "systematize the business on a sound and discriminating basis." Ultimately, he proclaimed, "such a record of measures for the welfare of the whole country as we present to you this day [1875] is rarely to be found in the annals of any other public body." The president's rhetoric transformed the National Board from a private lobbying interest to a great public body, inspiring its executives "with noble aims," promoting the "general interest," and constituting "a power for good."[38]

By the time Oakley began attending American Bible Society board meetings in 1871, Frederick Winston and his colleagues had placed the benevolent enterprise on a sound late nineteenth-century business basis. They had accomplished something else in their own private concerns as well. Thomas Eddy had worked as an insurance underwriter in the 1790s, but when he accumulated sufficient money he chose to devote the remainder of his life to benevolent concerns. A republican ideal of civic humanism informed his career, and Eddy effortlessly incorporated a broad range of religious, benevolent, and business enterprises into his life's work. By promoting broad civic improvements such as penitentiaries, hospitals, and the Erie Canal, Eddy both profited personally and advanced the "best" interests of the young republic. Single-mindedly pursuing private profit, without considering the public implications, would appear incomprehensible to this Federalist philanthropist.

Frederick Winston pursued narrower goals with a greater intensity. Christian insurance men in the 1870s lived in a fragmented, socially divided city. For sober Protestant Republican businessmen, "public life" implied Tammany corruption and Irish Catholic Democrats. A socially divided elite could no longer define, let alone pursue, a common "public interest." As New York's best men retreated into their private affairs and Victorian households, they transformed this withdrawal into a Christian virtue. In their minds, private concerns functioned as great corporate benevolences. Ag-

---

38. *Addresses as President of the National Board of Fire Underwriters of the United States on Several Occasions* (New York: N.p., 1876), pp. 4, 6, 8; *Address to the National Board of Fire Underwriters at the Decennial Meeting* (New York: Charles H. Clayton, 1876), p. 40.

gressively pursuing one's own selfish interest adequately served the general welfare. A compulsive, self-conscious devotion to the company was more than an employee's responsibility; it was a highly desirable social trait and a means of serving society as well. Businessmen such as Winston and Oakley aggressively defended their profits and presented their balance sheets as quantitative evidence of Christian virtue. If the dedicated Victorian Christian insurance salesman lined his own pocket in the service of the company, he might remain confident in the knowledge that he simultaneously advanced the interests of his Creator.

A new self-righteous business rhetoric announced the death of civic humanitarianism and the rise of corporate benevolence. On October 22, 1874, when the top executives of New York City's life and fire insurance companies gathered at Delmonico's, on Fifth Avenue and Fourteenth Street, this rhetoric was much in evidence. Cornelius Walford of London, a giant in the British insurance industry, had been touring the United States, and this banquet honored his contributions to the profession. As they paid tribute to themselves and their businesses, Oakley, Winston, and their corporate associates raised their glasses and drank to the following toast: "The Chamber of Life Insurance, representing interests that have the best claims upon the beneficent and humanitarian spirit of our age. This branch of underwriting should be fostered and encouraged by all as the true benefactor of the widow and fatherless, and the promoter of thrift and prudence!"[39]

39. *Banquet in Honor of Mr. Cornelius Walford of London, Given by the Fire and Life Insurance Companies of New York, at Delmonico's, 5th Avenue & 14th Street, October 22, 1874* (New York: New York Economical Printing Company, 1874), p. 20.

3

Local Particularism and National Interests: Creating the Agency System, 1816–1830

Administering a national philanthropy in the young republic presented formidable difficulties. Antebellum American culture was profoundly local and oriented toward the town. The American Bible Society's founders initially believed that they could effect their ambitious plans to Christianize the nation through a voluntary network of county and town auxiliaries, bound to the parent body but retaining some local autonomy. They soon found, however, that such a structure did not provide the regular, predictable cash flow necessary for printing the Scriptures and linking distribution with demand. Eventually, the board settled on a different administrative tool. In the 1820s, the Society began employing paid, traveling agents who argued their case in the growing cities, factory towns, and rural villages of early nineteenth-century America. The use of paid agencies was not an innovative idea. The British and Foreign Bible Society had used this technique early in its institutional life, and every national philanthropy associated with America's antebellum benevolent empire instituted some variation of the agent and auxiliary system.

The origins and growth of the agency system should be examined for several reasons. From a narrow, purely institutional perspective, agents and auxiliaries remained the principal administrative elements of the American Bible Society into the twentieth century. The dynamic relationship between semiautonomous aux-iliaries and paid agents reflects the tension between retaining the organization's loose, voluntaristic structure and adopting a more tightly coordinated bureaucratic plan of action. Most critically, it exposes an important struggle for authority. Protestant philan-thropic enterprises sent paid agents into towns and communities because they could not rely on traditional elites to exercise their moral oversight and leadership responsibilities effectively. Purely local institutions appeared inadequate in an age of mobile men from highly diverse social backgrounds. Benevolent societies in-creasingly relied on their own agents to plead their cause and per-suade others. They helped create an important new social type in nineteenth-century America: the rootless religious professional.[1]

"Concentrated action is powerful action." This deceptively sim-ple statement, issued by the Bible Society's board of managers in their first "Address to the Christian Public" in 1816, masked a radi-cal institutional strategy. United efforts to circulate the Scriptures

1. For general historical accounts of the agent and auxiliary systems see Charles I. Foster, *An Errand of Mercy: The Evangelical United Front, 1790–1837* (Chapel Hill: University of North Carolina Press, 1960), and Clifford S. Griffin, *Their Broth-ers' Keepers: Moral Stewardship in the United States, 1800–1865* (New Brunswick: Rutgers University Press, 1960). These works present a relatively static portrayal of the agent and auxiliary systems and do not examine their historical evolution over the course of the antebellum period.

David F. Allmendinger, *Paupers and Scholars: The Transformation of Student Life in Nineteenth Century New England* (New York: St. Martin's Press, 1975), pp. 65–70, shows that the American Education Society was more sensitive to historical change than Foster and Griffin suggest. His claim that this group (established in 1816) constituted a uniquely new type of organization should be read against the history of the ABS, American Sunday School Union, American Tract Society, and similar institutions, however. Allmendinger also claims that by 1826, "the bureau-cratic structure, the schedules and the loans began to appear as related parts of a single, grand system" (p. 71). I would argue that a much more informal system ex-isted within the American Bible Society, at least until the late 1830s. For a view that deemphasizes the rational, systematic, centralized nature of such organizations in the 1820s, see Paul H. Mattingly's discussion of the School Agents' Society in *The Classless Profession: American Schoolmen in the Nineteenth Century* (New York: New York University Press, 1975), pp. 33–41.

Internal American Bible Society histories include William P. Strickland, *History of the American Bible Society, from Its Organization to the Present Time* (New York: Harper & Brothers, 1849); Henry Otis Dwight, *The Centennial History of the Ameri-can Bible Society* (New York: Macmillan, 1916); and Creighton Lacy, *The Word-Carrying Giant: The Growth of the American Bible Society (1816–1966)* (South Pasa-dena: William Carey Library, 1977).

and Christianize the nation constituted a fundamentally new idea. Although 108 state, county, and town Bible societies functioned from Vermont to Louisiana in 1816, each operated as an independent local entity. Missionary labor traditionally ended at the town line, and few eighteenth-century ministers or pious laymen felt responsible for the unchurched masses outside their congregations.[2]

By 1816, however, some men in the nation's urban centers had begun thinking in new ways. Historian Thomas Haskell has argued that the market revolution that occurred after 1750 produced changes in *"perception* or *cognitive style,"* creating the structural preconditions necessary for the rise of a "humanitarian sensibility." The new entrepreneurial classes, dealing with each other on an international level through the impersonal medium of the market, paid closer attention to the remote consequences of their immediate actions and began feeling personally responsible for events and social conditions beyond the borders of their local communities. Religious historians have placed this consciousness within the context of the Second Great Awakening, linked it with the theology of Samuel Hopkins (1721–1803), and labeled it "disinterested benevolence."[3]

2. American Bible Society Board of Managers, "Address to the People of the United States," May 1816, ABS Archives. On this earlier conception of missionary labor, see Donald M. Scott, *From Office to Profession: The New England Ministry, 1750–1850* (Philadelphia: University of Pennsylvania Press, 1978), pp. 1–17; David Hall, *The Faithful Shepherd: The New England Ministry in the Seventeenth Century* (Chapel Hill: University of North Carolina Press, 1973); and Gregory Singleton, "Protestant Voluntary Organizations and the Shaping of Victorian America," in Daniel Walker Howe, ed., *Victorian America* (Philadelphia: University of Pennsylvania Press, 1976), pp. 47–58.

3. Thomas L. Haskell, "Capitalism and the Origins of the Humanitarian Sensibility, Part I," *American Historical Review* (April 1985), 339–361, and "Capitalism and the Origins of the Humanitarian Sensibility, Part II," *American Historical Review* (June 1985), 547–566. On "disinterested benevolence," the missionary impulse, and Hopkins, see especially Donald Matthews, "The Second Great Awakening as an Organizing Process, 1780–1830: An Hypothesis," *American Quarterly* (Spring 1969), 23–43; Earl R. MacCormack, "An Ecumenical Failure: The Development of Congregational Missions and Its Influence upon Presbyterians," *Journal of Presbyterian History* (December 1966), 266–285; George M. Marsden, *The Evangelical Mind and the New School Presbyterian Experience: A Case Study of Thought and Theology in Nineteenth-Century America* (New Haven: Yale University Press, 1970); Timothy L. Smith, *Revivalism and Social Reform: American Protestantism on the Eve of the Civil War* (Baltimore: Johns Hopkins University Press, 1980); and Oliver Wendell Elsbree, "Samuel Hopkins and the Doctrine of Benevolence," *New England Quarterly* (December 1935), 534–550.

The personal obligation many evangelicals felt by 1816 to create a pious national community of believers is evident in the early reports of the American Bible Society. The 1816 "Appeal" recognized no geographical or political limitations: the Society would extend its mission "to such parts of the world as are destitute of the blessing, and are within our reach." Moral responsibility for accomplishing this task rested with each individual: "Shall *you* hang back in indifference? . . . Let no heart be cold; no hand be idle; no purse reluctant." Ministering "to the blessedness of thousands and tens of thousands, of whom we may never see the faces nor hear the names" constituted a "duty" as well as a goal. Bible work possessed timeless significance, and its good influence would extend well beyond the managers' own lives. They hoped to "set forward a system of happiness" which would proceed with "accelerated motion and augmented vigor" and remain influential "after we shall have finished our career." Always, the board attempted to extend its benevolence as widely as possible and attribute the broadest significance to its words and deeds.[4]

Not all Americans—indeed, not even all pious and benevolently disposed Americans—thought in these terms. Small, parochial, idiosyncratic communities remained the norm in the young republic, and the new voluntary associations would have to respect the peculiarities of local life to enlist Christians in their crusade. Accordingly, the managers of the new religious philanthropies initially operated through the preexisting town and county societies. The American Bible Society's plan for uniting these local, independent organizations into a national federation appeared relatively simple. Each county or town Bible Society must adopt a formal constitution containing a commitment to circulate the sacred Scriptures "without note or comment" and a pledge to turn over its "surplus revenue, after supplying their own districts with the Bible," to the national agency.[5]

The first provision aimed to exclude sectarian associations seeking to promote particular denominational tenets. By reducing Protestant Christianity to its most basic level—the Bible "without note

4. ABS Board of Managers, "Address to the People of the United States," May 1816, ABS Archives.

5. *The Constitution, Charter, and By-Laws of the American Bible Society* (New York: American Bible Society's Press, 1853), p. 3; A Citizen of New York [William Jay], *A Memoir on the Subject of a General Bible Society for the United States of America* (N.p.: N.p., 1816).

or comment"—the ABS hoped to make itself broadly inclusive and avoid denominational and theological controversies. The second requirement reinforced local Bible societies' commitment to supply their own neighborhood needs. Their primary responsibility involved canvassing their localities and assisting the destitute. Only after their community's wants had been satisfied were these organizations required to aid the parent Society. Auxiliaries would unite in a federation of local societies, not subordinate their concerns to the dictates of a full-blown national philanthropy.

The New York office did not formally monitor local societies' progress or regularly examine their books. Joining the American Bible Society might give auxiliary officers a sense of participation in a national cause, but it also reinforced their localism and strengthened the parochial organizations they founded. At local meetings religious leaders could join to set moral policy in an intimate communal setting. The associations' interdenominational character reinforced local elite cohesiveness, and connection with a national philanthropy enhanced their local prestige. Exercising their traditional function of moral oversight, the Bible Society officers might continue perceiving themselves as the political, economic, and religious leaders of integrated, particularistic communities.[6]

In return for committing their surplus funds to the ABS, the auxiliaries could purchase Bibles from the national depository at 5 percent below cost and vote on resolutions at the Society's annual meeting. The latter benefit had little practical value because annual meetings served as public displays for demonstrating solidarity, not as serious policy-making sessions. Governance remained concentrated at the national level, but the records do not indicate that this was a problem in the 1820s. As long as they retained reasonable autonomy, the auxiliaries had little interest in the internal workings of the national society. They went about their business,

6. This discussion of local communities in antebellum America owes much to the synthetic work of Thomas Bender, *Community and Social Change in America* (Baltimore: Johns Hopkins University Press, 1982), esp. pp. 86–108. For a case study of an individual community, see Stuart Blumin, *The Urban Threshold: Growth and Change in a Nineteenth-Century American Community* (Chicago: University of Chicago Press, 1976). Matthews, "Second Great Awakening," suggests ways that national movements strengthened local feeling.

took advantage of the discount, and carried on their affairs much as they had before the American Bible Society was founded.[7]

The early history of one local Bible Society in New Jersey offers some insight into the workings and problems of the auxiliary system. Bloomfield, a small township on the outskirts of Newark, had been settled by pious New Englanders in the eighteenth century. Boasting a spacious and central town common, a dispersed population approaching three thousand by 1820, and sufficiently fertile farmland to support its predominantly agrarian inhabitants, Bloomfield also had a reputation for extraordinary religiosity. Presbyterianism became "identified with the name of the town and with the larger body of the people" by the second decade of the nineteenth century, according to one local historian. Bloomfielders laid their town green in front of the church's lot and built an academy in 1810 to educate pious young men for the Presbyterian ministry.[8]

One might expect the Bible movement to flourish in such a staunchly religious community. The Bloomfield Bible Society drafted its constitution and attained official auxiliary status in February 1817. The town's Presbyterian minister actively promoted Bible Society activities, and fifty-seven leading local churchmen contributed their annual dollar dues in support of the cause. The Society's "Constitution and Minute Book," however, suggests little local interest in affairs outside the township. The ABS defined each auxiliary's function as soliciting funds to circulate the Scriptures "without note or comment." Bloomfield's constitution added a second proviso: "particularly to provide a supply of Bibles for those within their own Neighbourhood who may be found destitute." Further, this New Jersey local established its dues schedule with the understanding that the money "shall be applied to furnish with Bi-

---

7. Report of "The Committee appointed to draft a notice to the Public explaining the principles upon which alone Bible Societies can become Auxiliary to this Society," Minutes of Meeting of the Board of Managers, October 1, 1819, ABS Archives. The founding of the American Bible Society was not greeted with universal support. Bishop John Henry Hobart especially expressed misgivings about the Episcopal church becoming involved in an interdenominational crusade. The Philadelphia Bible Society initially declined to join, largely because its managers objected to the institution being located in New York. See the exchange in *An Answer to the Objections of the Managers of the Philadelphia Bible-Society against a Meeting of Delegates from the Bible Societies in the Union* (Burlington: David Allinson, 1816). The Society seems to have had no serious internal schisms during its first decade.

8. William H. Shaw, *History of Essex and Hudson Counties, New Jersey* (Philadelphia: Everts & Peck, 1884), pp. 858–879, quote on p. 862.

bles such families or Individuals as may be found destitute in this Neighbourhood."[9]

In its first year of operation, the Bloomfield Bible Society purchased twenty-five Bibles and fifty Testaments from the parent Society, supplied the scripturally destitute within its boundaries, and dutifully remitted a $35 surplus to the ABS. Once they had supplied books to the locally needy, however, the managers appeared to lose interest. Contributions were small and irregular. In 1819, the ABS reported only a fifty-cent donation from Bloomfield corresponding secretary Zophar B. Dodd. The auxiliary's minutes for January 2, 1822, noted "but little money collected during the past year and no Bibles purchased." The treasurer reported only $11.38 in the coffers. By 1824, the society's managers could not secure a quorum.[10]

Yet the Bloomfield Bible Society's history should not be read simply as a record of steady decline. When some new and unknown families moved into a relatively unsettled portion of the community in 1820, the Bible Society voted "to make Enquiry in the Northern part of this Township and supply those indigent persons who may be found Destitute." The 1823 annual meeting recorded the purchase of twenty-one Bibles from the parent Society for circulation "among the people of Stone House Planes—a few for the benefit of schools and four or five to the poor in our own congregation." Local crises produced local responses. The Bloomfield Bible Society's records show little evidence, however, that the officers enthusiastically supported broader missionary efforts or that the township's small farmers felt compelled to participate in crusades beyond their own borders.[11]

The ABS's managers grew dissatisfied with auxiliary arrangements almost immediately. Local societies were generally lethargic in contributing to the national ABS. By 1819, the corporate minutes reflected a concern that "the payments from Auxiliaries are less punctual and the amount received on donations has considerably decreased" over the course of three years. Two and one-half years

9. American Bible Society, *Second Annual Report* (1818), provides a list of auxiliaries and dates of their accession. The Bloomfield Bible Society's constitution and minute book are located at the New Jersey Historical Society, Newark.

10. Minutes of Meetings of Bloomfield Bible Society, January 7, 1818, January 2, 1822, 1824, Bloomfield Bible Society Records; Zophar B. Dodd to John Nitchie, February 4, 1819, General Agent's Papers, ABS Archives.

11. Minutes of Meetings of Bloomfield Bible Society, January 10, 1821, January 1, 1823, Bloomfield Bible Society Records.

later, a special committee reported that many auxiliaries simply "hold their annual meetings, hear their reports, pass votes of thanks, disperse to their several places of abode, and engage in their various ordinary pursuits." Local Bible Society officers might appear "gratified upon the whole," but few experienced "that fervor of spirit" which resulted in continuous, regular, "active & vigorous exertions in the great cause of benevolence." Bible work did not occupy a central place in these men's lives. Annual meetings might publicly reaffirm elite solidarity and demonstrate their commitment to doing good, but relatively few auxiliary officers continued the work throughout the year. Indeed, when the Bible Society sought to relieve its financial distress in 1819 by writing "many respectable individuals in different parts of the country, with the hope of obtaining their assistance and cooperation," they received no responses.[12]

The managers recognized that they competed for support with other philanthropic and benevolent organizations. As was true in Bloomfield, on a local level they also competed with parish churches and town-based missionary endeavors. Societies to reform morals, support foreign missions, encourage temperance, foster education, and distribute tracts flourished along the Atlantic seaboard. The managers acknowledged in 1819 that even "the most liberal are scarcely able to answer every demand." The same people held offices in many of these societies, and, after all, benevolence was a part-time activity. A particular disadvantage, the ABS managers observed, was that "many of these institutions rise near home, and make early impressions and hold forth importunate claims upon the assistance of the pious and benevolent in their neighborhood." Local claims always took precedence, and the ABS, headquartered in New York, appeared "more remote, and of course, not so immediately in view, not much more than the gleanings of charity." Many town elites failed to respond to demands beyond their localities.

Further, the managers admitted, "the mode of address by epistolary correspondence" had proven a "less efficacious" fund-raising tool than anticipated. Authority in local communities still depended on face-to-face relationships and personal demonstrations of char-

12. Minutes of Meeting of the Board of Managers, June 3, 1819; Minutes of Meeting of the Auxiliary Society Committee, March 7, 1822, November 1819, ABS Archives.

acter. Perhaps the managers needed to make "a personal application" for money, rather than rely on their circulars and written
appeals. In sum, although the managers in New York had internalized the impersonal values and lessons of the marketplace and cultivated a broad "humanitarian sensibility," traditional notions of
status and custom held sway among local elites in smaller, more
isolated communities.[13]

Local particularism created a serious cash flow problem. The
ABS counted on a continual, regular, predictable flow of capital into
New York to carry on its work. It obtained market information from
the auxiliaries so that the managers might ship the Scriptures to
truly needy and destitute areas. Further, the ABS expected these
local organizations to provide approximately five-sixths of the parent Society's total annual income. Effective planning and bud-
geting clearly required a stronger auxiliary system.[14]

The managers' solution—paid, traveling agents who would
"pass through the U. States and their territories, soliciting donations and subscriptions, reporting on the State of morals and
religion, collecting information for the Board, and establishing
Auxiliary Societies"—eventually transformed the nature of Bible
work. Agents, the board hoped, would provide the personal touch
lacking in the Society's formal correspondence, dry financial appeals, and published monthly extracts. Their temporary presence
in a community might help contributors and auxiliary officers associate the distant, impersonal American Bible Society with a specific face and personality. The Society described its emissaries'
missions in personal, emotional terms: an agent "warms the feelings," "animates the zeal," and provides "a personal application."
Agents created public social events in the towns they visited. They
served as guest preachers in the churches, breaking the often dull
and formal Sunday routines. As strangers and objects of curiosity,
they linked local efforts with a vast and powerful national movement. Personally courting and soliciting the town's leading citizens, they offered the face-to-face contact essential for success in a

13. Minutes of Meeting of Auxiliary Society Committee, November 1819, ABS Archives.
14. Minutes of Meeting of the Auxiliary Society Committee, April 6, 1819, ABS
Archives.

predominantly oral culture. They linked the intimacy of the neighborhood with the needs of the national organization.[15]

Ultimately agents worked for the central office in New York. The auxiliary society committee reminded its first agent, Ward Stafford, in 1820 that his principal purpose was "to aid the American Bible Society, by enlarging their funds and multiplying their friends and assistants in accomplishing the great objects of their institutions." Historians have described antebellum America's national Protestant philanthropies as rational, systematic, and centralized. The actual workings of the agency system during the 1820s suggests a different vocabulary: informal, haphazard, idiosyncratic. Systematic organization came later in response to specific historical circumstances. In the beginning, things functioned quite differently.[16]

Between 1820 and 1830, the managers gradually defined and refined the agents' tasks and responsibilities. The ABS employed forty Bible agents during this decade. Their length of tenure with the Society tended to be very short. Only two remained for more than five years; 70 percent devoted less than two years to the Bible cause. Fifty-eight percent lasted less than a year, and terms were often considerably shorter. Robert Baird (1798–1863) received an appointment "for a few weeks" in 1827 to revive auxiliaries in New Jersey; Macaiah Fairfield (1786–1858) spent four and one-half weeks in the Miami, Ohio, area in 1830; Isaac Reed (ca. 1790–1858) offered his services "for part of his time in the quarter where he resides" and labored for twenty-eight days raising funds in Essex County, New York, in May 1830. Three-month and six-month appointments were most frequent. Bible work constituted a brief

15. Minutes of Meeting of the Board of Managers, October 1, 1818, ABS Archives. Minutes of Meeting of the Auxiliary Society Committee, November 1819. See Bender, *Community and Social Change in America*, pp. 88–92.

16. "Instructions of the Auxiliary Society Committee to the Revd. Ward Stafford," Minutes of Meeting of the Auxiliary Society Committee, November 15, 1820. For historians' characterizations of the "benevolent empire," see Griffin, *Their Brothers' Keepers;* Paul Boyer, *Urban Masses and Moral Order in America, 1820–1920* (Cambridge: Harvard University Press, 1978), pp. 3–64; David Paul Nord, "The Evangelical Origins of Mass Media in America, 1815–1835," *Journalism Monographs*, no. 88 (Columbia: University of South Carolina, 1984). For an analysis of the social control literature, see Lois W. Banner, "Religious Benevolence as Social Control: A Critique of an Interpretation," *Journal of American History* (June 1973), 23–41; and Ralph E. Luker, "Religion and Social Control in the Nineteenth-Century American City," *Journal of Urban History* (1976), 363–368.

interlude in a clergyman's career and implied no permanent commitment on the part of employer or employed. Agents typically returned to pastoral labor after concluding their Bible Society obligations. Only one received a very temporary administrative appointment with the ABS.[17]

The Society established no formal mechanism for selecting agents or defining their territories. A "Subcommittee on Procuring Agents" suggested in 1827 "that a correspondence be opened with our Theological Seminaries, or that they be visited by persons from

17. Much of the following discussion is based on biographical information for the forty Bible agents active between 1820 and 1830. The ABS kept no central list of agents. I compiled a list by combing the Minutes of the Board of Managers and Auxiliary Society Committee between 1816 and 1830. The minutes indicated when an agent was appointed and when he left, as well as summarizing any correspondence between him and the board or corresponding secretaries. Biographical information was obtained from biographical catalogs from colleges and seminaries, particularly those from Princeton Theological Seminary, Andover Theological Seminary, Auburn Theological Seminary, Colgate University, Union Theological Seminary, and Middlebury College. Franklin Bowditch Dexter's *Biographical Sketches of the Graduates of Yale College, with Annals of the College History* (New Haven: Yale University Press, 1912) was useful for pre-1815 Yale graduates. The clergy card file at the Methodist Commission on Archives and History at Drew University provided an index to obituaries in the General Conference minutes.

The forty Bible agents on which this analysis is based are Robert Baird (1798–1863), James C. Barnes (1789–1865), Isaac C. Beach (1803–1873), Samuel D. Blythe (1804–1843), Artemas Boies (1792–1844), George Boyd (1788–1850), Joseph S. Christmas (1803–1830), Richard Corwin (1789–1843), Samuel L. Crosby (dates unknown), George B. Davis (1790–1852), Patrick W. Dowd (1799–1866), Nathaniel Dwight (1770–1831), William Eagleton (dates unknown), Elias Riggs Fairchild (1801–1878), Macaiah Fairfield (1786–1858), Robert Gibson (1792–1829), Daniel Gould (1789–1834), Samuel Lyle Graham (1794–1851), Richard D. Hall (dates unknown), Samuel Carnahan Jennings (1803–1885), Andrew M. Keith (1802–1882), Eleazer Lathrop (?–1834), Jason Lothrop (1790–1870), Sumner Mandeville (1800–1880), Nicholas Patterson (1792–1865), John Mason Peck (1789–1857), Alexander M. Proudfit (1770–1843), Isaac Reed (ca. 1790–1858), Greenbury W. Ridgeley (1798–1883), Samuel Robinson (dates unknown), Henry A. Rowland (1804–1859), George Sheldon (of Ohio) (1797–1873), Thomas Shepard (1792–1879), Ward Stafford (1788–1856), William W. Stevenson (1768–1857), Herbert C. Thompson (dates unknown), Jared Bell Waterbury (1799–1876), Henry White (1800–1850), Simon Wilmer (1779–1840), and Denis M. Winston (1801–1840).

Quotations in this paragraph are from Minutes of Meeting of the Board of Managers, September 5, 1827; Macaiah Fairfield to John C. Brigham, July 20, 1830, and Isaac Reed to John C. Brigham, May 27, 1827, Corresponding Secretary's Papers; Minutes of Meeting of the Board of Managers, May 1, 1828, ABS Archives. Sumner Mandeville received an appointment in the ABS secretary's office in 1831.

the Board," but the ABS rarely solicited individuals. Typically, a theological student, settled pastor, or minister without a charge would approach the managers and request a temporary appointment. Applicants might present an introductory letter from a prominent clergyman or relation, but many appeared virtually unknown. Typically they defined their own territories and routines. Ward Stafford, for example, worked extensively with seamen and mariners in New York City before approaching the Society with his plan to form marine Bible societies along the Atlantic Coast in 1820. Joseph Christmas (1803–1830), a Presbyterian pastor in New York, planned to travel south on the advice of a physician in 1828 and requested a brief Bible agency in New Orleans to help defray his expenses. James C. Barnes (1789–1865), a clergyman in Paint Lick, Kentucky, received authorization "to act as the agent of the American Bible Society, as he may find time, in the region where he resided" in March 1827. Such initiatives came from outside the board and reflect a decentralized, haphazard approach to Bible work instead of the systematic, well-coordinated operation one might expect from historians' accounts.[18]

Informal arrangements persisted after the agency began. No contract bound Bible agent to Bible Society. An agent might stop work if he received a call to a parish or if contributions fell below expectations. The board required no record keeping, only asking the agent to "inform the chairman of the [auxiliary] committee from time to time, of the progress he makes and the success he meets with." A brief monthly narrative letter more than sufficed. Further, the Society kept no records relating to its own agents. As late as 1837, the committee on agencies found it necessary to prepare "a succinct statement of the present condition of the Agencies of the Society, the names of the Agents, the districts in which they are labouring, the date and duration of their commission, and their compensation." No such effort had ever been attempted, and the

18. Minutes of Meeting of the Auxiliary Society Committee, April 5, 1827, ABS Archives; Dexter, "Ward Stafford," in *Biographical Sketches of the Graduates of Yale College*, 6:496–499; Gardiner Spring, *Moses on Nebo: or Death a Duty: A Sermon Occasioned by the Death of the Rev. Joseph S. Christmas, Late Pastor of the Bowery Presbyterian Church in the City of New York* (New York: John P. Haven, 1830); Minutes of Meeting of the Board of Managers, March 19, 1827, ABS Archives.

ABS could not state with certainty, at any given moment in time, who labored in the field.[19]

Bible agents came from diverse backgrounds. Two-thirds claimed affiliation with the Presbyterian or Congregational church. Yet the predominantly "Presbygational" board of managers reached out to others as well: seven Baptists, four Episcopalians, and two Methodists also worked in the Bible movement. Nearly half of the thirty-three agents whose place of birth is known were from New England or upstate New York. Six others had been born in rural sections of New Jersey and Pennsylvania, and three grew up in Kentucky. Few southerners appeared interested in Bible work, and only three agents were born in a city. Twenty-seven of the forty received formal theological training; Princeton (eleven) and Andover (seven) were the most popular seminaries. The twenty-nine agents for whom a college choice is known attended seventeen different institutions. Only Yale (six) and Hamilton (three) produced more than two agents. Common stereotypes about missionary workers fresh out of theological school who sought some experience before embarking on a lengthy pastorate do not hold up completely. Agents ranged in age from twenty-two to sixty-two, with thirty-four as the average beginning age. Still, the median age was thirty-one, and approximately one-third were under twenty-seven when they entered the Society's employ. Eight agents began their ecclesiastical careers with the American Bible Society.[20]

The composite portrait that emerges from these statistics is one of a Bible agent who grew up in a rural northern town, attended college near his home, received some theological seminary training, undertook a Bible agency relatively early in his career, served for a very short time, and subsequently returned to pastoral labor. This overview, however, simplifies reality, fails to address adequately the profound changes affecting young men entering religious life in the 1820s, and conveys little sense of the complex social dynamics that prompted some men to work for the Bible cause. After carefully surveying the lives and careers of the forty ministers and preachers who successfully sought Bible agencies in the 1820s, I have selected three for more detailed scrutiny.

Alexander Proudfit, Sumner Mandeville, and Robert Baird do not

19. "Instructions of the Auxiliary Society Committee to the Revd. Ward Stafford," Minutes of Meeting of the Auxiliary Society Committee, November 15, 1820; Minutes of Meeting of the Committee on Agencies, May 19, 1827, ABS Archives.

20. This analysis is based on the careers of the men mentioned in note 17.

constitute "typical" agents. Rather, they represent the diversity and broad spectrum of men who labored for the Bible cause in the 1820s. Further, each illustrates an important experience shared by many contemporaries in religious work. Proudfit's life and work appear profoundly atypical in the world of Jacksonian America. His story begins in the eighteenth century, and his reaction was that of an older ministerial generation responding to new notions of "disinterested benevolence." Mandeville and Baird illuminate the educational and social diversity of men entering the ministry in the early nineteenth century, and their careers contain suggestive implications for the future of nineteenth-century Protestantism. Considered together, these three American lives chart the beginnings of a "great transformation" that would affect religion, no less than every other aspect of American life, in the decades ahead.

Alexander Moncreif Proudfit was born in Pequa, Pennsylvania, the son of a Scotch Presbyterian minister, in 1770. His father, James, who emigrated from Perth in 1754, was in the midst of a twenty-four-year pastorate at Pequa when Alexander was born. In 1783, the elder Proudfit accepted a call from Presbyterians in Salem, New York, and he remained pastor in that town until his death in 1802. James Proudfit emphasized traditional education, and Alexander began studying ancient languages at a classical school opened in Salem by Thomas Watson, another Scottish émigré. In 1785, the younger Proudfit was sent to Hackensack, New Jersey, where Peter Wilson (1746–1825), a graduate of the University of Aberdeen, conducted a famous academy and elite training school. Proudfit moved to New York City in 1789 to enter the sophomore class at Columbia College and board with Wilson's family.[21]

Around this time, Proudfit publicly professed his religion and announced his intention to study for the ministry. After graduating from Columbia in 1792, he returned home to Salem and spent one year "in quiet study and devotion among his father's old books." The Presbyterian Synod of 1786 had recommended that young men interested in the ministry "procure from their teachers proper testimonials of their acquaintance with human literature, and that they attend the lectures of the Reverend Dr. Livingston." Accordingly, Proudfit returned to New York in 1793 to attend John H.

21. The principal source on Alexander Proudfit is John Forsyth, *Memoir of the Late Rev. Alexander Proudfit, D.D., with Selections from His Diary and Correspondence, and Recollections of His Life &c. by His Son* (New York: Harper & Brothers, 1846).

Livingston's divinity lectures at the Dutch Reformed Protestant Church and continue his study. In 1794, he received a license to preach from the Washington, New York, Presbytery and began work as his father's assistant at the Salem parish. Proudfit would remain at Salem for the next thirty-nine years.[22]

Several aspects of Proudfit's ministerial training merit attention: the use of a Scottish immigrant educational network to train promising young men for elite leadership, the relatively informal and unsystematic nature of theological education, and the prospective theologian's immersion in secular institutions and communities. Proudfit was not secluded in a theological seminary with like-minded young men. He subsequently described "the state of religion among his fellow-students" at Columbia as "wretchedly low" and recalled that the environment produced "a sad declension in his own spiritual life." The eighteenth-century minister remained exposed to, and constantly cognizant of, such evil secular influences throughout his youth and early adulthood. Proudfit's father continued performing all the regular duties of a country pastor while instructing his son, thus providing a practical introduction to church life. Study under Livingston involved residence in a major metropolitan and commercial center and exposure to the demands of an urban ministry. The entire course of ministerial training prepared the young man for practical church work in a broad community context.[23]

The eighteenth-century pastor also pursued a broad range of intellectual interests. The heavy classical emphasis might seem narrow to a twentieth-century observer, but Proudfit's mind wandered over a wide philosophical terrain. In a sermon before the Middlebury College Charitable Society for Educating Indigent Youth for the Gospel Ministry in 1817, he outlined his recipe for an adequate theological education: knowledge of languages, a "profound acquaintance" with natural history, and broad attention to civil as well as ecclesiastical history. Deprecating "the opinion entertained and avowed by some, that human literature is unnecessary for those who 'labor in the gospel,'" he cast his lot with the advocates of a learned and broadly educated ministry. All knowledge, of course, served to reinforce biblical truth, and the Good Book functioned as "the Sun which enlightens and cherishes the whole system." Other

22. Ibid., pp. 27–28.
23. Ibid., p. 22.

branches of knowledge served as "satellites revolving and shining in their respective orbits." Still, comprehensive knowledge of the physical sciences and secular pursuits was essential for a man entering religious life in the 1790s.[24]

Ultimately, all this education constituted preparation for a public role firmly rooted in community and locality. When John Forsyth, pastor of the Union Church in Newburgh, New York, compiled his *Memoir of the Late Rev. Alexander Proudfit, D.D.* in 1846, he shrewdly began with a description of the town of Salem. Located in "one of the loveliest valleys of Northern New-York," this quiet farming village skirted the Vermont border. Proudfit drew liberally upon "the objects and occupations of rural life" in his sermons and spent nearly fifty years amid this scene "of rich and quiet rural beauty" surrounded by the Green Mountains. After his father's death in 1802, Alexander Proudfit immediately succeeded to the same pulpit. Proudfit ministers thus communed with Salem residents for fifty consecutive years at this Presbyterian altar. Alexander further cemented his civil standing and social status by marrying Susan Williams, daughter of the wealthiest man in Salem and the largest landholder in Washington County. Contemporaries remembered their household as a center of local culture and intellectual life. Proudfit expended considerable energy in his ministry, moving beyond the church to exert influence in town and county affairs. He watched over Salem's common schools, emphasized pastoral visitation, conducted outdoor prayer meetings, and traveled the county saving souls. Proudfit derived his social authority from traditional sources: lengthy residence in the community, rigorous yet informal intellectual training, a well-chosen marriage into a prominent family. The stable, orderly village of Salem paid Proudfit the requisite deference, and he proudly presided over its public rituals.[25]

In his sermons, Proudfit frequently spoke on the theme of public service, including participation in the great benevolent enterprises of the age, all of which Proudfit enthusiastically supported. He

24. Alexander Proudfit, *The Extent of the Missionary Field: A Call for the Increase of Missionary Labourers* (Middlebury Vt.: Frederick P. Allen, 1817); Proudfit, *Ministerial Labour and Support: A Sermon Preached at Middlebury, Vermont, February 21, 1810, at the Ordination of Mr. Henry Davis, and His Induction as President of the College* (Salem, N.Y.: Dodd & Ramsey, 1810), p. 8.

25. Forsyth, *Memoir,* p. 9; *The Salem Book: Records of the Past and Glimpses of the Present* (Salem, N.Y.: Salem Review Press, 1896), pp. 84–85.

helped found the Northern Missionary Society at Troy and the American Tract Society. He served as a manager of the American Board of Commissioners for Foreign Missions, the United and Foreign Missionary Society, and the Washington Bible Society, as well as being "one of the earliest and warmest friends of the American Society for meliorating the condition of the Jews." Such efforts constituted part of his public responsibility to serve as an effective community "watchman." The managers of the American Bible Society acknowledged his social leadership and status by asking Proudfit in 1829 to help them raise funds in their two-year campaign to supply the world with the Word of God. Characteristically, he accepted their call.[26]

Venturing forth into New England, upstate New York, and Ohio with his ABS Commission, Proudfit exercised another public responsibility. But the benevolent world of 1829 differed significantly from late eighteenth-century Salem. Henry Augustus Rowland (1804–1859), a much younger Bible agent, who chose to spend his ecclesiastical career in a series of large and prestigious urban parishes, greeted Proudfit's efforts with cynicism. Writing from Bridgeport, Connecticut, in July 1829, he suggested that "much more good might be effected by the *Great Agent* Dr. Proudfit" if he were accompanied by an agent "who is acquainted with the *practical business* of organizing these Societies." Stirring discourses, in Rowland's view, accomplished little if not accompanied by *"systematic exertion."* Proudfit proved extraordinarily successful in presenting the Bible cause at Salem and Washington County; outside his immediate milieu he received a less enthusiastic reception. A

26. Proudfit outlined his public conception of the ministry in *Ministerial Labour and Support*, pp. 19–20; "An Address Delivered to the Students of Theology at the Seminary in New York," ibid., pp. 31–35; and especially *The Duties of the Watchman Upon the Walls of Zion* (Salem, N.Y.: H. Dodd, 1822). Forsyth, *Memoir*, p. 232. Financial arrangements for Proudfit's agency are not clear. Corresponding Secretary John Brigham, summarizing a letter he wrote to Proudfit on May 5, 1829, noted only that the "Aux[iliary]. Soc[iety]. Com[mittee]." would address the issue of compensation and "settle this point when he comes to New York in May" (Letter Book, Corresponding Secretary's Papers, ABS Archives). The ABS's standing committee, which approved all the agency's disbursements, noted only one $100 remittance to Proudfit on October 9, 1829, suggesting that he received minimal compensation, primarily to defray traveling expenses. Agency expenditures were a small percentage of the Society's overall budget at this time, accounting for slightly over $5,000 of approximately $170,000 in expenditures in 1829 (Minutes of Meeting of Standing Committee, 1817–1836, ABS Archives; ABS, *Fourteenth Annual Report* [1830], pp. 60–61).

younger ministerial generation was beginning to find that traditional notions of deference and public duty did not secure their parishioners' submission. More "systematic" techniques of persuasion appeared to be in order.[27]

Public guardianship transcended one's own town and parish, and the new generation willingly abandoned their ministerial charges to realize broader evangelical goals. Alexander Proudfit's generation, of course, created the new national philanthropies in which many of these young men found homes. Yet his contemporaries did so without sacrificing their traditional notions of hierarchy and community. Proudfit's biographer captured the essential paradox: "He was the pastor of what was then a secluded country congregation. Yet, in the comparative solitude of Salem, he seems to have been awake to the calls of the stirring age in the midst of which we now [1846] are [and] deeply sensible of the responsibilities growing out of the character of the times in which he lived." Proudfit died in 1843. He spent the last nine years of his life as secretary of the New York Colonization Society, which had become socially irrelevant by the time of his death.[28]

Sumner Mandeville (1800–1880) possessed little sense of place and few roots. For most of his life, he did not know the town of his birth but remembered only "the howling of wolves, and seeing deer and other wild animals" in "an almost unbroken wilderness" somewhere in south central New York. His father's marginal farm proved inadequate to support the family, and from age six Mandeville boarded with a series of friends and distant relatives in the area of Granby and South Hadley, Massachusetts. He subsequently recalled that from 1806 through 1813 "I knew not what it was to have a home" and could "scarcely refrain from weeping" when other children spoke of their mothers. He did learn the lessons of hard physical labor. At age seven, he recalled "having to ride a horse before oxen in ploughing or dressing out corn, until I had sores as large as my hands, and could scarcely walk." Formal edu-

27. Henry A. Rowland to John C. Brigham, August 22, 1829, Corresponding Secretary's Papers, ABS Archives. On Rowland, see *Memorial of the Life and Services of the Late Henry A. Rowland, D.D., Pastor of the Park Presbyterian Church, Newark, N.J., with the Sermon Preached at His Funeral by E. R. Fairchild* (New York: M. W. Dodd, 1860).

28. Forsyth, *Memoir*, p. 105.

cation proceeded haphazardly; occasionally he attended Massachusetts district schools during unproductive winter months.[29]

By 1813, the elder Mandeville had remarried and settled on a three-hundred-acre farm in Bradford County, Pennsylvania. Sumner and two sisters left Granby to join him that winter, but the family patriarch soon "met with some heavy afflictions, and sunk down in despondency, scarcely leaving the house for months." Sumner Mandeville assumed charge of the Pennsylvania farm for the next four years, managing also to spend a few more months in district school and take advantage of a lending library in nearby Wysox. In 1817, he convinced his father to let him return to Massachusetts and began a three-hundred mile journey on foot with but "a loaf of bread, and cheese, and all I possessed in a pack on my back," as well as fifteen dollars in shinplasters which "were issued for local circulation, and had no value far from home."[30]

Upon his arrival in Granby, Mandeville immediately hired out to work on a farm for a year, boarded with his uncle, and used his earnings "to pay some debts of father's, he having moved down the Susquehanna below Harrisburgh, to a place called Bainbridge." In 1818, he walked from Granby to Bainbridge, stayed a few months, then returned to Massachusetts. Spring 1819 found him back at Bainbridge, having been hired out by his father to labor for "a Mr. Salderman." One year later, he returned to Bradford County. At Wysox, Mandeville obtained a job carding wool, was "engaged to cut cord wood," and conducted a district school in his spare time. There, in the Pennsylvania woods, at age twenty-one, he found religion.[31]

Mandeville's life contained none of the stability, rootedness, or sense of place so evident in the biography of Alexander Proudfit. Born into rural poverty, he worked hard from age six and kept on the move. He remained bound to his father in a precarious state of semidependence. Mandeville assumed responsibility for the family debts, and his father often hired him out to ease his own burdens. Rather than the ambitious young man on the make so central to Jacksonian mythology, Mandeville was a young man who barely made ends meet. Historians working with antebellum census data have discovered remarkably high geographical mobility in early

29. *Autobiography of Rev. Sumner Mandeville, Masonville, N.Y.*, Intro. by Rev. G. P. Nichols (Bainbridge, N.Y.: Republican Power Presses, 1882), pp. 7, 9.
30. Ibid., pp. 10–12.
31. Ibid., pp. 13, 16.

nineteenth-century America and have hypothesized the existence of a migratory underclass, floating from town to town but failing to find economic success. The last place one might expect to find such a person would be in a Presbyterian pulpit. But the social composition of the American ministry underwent a profound transformation in the 1820s. Organizations like the American Education Society (founded in 1816) began recruiting poorer men from marginal agricultural areas in New England and upstate New York. In the process, they helped unravel the delicate weave of family, community, and elite deference that bound the social world of Alexander Proudfit.[32]

Sumner Mandeville's problems did not end when he decided to pursue a religious vocation. He balanced a tiring regimen of farming, district school teaching, and classical studies. His father, now living on a seventy-acre farm in Monroeton, again asked Sumner to "come home and help him" in 1822, but the young man decided he must pursue a steady course if he hoped to realize his religious plans. Finally, a revival preacher who had been instrumental in Mandeville's conversion put him in touch with a Northumberland parish that wanted to sponsor some poor young man for the ministry. After a few more years of part-time study at a classical school, part-time teaching, and organizing prayer meetings in western Pennsylvania, he placed himself under the Northumberland Presbytery and commenced the formal study of theology. In 1826, however, the presbytery refused to grant him a license. As Mandeville noted, the elders found that "I held a general, instead of a limited, atonement." Not completely discouraged, he set out for Maryville Seminary in Tennessee for further formal study.[33]

Young men like Sumner Mandeville created a serious problem for early nineteenth-century presbyteries and congregations. Indigent youth from throughout the United States, moved by the spirit of revival after 1790, sought careers in the ministry. Because they

32. On geographical mobility, see Michael B. Katz, *The People of Hamilton, Canada West: Family and Class in a Mid-Nineteenth-Century City* (Cambridge: Harvard University Press, 1975), pp. 94–175. See also Stephan Thernstrom and Peter Knights, "Men in Motion: Some Data and Speculations about Urban Population Mobility in Nineteenth-Century America," *Journal of Interdisciplinary History* (Autumn 1971), 7–35; Joseph F. Kett, *Rites of Passage: Adolescence in America, 1790 to the Present* (New York: Basic Books, 1977), pp. 96–102.

For the social composition of the ministry see Allmendinger, *Paupers and Scholars*, and Scott, *From Office to Profession*, pp. 52–62.

33. *Autobiography of Sumner Mandeville*, pp. 29–33.

were not bound by ties of family and community, occupied a marginal social status, and possessed none of the traditional trappings of ministerial authority, their suitability for the work could not be judged in conventional ways. A crisis of character ensued. Just as antebellum advice books warned young men entering the cities about the dangers of confidence men, hucksters, and hypocrites, the religious world required a new standard by which to gauge orthodoxy. After Presbyterians and Congregationalists created theological seminaries, young men could not prepare for religious labor in traditional ways. Now they were isolated in formal temples of learning, absorbed lectures in a "systematic theology," and pursued their studies far removed from community and family. Upon completing his course, the seminarian emerged as a man of character, objectively qualified to practice his craft. He became reliable.[34]

Officers of benevolent societies, as well as congregations and presbyteries, began looking to the seminary for help. ABS corresponding secretary John C. Brigham wrote to Maryville Seminary in December 1828 seeking a Bible agent for the upper South. One professor recommended Mandeville, who had been licensed and ordained earlier that year, and the young man took to the road to begin a new challenge. During the next two years he covered seven hundred miles on horseback, traveling through Tennessee, Arkansas, and West Virginia. Mandeville proved a reliable agent, communicating frequently with New York and making an earnest effort to help supply the nation with Bibles. His letters offered vivid testimony to the difficulties facing a stranger attempting to establish his authority in a foreign land. In Hardiman County, Tennessee, "I likewise met with a good deal of opposition. The wealth, talent & influence of this place are almost wholly on the infidel side"; at Paperville, in the same state, "11 o'clock was the hour—only three individuals besides females attended"; in Sullivan County, visited "the farmers in their fields—& met with more virulent abuse, than in any other place." By 1830, he acknowledged the hard life of the agent: "It would not be a very pleasant undertaking, to one whose heart was not fully in the cause—to go to a man's hut & ask him if

34. Antebellum advice literature is treated in Kett, *Rites of Passage*, pp. 102–107; Allan Stanley Horlick, *Country Boys and Merchant Princes: The Social Control of Young Men in New York* (Lewisburg: Bucknell University Press, 1975), pp. 147–178; and Karen Halttunen, *Confidence Men and Painted Women: A Study of Middle-Class Culture in America, 1830–1870* (New Haven: Yale University Press, 1982), pp. 1–55. On seminaries, see Scott, *From Office to Profession*, pp. 63–64.

he had a Bible, when you know that if he is offended—he would almost as soon shoot you—as to shoot one of the wild beasts that prowls in the forest around his dwelling."[35]

In May 1831, Mandeville visited Perth Amboy, New Jersey, where his father now resided. He took advantage of his proximity to New York to attend an American Bible Society annual meeting. The managers, impressed with this young man, offered him a position in the secretary's office conducting the correspondence and preparing for board meetings. He accepted and labored out of the New York office for the next year or so. A more modern man might have seized the main chance, worked his way up through the Bible Society hierarchy, and eventually become a corresponding secretary. Mandeville did not. Within a year he was on the road again, stimulating auxiliaries and starting revivals. A string of pastorates followed: Hanover, New Jersey; La Grange, New York; Poughkeepsie, New York. Finally, in 1866, he found himself in Masonville, Delaware County, New York. Visiting some family in Chenango County, he discovered "to my utter surprise . . . that [Masonville] was the very place where I was born—some persons were living who knew my father." He began a ministry in Masonville and spent the last fourteen years of his life there. At age sixty-six, Mandeville finally found the town of his birth.[36]

Mandeville's life teaches several important lessons. The random, idiosyncratic nature of his movements appears foreign to the modern sensibility. He had no notion of career as a series of related, upward movements through hierarchically arranged occupations and statuses. He sought a ministerial life but rejected the earlier ideal of the settled pastorate, moving constantly and attaching himself permanently to no community. His attempts to establish authority and leadership as a Bible agent met with limited success. Mandeville never perfected the techniques of gaining confidence and arousing a community of strangers. Ultimately, he found a home in the town of his birth. Family and local connections meant something, even in 1866. He appears in our story as a transitional figure. His world differed radically from the ordered, hierarchical eighteenth-century society of Alexander Proudfit. He had not com-

35. Sumner Mandeville to John C. Brigham, July 22, 1829, and February 23, 1830, Corresponding Secretary's Papers, ABS Archives.
36. *Autobiography of Sumner Mandeville*, pp. 49–50.

pletely made the accommodation to modernity so evident in the life of the next Bible agent we will examine.[37]

Robert Baird was born in rural Fayette County, Pennsylvania, in 1798. Like Mandeville, he "was introduced to the rugged labors of the field as soon as he was capable of being thus employed," and his early formal training consisted of some irregular attendance at district schools. Baird enjoyed material comfort and family stability unknown to Mandeville, but his father's middling farm did not carry the social weight of James Proudfit's ministry. When he attended Uniontown Academy at age sixteen, Baird's classmates taunted him, and he "recoiled so much at the ungracious treatment he received from his fellow students, that he broke away from the scene both of his studies and of his troubles, and went home." Baird subsequently returned to Uniontown and completed his course work, but he received no deferential treatment from his classmates. Respect, he found, must be earned. His devout parents sent him to nearby Washington College, where he matriculated between his twentieth and twenty-second birthdays. Baird completed his studies at Jefferson College in Canonsburg in 1818. Both colleges encouraged promising farm boys to enter the Presbyterian ministry, and Baird decided to pursue a course at Princeton Theological Seminary shortly after graduation. Princeton attracted students from throughout the nation and served as a training ground for many leaders of the new philanthropies. Baird graduated with the Class of 1822 and looked forward to finding a mission in life. He never thought of returning to western Pennsylvania to accept a pastoral position.[38]

37. See William H. Form, "Occupations and Careers," in *International Encyclopedia of the Social Sciences,* ed. David L. Sills (New York: Macmillan, 1968), 11:245–253.

38. Major sources on the life of Robert Baird include Henry M. Baird, *The Life of the Rev. Robert Baird, D.D.* (New York: Anson D. F. Randolph, 1866); Paul Van Dyke, "Robert Baird," *Dictionary of American Biography,* 20 vols., 8 supplements (New York: Charles Scribner's Sons, 1927–36), 1:511–512; William B. Sprague, *A Discourse Commemorative of the Late Rev. Robert Baird, D.D.* (Albany: G. Van Benthuysen, 1863); Michael Richard H. Swanson, "Robert Baird and the Evangelical Crusade in America, 1820–1860" (Ph.D. dissertation, Case Western Reserve University, 1971); and his obituary in the *New York Times,* March 17, 1863.

The quotes are from Sprague, *Discourse,* pp. 30–31. Henry M. Baird, Robert's son and a professor at the University of the City of New York, is especially good on family background and the incident at Uniontown Academy (*Life of the Rev. Robert Baird,* pp. 9–18). Henry M. Baird based his remarks largely on Robert Baird's autobiographical manuscript account of his early years.

Baird hoped to avoid traditional parish labor. Education especially attracted him. He had taught district school near his home to pay his early educational·expenses, lectured at an academy in Bellefonte, Pennsylvania, after receiving his baccalaureate, and tutored in Princeton College while attending the seminary. In 1822, an academy at Princeton engaged him as principal, and he remained there six years, "preaching as opportunity afforded in the churches of that city and vicinity."[39]

William Buell Sprague (1795–1876), an insightful clerical biographer and fellow Princeton Seminary graduate (Class of 1819), observed that "it is doubtful whether, when [Baird] left his school at Princeton, he expected ever to become a settled Pastor." Rather, he wished to exert his influence over a "much wider field." The ideal of pastoral permanence no longer attracted Baird's generation. Infused with missionary zeal, young ministers cast their nets widely, seeking participation in the thrilling crusade to convert the nation. Seminary professorships, agencies, and mission work carried much greater prestige than the dreary duties of a routine rural pastorate. Increasingly, men like Baird looked to their ministerial colleagues, rather than their local communities, for approval.[40]

Missionary labor always attracted Baird. He had been active in the Nassau Hall Bible Society, a collegiate affiliate of the ABS. In 1827, he accepted a brief ABS agency to supply New Jersey with the Scriptures. Baird did not view Bible work as a brief interlude in his career. Rather, it marked the beginning of his missionary association affiliations. With each career move, the sphere became wider, the stakes higher. In 1828, he secured employment with the New Jersey Missionary Society. Baird used this opportunity to promote his scheme for a statewide common school system. He became visible as a legislative lobbyist and spokesman for education. Baird wished to replace the informal, haphazard, locally controlled district schools with a more orderly, integrated, and centralized sys-

On Washington College, Jefferson College, and Princeton Theological Seminary, consult Howard Miller, *The Revolutionary College: American Presbyterian Higher Education, 1707–1837* (New York: New York University Press, 1976), pp. 247–254.

39. Baird, *Life of the Rev. Robert Baird*, pp. 26–35; *New York Times*, March 17, 1863.

40. Sprague, *Discourse*, p. 18. On Sprague, see *Dictionary of American Biography*, 17:476–477. Sprague's multivolume *Annals of the American Pulpit* remains a major source of nineteenth-century clerical biography, and he published more than 150 sermons and addresses during his lifetime. On the decline of pastoral permanence, see Scott, *From Office to Profession*, pp. 74–75, 117–118.

tem. His proposals helped lay the groundwork for New Jersey's educational reform and, more important from his personal standpoint, gained him considerable attention within the evangelical community.[41]

In 1829, Baird abandoned state missionary work and began operating on a national level. A five-year tenure as agent for the American Sunday School Union dramatically increased his visibility. Sprague summarized his accomplishments noting that when he began "the revenue of the Society did not exceed five thousand dollars, and the labourers employed were not more than half a dozen, when he retired from it in 1835, its revenue had become twenty-eight thousand, and the number of its laborers had increased to fifty." Successful fund-raising ability and sound organizational acumen proved valuable talents in the new evangelical world.[42]

Baird outgrew the American Sunday School Union in 1835 and began operating in the international arena. A French Association had been formed in New York, with the aim of helping the Protestant church of France. Bankrolled by wealthy Huguenot émigrés, the association named Robert Baird as its agent, and he spent the next eight years in Paris and other world capitals. Baird attempted to begin an international temperance movement, lectured widely from Brussels to Moscow, and through his prolific writings interpreted American evangelicalism for a European audience. He remained with the French Association through various corporate mergers and eventually became secretary of a successor organization, the American and Foreign Christian Union, which stationed agents in Roman Catholic countries in an effort to convert the world to Protestantism and assert the hegemony of American evangelical culture. Although it never achieved many conversions, the Christian Union was an unqualified success by other increasingly important Victorian standards: it possessed a smooth internal administrative structure and it accumulated massive capital resources. Baird remained in its service until his death in 1863 and found time to bring another favorite project to fruition: the international Evangelical Alliance.[43]

41. Baird, *Life of the Rev. Robert Baird*, pp. 40–67.
42. Sprague, *Discourse*, p. 19.
43. Baird, *Life of the Rev. Robert Baird*, pp. 87–313. Some of his more influential writings included *A View of the Mississippi Valley* (Philadelphia, 1832); *Histoire des sociétés de temperance des Etats-Unis d'Amerique* (Paris, 1836); *Religion in America*

Robert Baird found community far removed from the town of his birth among the international evangelical elite. He never experienced the hostility of bringing a Bible to an unreceptive Kentucky frontiersman, but he did know the pleasure of dining with Louis Philippe in Paris. He chose his career moves carefully, always finding a wider sphere for his endeavors. What made him successful? William Sprague's eulogy contains some clues. Thrift, industry, diligence, and perseverence defined Baird's character. Most important, he managed time effectively. "You would never find him unemployed, and yet you would never find him in a hurry." He remained "a rigid economist of time . . . frugal in respect to moments as well as hours and days." Although Baird "read the daily papers with intense interest . . . he read them chiefly in the rail-car, as he was going to and from his work, when he could do nothing else." Every moment counted. He anticipated an age governed by the factory whistle, the standard time zone, and the railroad conductor's meticulously accurate timepiece. The successful benevolent agent and religious missionary had become a man of the new middle class.[44]

Baird especially excelled in "the personal solicitation of pecuniary contributions." He "enjoyed the friendship and confidence of a large part of the notables and best men in his own country, and of many in nearly every country in Europe." Cultivating friendships and gaining the confidence of strangers assumed new importance in the impersonal market world of the mid-nineteenth century. A new social geography existed in the democratic society of equals, and Baird mastered the required personal techniques. He prodded potential philanthropists with "marked discretion and gentlemanly propriety." Donors enjoyed his solicitations to the point that "it was generally felt to be a pleasure rather than a sacrifice to respond to them." This successful fund-raiser possessed "an ingenuous simplicity and guilelessness that revolted at even the sem-

(Edinburgh, 1843; New York, 1844; rev. ed. New York, 1856); and *The Progress and Prospects of Christianity in the United States* (London, 1851). Ray Allen Billington, *The Protestant Crusade, 1800–1860: A Study of the Origins of American Nativism* (New York: Macmillan, 1938), discusses the American and Foreign Christian Union on pp. 264–272.

44. Sprague, *Discourse,* pp. 35–36. On the new Victorian middle class and the central importance of time, see Daniel Walker Howe, "Victorian Culture in America," in Howe, ed., *Victorian America* (Philadelphia: University of Pennsylvania Press, 1977), pp. 3–28; and Alan Trachtenberg, *The Incorporation of America: Culture and Society in the Gilded Age* (New York: Hill and Wang, 1982), pp. 59–60.

blance of double dealing." Baird moved cautiously but effectively among the wealthy, convincing them of his honesty and sincerity. He "never obtruded himself any where; never sacrificed courtesy or delicacy ... never urged his own claims at the expense of the slightest interference with those which were most imperative." Success came remarkably often. Denominational barriers disintegrated. Baird passed from one to the other "with the most genial and graceful felicity" and enlisted "the sympathies and cooperation of each." In a world of strangers, he provided a personal touch.[45]

The American Bible Society and other national philanthropies gradually found that they could not rely on traditional elites and a loose network of local communities to support their activities. By 1830, an Alexander Proudfit could not inspire the necessary confidence or secure sufficiently widespread patronage. Increasingly, the managers turned to men such as Baird, who gained their status by loosening purse strings and relying on the kindness of strangers. Eventually, charismatic Bible fund-raisers would create another institutional crisis. Independent agents, pursuing an ethic of career advancement and seeking approval from their professional peers, did not always find their interests coincident with particular organizations. Baird evidenced little loyalty to any of his employers. Later in the century, large organizations found ways to harness men and create a sense of corporate community. But in 1830, the Bible Society still supported agents as socially diverse as Alexander Proudfit, Sumner Mandeville, and Robert Baird. The challenges and crises in the coming decade would not come from within but from external political and social forces.

45. Sprague, *Discourse*, pp. 33–35, 40.

4

The Limits of Consensus in a Capitalist Metropolis: The Problem of Mariners and "Papists"

Early nineteenth-century evangelicals increasingly realized that an aggressively expansive commercial capitalism created serious social problems as well as lucrative investment opportunities. Between the outbreak of the Anglo-French wars in 1793 and the imposition of Jefferson's Embargo in 1807, commerce yielded extraordinarily high profits. Seaboard cities prospered, shipbuilding emerged as a major American industry, and New York's merchant princes accumulated unprecedented capital from far-flung overseas trading ventures. Initially, the nation's religious leaders welcomed such commercial expansion. Unprecedented wealth, concentrated in the hands of pious and respectable merchants, had great potential for accomplishing good works. Such capital fueled large-scale benevolent enterprises. Mercantile fortunes provided the financial base for the great Protestant philanthropies that flourished during the second decade of the nineteenth century.[1]

God-fearing men soon discovered, however, the ambiguous legacy of commercial capitalism. By the early nineteenth century, simple family partnerships began evolving into more complex, impersonal enterprises. Merchants traded in numerous foreign

---

1. James A. Henretta, *The Evolution of American Society, 1700–1815: An Interdisciplinary Analysis* (Lexington, Mass.: D. C. Heath, 1973), pp. 189–193.

ports, vessels frequently remained at sea for several years, and a commercial economy based on the forces of credit and capital threatened to replace a trading world still governed by family ties and intimate social relationships. The nation's wealthiest and most sophisticated mercantile community was located in New York City, but it depended heavily on the availability and exploitation of unskilled urban workers. Mariners, stevedores, and dockworkers composed an increasingly significant population in the port. Demand for other forms of unskilled labor also grew during the antebellum years as New York began its transformation into what Sean Wilentz has described as "the most productive manufacturing city in the United States." By 1850, unskilled and underpaid immigrants dominated many leading trades.[2]

Merchant princes and small masters needed these unskilled laborers, but few knew them personally. Abstract economic relationships, unfettered by social networks and cultural ties, developed between employers and employees. Men who manipulated capital and men who labored for wages lived in dramatically distinct social and cultural worlds. Mobile, transient workers, prone to periodic underemployment and highly susceptible to shifting economic forces, strained the city's traditional social relationships. Authority based solely on the ties of kinship, community, deferential behavior, and paternalistic clientage proved virtually impossible to enforce in the mid-nineteenth-century metropolis. Ensuring that one's employees behaved in a loyal, reliable, and respectable manner presented an increasingly complex challenge.[3]

When pious merchants and evangelicals met in City Hall to form the American Bible Society in May 1816, these divisions were barely perceptible. Many of the socioeconomic forces that would

2. Sean Wilentz, *Chants Democratic: New York City and the Rise of the American Working Class, 1788–1850* (New York: Oxford University Press, 1984), p. 107. On the rise of New York's merchants, the classic study remains Robert G. Albion, *The Rise of New York Port, 1815–1860* (New York: Charles Scribner's Sons, 1939).

3. See, for example, the discussions in Gary B. Nash, *The Urban Crucible: Social Change, Political Consciousness, and the Origins of the American Revolution* (Cambridge: Harvard University Press, 1979), pp. 382–384, on the shattering of the "habit of obedience"; Paul A. Gilje, *The Road to Mobocracy: Popular Disorder in New York City, 1763–1834* (Chapel Hill: University of North Carolina Press, 1987), pp. 175–202, on labor tension in New York; Graham Russell Hodges, *New York City Cartmen, 1667–1850* (New York: New York University Press, 1986), pp. 108–128, on the breakdown of "clientage" relationships between cartmen and merchants; and Wilentz, *Chants Democratic.*

transform New York from a traditional provincial port into a socially diverse and differentiated capitalist metropolis remained in the future. Large-scale European immigration had not yet begun, New York was physically compact, evangelical Protestantism dominated the city's religious life, and divisions between master artisans and journeyman helpers had not yet hardened. New York City's religious leaders confidently maintained that simple fidelity to the Scriptures would unite the disparate elements of the growing commercial city. Good men needed only to place the Old and New Testaments in the hands of their less fortunate brethren.[4]

Ultimately, this vision proved flawed. Those the reformers hoped to reach had their own strong traditions and beliefs. Further, the new Jacksonian set of values shattered established patterns of deference and clientage and destroyed elite traditions of noblesse oblige. Evangelicals made relatively few inroads among those whom they defined as most dangerous and alien: merchant seamen and Irish Catholics. The Bible Society's work with these groups, however, was significant. The ways early ABS leaders defined social problems and attempted to reform them reveal their increasing insecurity and trepidation about the direction of unfettered capitalist growth. Further, the Bible Society's failure to bring "outsiders" into the evangelical fold ultimately contributed to a redefinition of the institution's mission. Reluctantly and bitterly, the managers acknowledged the inevitability of social and cultural divisions and abandoned their rhetoric of Christian harmony. By the 1840s, they applied the language of confrontation to dissenting social groups. Those who rejected the Bible "without note or comment" no longer seemed merely misguided and neglected persons in need of reform. They had evolved into dangerous classes and permanently divisive enemies of order.

Efforts to reform the unchurched began optimistically. John B. Romeyn (1777–1825), an American Bible Society founder and the secretary for domestic correspondence, embraced the rise of com-

4. Clifford S. Griffin, *Their Brothers' Keepers: Moral Stewardship in the United States, 1800–1865* (New Brunswick: Rutgers University Press, 1960); Charles I. Foster, *An Errand of Mercy: The Evangelical United Front, 1790–1837* (Chapel Hill: University of North Carolina Press, 1960); and Raymond A. Mohl, *Poverty in New York, 1783–1825* (New York: Oxford University Press, 1971), address the evangelicals' fear of cultural diversity. One should not read modern urban developments too far back into the past. See Thomas Bender, *Community and Social Change in America* (Baltimore: Johns Hopkins University Press, 1978), pp. 65–120.

mercial capitalism uncritically and enthusiastically in an 1819 sermon to benefit the New York Missionary Society. The pastor of New York's Cedar Street Associate Reformed Church began by praising those who "enrich themselves, and the community with who they are connected," through participation in trade. International commerce provided an arena in which fruitful "connexions are formed between countries far removed from each other," he observed. Through the exchange of commodities "an interchange of opinions and feelings takes place, which, in the issue, is productive of important consequences." Commercial capitalism complemented and nurtured America's virtuous republican political institutions. Nations committed to trade, argued Romeyn, even when engaged in imperialist acts and hostilities, "carry with them to their conquered countries the spirit of liberty ... the genius of commerce is hostile to absolute subjection." When agriculture and industry dominate commerce, however, "you will find patrician families, and aristocratic power."[5]

Romeyn enthused that commercial life "makes those engaged in its pursuits citizens of the world." Trade promoted a healthy cosmopolitanism among merchants: "It subdues their national prejudices, and overcomes their local feelings." A commercial people also possessed important moral responsibilities. Traders "must send the Gospel to the remote heathen" and use their fortunes to glorify God and benefit mankind. Indeed, Romeyn cheerfully concluded, commerce constituted the "great means of fulfilling the Scriptural prophecy of the latter day glory." Merchants had entered upon a holy labor. Romeyn, of course, drew his salary from the prosperous urban merchants who filled the pews at his Cedar Street Church each Sunday. He found little to criticize in the behavior, life's work, or Christian commitments of his flock. The port's prosperity offered seemingly unlimited potential. New York was the nation's principal commercial entrepôt, and its citizens could exert an international Christianizing influence. The dynamic, relatively cohesive evangelical elite who directed municipal affairs and worshiped in the city's most fashionable temples had the potential to play a critical role on the world stage.[6]

Romeyn realized, however, that New York City's commercial

5. John B. Romeyn, *A Sermon Delivered in the Middle Dutch Church, on the Evening of the Lord's Day, March 21, 1819, for the Benefit of the New York Missionary Society* (New York: J. Seymour, 1819), pp. 11–12.

6. Ibid., pp. 13–15.

expansion also owed much to another "long neglected but highly useful class of men." Seamen, notoriously impious and seemingly addicted to vice, presented a dramatic contrast to the respectable urban mercantile community. Yet economic prosperity depended no less on the labors of Jack Tar than on the financial prowess of merchant princes. Merchants accumulated the capital necessary to link nations into a new political economy, but mariners provided the muscle. Romeyn bemoaned the seamens' spiritual and temporal plight: their dangerous, reckless life-style encouraged a "peculiar fearlessness of life," which resulted in wild binges to gratify their "corrupt passions and appetites." But their impiety did not suggest any flaw or weakness in the structure of commercial capitalism. The mariners' irreligion was "not so much the result of their occupation." Rather, the "Church of God" deserved blame for its "negligence in not attending to their situation." If pious evangelicals aggressively proselytized to the unchurched and wealthy merchants opened their purse strings to support these efforts, conversion seemed inevitable. In fact, however, the problem proved much more complex than Romeyn conceded or realized.[7]

Seamen, as Romeyn acknowledged, constituted an unsettling force in seaport cities. Sailortown districts, with their cheap lodging places, gambling dens, grog shops, and bawdy houses, developed near the docks and wharves of colonial America's commercial towns in the early eighteenth century. By all accounts, seamen pursued a fast, brawling existence during their short stays in port. Extraordinarily high mortality rates, the constant specter of impressment and mutiny, low wages and heavy labor, harshly enforced discipline, underemployment, and the fierce ravages of unpredictable weather characterized life at sea. Consequently, on shore, mariners led lives of excess. Complaints concerning their riotous behavior, heavy drinking, voracious sexual appetites, and spendthrift living provided regular themes for Anglo-American reformist tracts throughout the seventeenth and eighteenth centuries.[8]

7. Ibid., pp. 19–21.
8. Relatively few secondary historical works deal with American seamen. See Marcus Rediker, *Between the Devil and the Deep Blue Sea: Merchant Seamen, Pirates, and the Anglo-American Maritime World, 1700–1750* (New York: Cambridge University Press, 1987), for an earlier period. See also Jesse Lemisch, "Jack Tar in the Streets: Merchant Seamen in the Politics of Revolutionary America," *William and Mary Quarterly* (July 1968), 371–407; Paul A. Gilje, "On the Waterfront: The

Quarter Deck of the Receiving Ship, Fulton, Navy-Yard, New-York, July 18, 1828.

The Sailor's Magazine and Naval Journal, American Seamen's Friend Society, September 1828. Mariners were a favorite target of evangelical reformers. This idealized representation of a prayer service aboard the *Fulton* in New York's Navy Yard suggests an orderly and receptive clientele. The reality often proved far different. *Courtesy of the General Research Division. The New York Public Library. Astor, Lenox and Tilden Foundations.*

By the early nineteenth century, such behavior seemed especially sinister. Evangelicals perceived and defined disorderliness in new ways and proposed novel remedies. Romeyn and his colleagues optimistically declared that the Word of God would eventually reform seamen, but they took steps to speed and ensure the process. Concerned preachers developed a special ministry for mariners, creating mariners' churches, marine Bible societies, seamens' savings banks, and similar special-purpose institutions. John Truair, a British-born evangelical preacher who spent much of his life spreading the Good News from his Mariner's Church

World of Sailors and Stevedores in New York City, 1783-1834," paper delivered at Organization of American Historians meeting, New York City, April 1986; Nash, *Urban Crucible,* pp. 63–64; and Gilje, *Road to Mobocracy,* 178–188.

near the East River wharves, articulated the problem in an 1826 sermon. The core of the dilemma, as this perceptive Presbyterian pastor defined it, was that "men who do business in great waters" formed "a class distinct from other men."[9]

By "class," Truair meant that sailors constituted a separate cultural group; their work experiences aboard ship, travels to distant corners of the globe, and life in port produced a manner of living and a pattern of behavior which separated them from landed society. Ward Stafford, the Bible agent who founded the New York Marine Bible Society (1817), Society for Promoting the Gospel among Seamen (1818), and Mariner's Church (1819), agreed. Seamen "regard themselves, and they are regarded by others, as an entirely separate class of the community," he argued in 1817. When in port, sailors associated almost exclusively with each other. A tight-knit camaraderie characterized their social relations. Mariners patrolled the seedy streets near the East River in groups, visiting the same rum holes and bedding down in the same cheap boarding-houses. Unfortunately, concluded one group of merchants concerned with seamens' spiritual state in 1818, "they almost necessarily associate with those who neglect public worship." They possessed "no friends to conduct them to the house of God."[10]

Seamen dressed alike: they wore baggy breeches, checked linen shirts, heavy jackets, gray stockings, and sailor caps. Dress, according to the founders of New York's Mariner's Church, proved "another barrier" to their conversion. On the infrequent occasions when they attended Sunday services, "they are noted and marked as Sailors." Nervous middle-class parishioners were revolted at the sight of men they perceived as having "a depraved, worthless character" entering their sanctuaries. Accordingly, Christians "felt

9. Roald Kverndal, *Seamen's Missions: Their Origin and Early Growth* (Pasadena: William Carey Library, 1986), provides an encyclopedic, but largely undigested, account of Anglo-American evangelical work among mariners. See pp. 407–536 for ministerial efforts in the United States. John Truair, *A Call from the Ocean, or An Appeal to the Patriot and the Christian in Behalf of Seamen* (New York: John Gray, 1826), p. 3.

10. Ward Stafford, *New Missionary Field: A Report to the Female Missionary Society for the Poor of the City of New-York and Its Vicinity, at Their Quarterly Prayer Meeting, March 1817* (New York: J. Seymour, 1817), p. 34; "A Meeting of Merchants and Others connected with the Commerce of the Port of New York, held on the 29th May, 1818, for the purpose of adopting measures for supplying Seamen with the Preaching of the Gospel" (New York, 1818), p. 4, manuscript in New-York Historical Society.

themselves at liberty to close their pews against them, and not un-
frequently to inform them, that there was no room for *Seamen.*"
Mariner language, with its technical nautical terms and salty, blas-
phemous oaths, appeared virtually incomprehensible to sophisticated city dwellers and further alienated the pious. Ultimately, the
tattoo, sewn into the forearm and proudly displayed in port, permanently marked its bearer as a denizen of the deep and a special
breed of man. Because of their radical and explicitly public attempts to differentiate themselves from others, sailors must be
treated "as a class of men by themselves," Ward Stafford and his
fellow evangelicals concluded.[11]

Such self-conscious social differentiation appeared more threatening in the complex and growing metropolis than in the intimate
and relatively well-ordered port town of the previous century. By
1820 New York City's social and religious leaders were groping for
ways to restore a consensual social vision to city life. Taming the
sailors provided one challenge. Seamen, recognized Stafford, were
"strangers in a strange place." Edward Dorr Griffin, delivering a
sermon for the benefit of the Marine Missionary Society at Brick
Presbyterian Church in 1819, described them as "a mass of people,
mostly strangers, and constantly changing." Estimating that mariners spent only six or seven weeks a year in their home port, Griffin
bemoaned their "roving way of life," which, he believed, "kept seamen away from the house of God when on shore."[12]

The New York City merchants who met on May 29, 1818, to organize the Mariner's Church agreed that seamen lacked a sense of
order "on account of their having no fixed residence," which prevented their "com[ing] under the immediate observation of the benevolent and pious." Spending the bulk of their time "either on the
sea or in the ports where they are strangers," they lacked the regular habits, the sense of stability and hierarchy, and the orderly manners a more rooted life might provide. "The vast republic of men
who have their dwellings on the sea," warned Griffin, "constitutes
in many respects a world by itself; governed by different laws, connected by a different language, and not likely to fall under the in-

11. "Meeting of Merchants and Others," p. 4; Rediker, *Between the Devil and the
Deep Blue Sea*, pp. 11–12.
12. Stafford, *New Missionary Field*, p. 34; Edward D. Griffin, *The Claims of Seamen: A Sermon Preached November 7, 1819, in the Brick Church, New-York, for the
Benefit of the Marine Missionary Society of That City* (New York: J. Seymour, 1819),
pp. 8, 10.

fluence of those plans which are set on foot for the reformation of landsmen.[13]

Fear of the stranger, the rover, and the rootless who had no familial or social ties to the community fueled elite anxieties. The impersonal mechanism of the market altered traditional social relationships. The scale and nature of life in New York changed as unknown young men arrived from the countryside, businesses grew larger, and the tightly knit world of the colonial merchant fragmented. Kinship and established social networks remained important, but an urban order based on family ties, deferential relations, and paternalistic clientage faced new challenges. Sailors personified these potentially disruptive forces. *Individual* mariners moved through the port constantly, rarely staying for more than a few weeks. Seamen as a *group* persisted and behaved in remarkably consistent ways. A stark division existed between landed men and seafarers. The docks were off-limits to stable city residents. Seamen defined their life by their labor, exhibited little deference to their employers, and lived completely outside the framework of family, church, and city. For nervous elites and troubled evangelicals, they presented an unruly vision of a future in which horizontal social groupings threatened vertical order, uncontrolled mobility produced dangerous rootlessness, and a society of strangers lived for the thrill of the moment.[14]

Jack Tar's dangerousness stemmed from both his rootless anonymity and his propensity for riotous behavior. New York's waterfront became a battleground in the popular disturbances directed against British rule in the 1760s and 1770s. Dockworkers occasionally rioted over labor competition from off-duty English soldiers who attempted to supplement their salaries with day laboring jobs on the wharves. Other tensions grew from the colonial American seaman's constant fear of impressment. Violence and rioting against the Royal Navy regularly erupted in Atlantic seaports. Colonial seamen, in the view of Jesse Lemisch, were society's outcasts. They developed a radical oppositional culture designed to protect their life, liberty, and meager property through violent acts and

13. "Meeting of Merchants and Others," p. 2; Griffin, *Claims of Seamen*, p. 7.

14. Allan Stanley Horlick, *Country Boys and Merchant Princes: The Social Control of Young Men in New York* (Lewisburg: Bucknell University Press, 1975); Karen Halttunen, *Confidence Men and Painted Women: A Study of Middle-Class Culture in America, 1830–1870* (New Haven: Yale University Press, 1982); Gilje, "On the Waterfront."

physical intimidation. In the eighteenth-century world such rioting served generally accepted and legitimate social purposes. When colonial seamen lashed out against imperial authority, they often made common cause with local merchants who viewed English rule as intrusive and illegitimate. Rioting served as a means of purging the social order of outside deviants and asserting legitimate communal power and sanctions.[15]

By the early nineteenth century, urban elites began to perceive riotous behavior differently. As the historian Paul Gilje has argued, acceptable traditions of popular disorder appeared as dangerous threats to social order in late Jeffersonian and early Jacksonian New York. Rioting seemed the tool of "special interests" intent on disrupting the delicate balance of power rather than a method of affirming and enforcing accepted social norms. Seamen figured prominently in crowd actions during the first three decades of the nineteenth century, but low wages and lack of work were more likely reasons than impressment, and the extralegal attacks were punished harshly. Both merchants and mariners realized that their interests in the expansive commercial economy differed greatly. Perhaps, evangelicals prayed, bringing sailors to truths of revealed religion might transform them into steady and reliable workers, less prone to rioting and divisive behavior.[16]

Converting seamen offered evangelicals direct benefits as well. As early as the mid-eighteenth century, mariners occupied a central and unique place in an increasingly global economy. They had cohered into a mobile, cosmopolitan, international laboring force with an impressive familiarity with foreign lands and cultures. Except for merchants and missionaries, no other group of Americans in the second decade of the nineteenth century possessed such an extraordinarily global outlook. Seamen moved goods through far-flung trade routes and helped unify distant corners of the world. As John Romeyn had shrewdly observed, men who took the fruits of commerce to distant ports were potential carriers of the Word of the Lord to heathen lands.[17]

The Christian challenge, according to Romeyn, was to convert the seamen so they might assume these international Christianizing responsibilities and distribute "Bibles and . . . Tracts from port

---

15. Lemisch, "Jack Tar in the Streets"; Nash, *Urban Crucible*, pp. 266, 371; Gilje, *Road to Mobocracy*, pp. vii, 178–179.

16. Gilje, *Road to Mobocracy*, pp. vii, 183–188.

17. Rediker, *Between the Devil and the Deep Blue Sea*, pp. 77–82.

to port, from clime to clime." Eventually, the ABS secretary for domestic correspondence predicted, "every vessel you dispatch will
be a Bethel on the deep, and its hands messengers of good to their
fellow-men." Yet sailors continued to behave in unruly ways. Too
often, the heathen in India, Africa, and the Far East received the
wrong messages. John Truair claimed that seamen's behavior frequently placed "innumerable and constant hindrance in the way
of [missionaries'] progress." Upon entering a foreign port, seamen
frequently "swindled and oppressed, robbed and spoiled" the unsuspecting natives. Their "vicious" acts and immoral behavior
turned "the minds of the heathen against the Christian religion."
An effective ministry to reform mariners seemed critical. The
global stakes appeared very high indeed.[18]

Seamen's working conditions and socioeconomic standing, in
the rhetoric of evangelical churchmen, did not erect significant
barriers to reform. Religious reformers believed that more aggressive proselytizing and new benevolent techniques would produce
a massive moral reformation. Armed with Christian optimism and
enamored of commercial capitalism, Protestants in the late 1810s
and early 1820s created a network of institutions to bring stability
and order to the seamen. The American Bible Society moved aggressively into this new ministry. In August 1820, the managers engaged Ward Stafford to tour the Atlantic seaboard, meet with
prominent merchants and sea captains, and encourage the establishment of marine Bible societies. By November, Stafford had traveled over fourteen hundred miles, societies had sprung up in
seaboard communities from Charleston to Portland, and the ABS
had given over twelve hundred Bibles and six hundred Testaments
to these local auxiliaries. That same year, the first mariner's church
in the United States opened on Roosevelt Street in New York. By
1825, seventy Bethel unions, twenty-three marine Bible societies,
and fifteen floating chapels and churches dispensed the Christian
message to sailors in North American ports.[19]

18. Romeyn, *Sermon Delivered in Middle Dutch Church*, p. 23; Truair, *A Call
from the Ocean*, p. 9; Kverndal, *Seamen's Missions*, pp. 407–460.
19. Ward Stafford, "Account of formation of Marine Bible Societies," manuscript,
November 12, 1820, Agents' Papers, ABS Archives; ABS, *Fifth Annual Report* (1820),
p. 127; "American Missions to Seamen," in *The Encyclopedia of Missions: Descriptive, Historical, Biographical, Statistical*, edited under the auspices of the Bureau of
Missions by Henry Otis Dwight, H. Allen Tupper, and Edwin Munsell Bliss, 2d ed.
(New York: Funk & Wagnall's, 1904).

This evangelical crusade branched out in other directions as well. In 1829, New York merchants created the Seamen's Bank for Savings to collect the mariners' earnings and undercut the influence of the boardinghouse operators who frequently held their money during stays in port. The bank, the directors hoped, might encourage industry, thrift, and frugality among seamen, while not incidentally pooling previously inaccessible capital resources for reinvestment by local merchants. Bank directors further planned to create "an efficient Register Office" at 49 Wall Street, based on a similar institution organized in Boston the year before. A network of registries in Atlantic ports would collect personal information concerning individual seamen: their dates of arrival in and departure from port, employment record, testimonials from merchants and shipmasters, and evidence of good moral character. Such registries might help potential employers form "a very correct judgment ... respecting the character of the person in question" and exercise a controlling influence over these anonymous floating laborers.[20]

By the time the Seamen's Bank for Savings opened its vault in 1829, however, the ministry for mariners was on the decline. As early as 1824, the American Bible Society learned that the organizations established by Stafford seemed in disarray. Phineas Pratt, corresponding secretary of the Saco and Biddeford, Maine, Marine Bible Society, observed in January of that year that "we have not accomplished very much, the last season ... the field of our exertion is so small, that it hardly keeps us awake to what is to be done." That same month, the secretary of the Newburyport, Massachusetts, Marine Bible Society admitted that "our operations have been so limited that we feel almost ashamed to have an account of them go abroad." The Wiscasset, Maine, Marine Bible Society ceased operations in February 1824, though recognizing that "no class of Sailors is probably so necessitous" of the Scriptures as "the Fishermen of this District.[21]

In 1825, traveling Bible agent Nathaniel Dwight reported the dissolution of the Providence, Rhode Island, Marine Bible Society. The

---

20. *One Hundred and Fifteen Years of Service, 1829–1944: The Seamen's Bank for Savings in the City of New York* (New York: Seamen's Bank for Savings, 1944); *Sailor's Magazine and Naval Journal*, May 1829, December 1830, May 1831, September 1831, and May 1833.

21. Phineas Pratt to Selah Strong Woodhull, January 19, 1824; L. F. Dimmick to Selah Strong Woodhull, January 21, 1824; Nathaniel Coffin to Selah Strong Woodhull, February 10, 1824, Corresponding Secretary's Papers, ABS Archives.

former president of that body observed that "there is a coldness on the part of the Mariners respecting the Bible. Few call for a Bible. Some of these few pay a part of the price, and others, if it is proposed to them to do so go off without the book." By 1828, the ABS complained that 35 percent of the marine Bible societies established by Stafford never contributed anything to the cause. Two years later, even the thriving whaling port of New Bedford reported apathy: at the 1830 annual meeting "but a fraction over sixteen dollars was collected . . . there were not as many persons present as the constitution requires for officers of the society!"[22]

Other efforts at reforming the mariners also met disillusionment and failure. The planned registry office never functioned effectively. Five years after its founding, the Seamen's Bank abandoned its original plan to accept money only from "seamen and those connected with a seafaring Life" and broadened its depositor base to remain financially solvent. Between 1825 and 1829, the ABS granted no Scriptures to marine Bible societies. Even the New York Marine Bible Society, the earliest and strongest seamen's auxiliary, began a long decline, receiving remarkably few mercantile contributions. In 1840, it quietly suspended operations when the American Bible Society and New York Bible Society agreed to assume responsibility for its substantial and growing debt. In the future, marine Bible work would be a small adjunct of local auxiliary society labors.[23]

Why had this mariner ministry, begun with such high hopes and great expectations, accomplished so little? In its 1817 address to "Merchants and Masters of Vessels," the New York Marine Bible Society anticipated one critical problem. "We cannot condescend to reason with those," its officers disdainfully remarked, "who, at this day, venture to assert, that were our Seamen enlightened by human and divine knowledge, they would be less active, courageous, and useful in their station." Romeyn touched on this same theme in his 1819 sermon. He criticized "the mistaken, the *grossly*

22. Alexander Jones, Esq., quoted in Nathaniel Dwight, "Journal," July 5, 1825, Agents' Papers, ABS Archives; *Sailor's Magazine and Naval Journal*, December 1828, October 1830.

23. Alan L. Olmstead, *New York City Mutual Savings Banks, 1819–1861* (Chapel Hill: University of North Carolina Press, 1976), p. 13; Eric M. North, "Distribution, 1821–1830," American Bible Society Historical Essay 14, Part II (1964), pp. 112–113; Minutes of Meeting of the American Bible Society's Board of Managers, March 19, 1840, ABS Archives.

mistaken idea, that no one can be a good seaman who does not indulge" in immoral acts and acknowledged that mariners' "employers have rather encouraged these habits."[24]

Yet employers' concerns arose from a legitimate attention to self-interest. Evangelicals preached a gospel designed to promote individual self-control, prudence, caution, moderation, temperate behavior, and steady reliability. They advocated total submission of the self to Divine authority. Such virtues certainly guaranteed success in the countinghouse. Occasionally, this message stimulated some segments of the urban work force to adapt themselves better to factory labor. Seamanship, however, attracted a very different and much wilder breed of man. Mariners pursued an adventurous life-style, eschewing landed stability for a world of random movement, life-threatening danger, and constant conflict with the forces of man and nature. Sea masters needed men willing to place their bodies and souls in jeopardy to protect a merchant's cargo from raging storms and ravaging pirates. Sea captains demanded absolute authority aboard their vessels; a Christian moral sensibility and an unyielding adherence to Divine dictates could not be allowed to interfere with a captain's commands.[25]

Selfless Christianity did not prepare men for the physical brutalities and social degradations of the mariner's world. Some merchants and captains, expressing guilt and remorse over the seamen's condition and wishing to soften the harsh quality of the unskilled laborers' life, did contribute substantial sums to the Bible cause. Ultimately, though, such donations proved too meager and too scattered to sustain an ongoing effort. Most captains of commerce accepted the mariners' plight and chose not to inquire too deeply into the conditions that characterized their existence. Turning the cat-o'-nine-tails on a "deserving" unregenerate seaman, after all, produced few moral misgivings. Meting out harsh punishment to a Soldier of Christ, however, carried more troubling implications. Evangelical reform, masters feared, might threaten or at least soften the established and brutally effective disciplinary

24. *Constitution of the Marine Bible Society of New York, Auxiliary to the American Bible Society: Together with an Address to Merchants and Masters of Vessels, and an Address to Seamen* (New York: J. Seymour, 1817), p. 5; Romeyn, *Sermon Delivered in Middle Dutch Church*, p. 21.

25. Paul E. Johnson, *A Shopkeeper's Millennium: Society and Revivals in Rochester, New York, 1815–1837* (New York: Hill and Wang, 1978), provides an overview of the evangelical message and its relevance to antebellum urban life.

system operative aboard ship. It could encourage a more submissive, prudent work force whereas sea captains demanded bold and daring men of action. Ultimately, merchants and masters preferred to view the mariners' religious indifference as an unpleasantly ugly but necessary by-product of an expansive commercial capitalism that provided grand estates and unprecedented wealth for a fortunate few.

Another reason for the failure to convert mariners was that the evangelical message was not meaningful to its intended recipients. Most mariners consciously and willingly turned their backs on the stability and security of life on shore. They carved out a social world with a well-defined set of values. Evangelicals viewed their behavior as disorderly and sought to persuade them to abandon nearly every ritual, tradition, and social form practiced at sea. To the men aboard ship, crusades against drinking, gambling, and dancing were meddlesome efforts to restrict the simple pleasures that helped make life at sea bearable. By focusing exclusively on symptomatic behavioral issues and ignoring the socioeconomic realities of the sailor's world, evangelicals undermined their own credibility.[26]

Religious reformers, for example, regularly decried the "superstitions" prevalent among mariners. Over the centuries, seamen had proudly developed and carefully crafted a complex and unique set of traditions, beliefs in supernatural forces and omens, and cultural customs. Elaborate rituals integrated new men into seafaring life. Sailors had constructed their own "popular" religion created partly from official church teachings, partly from their practical experiences and observations, and partly from a mystical respect for the forces of nature. This traditional belief system served them well, offering coherent explanations for the fragility of life at sea, the random and unpredictable natural disasters, and the harsh qualities of their laboring existence. Organized religious bodies, denominational tenets, ministerial authority and formal Bible study occupied little place in this complex belief system. They appeared much more applicable to the relatively reliable, stable, ordered world inhabited on shore by urbanites of middling and upper ranks.[27]

Herman Melville, a keen observer of maritime life and no friend

---

26. Rediker, *Between the Devil and the Deep Blue Sea*, pp. 189–194.
27. Ibid., pp. 169–204.

to Protestant missionaries, summarized the place of the Bible aboard ship in his novel *White Jacket,* published ten years after the New York Marine Bible Society declared bankruptcy. "By the regulations of the Navy," he recalled, "each seaman's mess on board the Neversink was furnished with a Bible." The Holy Oracles, according to Melville, "were seldom or never to be seen, except on Sunday mornings, when usage demands that they shall be exhibited by the cooks of the messes, when the master-at-arms goes his rounds on the berthdeck." During such inspections, the author noted, Bibles "usually surmounted a highly polished tin-pot placed on the lid of the chest." Jack Tar paid this little mind. Fighting for survival in an individuated capitalist economy that offered seamen few rewards and little real benevolence, mariners had discovered a seemingly irrefutable lesson: "Our own hearts are our best prayer-rooms," and "the chaplains who can most help us are ourselves."[28]

Irish Catholic immigrants introduced an even more alien and divisive cultural element into the commercial metropolis than did mariners. Seamen moved through the port rapidly and anonymously, barely participating in New York's institutional life. Labor aboard ship defined the sailor's existence, and his ties with the city were temporary and tenuous. Irish immigrants, in contrast, began exerting political and social influence in New York as early as the 1820s. By the 1840s, they had created their own largely separate rich urban associational life, built around a series of well-defined ethnoreligious institutions. Patrician elites nervously contemplated the immigrants' growing political influence, and native-born artisans linked the Irish presence with the degradation of specific crafts and the general depression of wages. Particular sections of the city, such as the "Bloody Ould Sixth" Ward, assumed a distinctively Gaelic character. The Irish appeared to be constructing a separate social system within the city, and no institution appeared more separate and central than the ethnic-based Roman Catholic parish. Bringing Roman Catholicism within the city's religious mainstream arose as an especially important task for an elite desirous of maintaining an organic social order.[29]

28. Herman Melville, *White Jacket or The World in a Man-of-War* (New York: New American Library, 1981), p. 160.

29. Jay P. Dolan, *The Immigrant Church: New York's Irish and German Catholics, 1815–1865* (Baltimore: Johns Hopkins University Press, 1975), discusses ethnic parish life in New York. Wilentz, *Chants Democratic,* pp. 118–119, 266–271, and 315–324

During its early years, the American Bible Society carefully avoided direct public criticism of Roman Catholicism, adopting instead a nonconfrontational, cooperative stance. Samuel J. Mills, the Williams College-trained missionary whose *Communications Relative to the Progress of Bible Societies in the United States* constituted a seminal document in the Bible movement, praised the administrator of the diocese of New Orleans in 1813. Bishop Louis William Dubourg (1766–1833), the French émigré who had ecclesiastical jurisdiction over New Orleans, pledged his cooperation with the Bible movement and assured Mills that the hierarchy offered "not the least objection to it." Dubourg even volunteered to coordinate the distribution of French Scriptures through "the convent of Ursuline Nuns," at which "are still educated the daughters of the principal catholic families of Louisiana."[30]

The Quaker philanthropist Thomas Eddy, attending the May 10, 1816, meeting that resulted in the formation of the ABS, asked whether "there was nothing to exclude the Roman Catholics" in the proposed constitution and observed that "several serious men among them" wished to participate in the Bible movement. Following Eddy's lead, the gathering dispatched "a deputation . . . to request the Roman Catholics to join us." Within one year of its founding, the ABS announced plans to print a Roman Catholic version of the Spanish Bible. Father Felipe Scio de San Miguel, a Spanish Catholic priest, had prepared this translation and it bore the necessary ecclesiastical imprimatur. French, Gaelic, and German Scriptures, which included the controversial Apocryphal Books and received authorization from the Roman Catholic hierarchy, also constituted important components of the Society's distribution efforts after 1817. In 1825, the managers seriously debated a recommendation from a Baptist Bible agent in Missouri, who sug-

---

addresses the changing ethnic nature of New York crafts and perceptions of the Irish as an alien threat; Amy Bridges, *A City in the Republic: Antebellum New York and the Origins of Machine Politics* (Ithaca: Cornell University Press, 1984), pp. 70–77 and 90–98, considers the withdrawal of the elite from New York politics and the rise of nativism. On the "Bloody Ould Sixth," see Carol Groneman Pernicone, "'The Bloody Ould Sixth': A Social Analysis of a New York City Working-Class Community in the Mid-Nineteenth Century" (Ph.D. dissertation, University of Rochester, 1973).

30. Samuel J. Mills and John F. Schermerhorn, *Communications Relative to the Progress of Bible Societies in the United States* (Philadelphia: Philadelphia Bible Society, 1813), pp. 7–8.

gested "the expediency of printing the Scriptures in English of the Roman Catholic version."[31]

Publicly, the managers took special care to praise priests and bishops who supported their efforts. In 1822, the board lauded a South American "Roman Catholic ecclesiastic" who received a shipment of Spanish Testaments and "proceeded immediately to a judicious distribution of them . . . with lively pleasure." The annual report for that year outlined plans to place the Word of God "in the hands of many of the catholic citizens" of Louisiana. Scriptures intended for Spanish Catholics arrived in South America in 1825, and the board noted "the cordial and affectionate co-operation of many of the most influential clergymen and laymen," which made the effort possible. By 1827, distribution in Cuba had been "mostly entrusted to Catholic clergymen . . . who have manifested a kindness and cordiality in disseminating [Bibles], which cannot but be viewed with grateful satisfaction by the friends of revealed truth." These public statements oozed with the language of harmony and cooperation.[32]

Some prominent leaders of the benevolent empire privately expressed a surprising sympathy for Romanism. John Pintard, the ABS recording secretary and a devout Episcopalian, suggested in 1818 that Protestants should "endeavour to exercise a little liberality" toward "that Church which for so many ages included every believer in Christianity." Three years later, Pintard criticized the "Protestant prejudices" that prevented the establishment of a proposed monastery, college, and convent in New York City. The failure of the "Nunnery" particularly annoyed him because he believed that the "strict attention paid to morals, health, & neatness of the pupils" at this institution would produce general social benefits.

31. Samuel Bayard to Elias Boudinot, May 11, 1816, and Elisha Boudinot to Elias Boudinot, May 11, 1816, Elias Boudinot Papers, ABS Archives. On Roman Catholic-approved versions, see Ivan H. Nothdurft, "The American Bible Society and Roman Catholicism, 1816–1979," ABS Historical Essay 23, Part VII, 1980. The suggestion concerning an English Roman Catholic version came from the Reverend John Mason Peck. See Minutes of Meeting of the Board of Managers, September 1, 1825, ABS Archives.

The ABS followed the lead of the British and Foreign Bible Society and ceased circulating Scriptures containing the Apocrypha in 1828. The managers did so with hesitation, however, and primarily in deference to the British society. See James Milnor to Rev. Andrew Brandram, August 31, 1826, Letter Book, Secretary for Foreign Correspondence, ABS Archives.

32. ABS, *Sixth Annual Report* (1822); *Ninth Annual Report* (1825); *Eleventh Annual Report* (1827).

Indeed, Pintard recalled that one of his nephews had been trained at a Roman Catholic college for young men. When his daughter Eliza announced plans to educate his niece in the academy conducted by Ursuline Sisters at New Orleans, John Pintard enthusiastically endorsed the arrangement.[33]

American Catholic historian Jay Dolan has described the early Federal era as "a prolonged period of cordial relations between Catholics and Protestants," and the American Bible Society's cooperative efforts support this view. Early nineteenth-century American Catholicism had a genteel character. Native-born patricians and aristocratic French émigrés ruled the principal American sees, and such men moved easily in polite Protestant circles. Bishop John Carroll (1735–1815) of Baltimore, for example, had been born into colonial Maryland's gentry society and counted Chesapeake aristocrats among his closest associates. A committed supporter of the American Revolution, Carroll attempted to blend its republican legacy with Roman Catholic institutional structures. During the 1780s, he advocated an English-language liturgy, supported election of bishops by the clergy, and argued for the separation of church and state. The administrative demands created by his 1790 episcopal ordination tempered his Enlightenment liberalism, but Carroll remained committed to extensive lay participation in local church administration. He opposed separate national parishes, insisted on a native-born clergy, discouraged Roman meddling in American affairs, and maintained a minimal bureaucratic structure. American Catholicism in the hands of Federalist patricians such as John Carroll impressed some Protestants as compatible with republican institutions.[34]

Catholicism in New York appeared equally genial and nonthreatening during the early Federal period. Roman Catholics established only two parishes within the city limits between 1785 and 1825, and neither thrived. The early history of St. Peter's on Barclay

---

33. John Pintard to Eliza Pintard, April 14, 1818, and April 20, 1821, in Dorothy C. Barck, ed., *Letters from John Pintard to His Daughter Eliza Noel Pintard Davidson* (New York: New-York Historical Society, 1940), 1:116, 2:31.

34. Jay P. Dolan, *The American Catholic Experience: A History from Colonial Times to the Present* (Garden City: Doubleday, 1985), p. 102. See also Dolan, "Catholic Education in the Early Republic," *History of Education Quarterly* (Summer 1981), 205–211, for more on Carroll; and Donna Merwick, *Boston Priests, 1848–1910: A Study of Social and Intellectual Change* (Cambridge: Harvard University Press, 1973).

Street consisted largely of internal bickering between French and Irish communicants. Six years elapsed between the founding of St. Patrick's on Mott Street in 1809 and the first mass celebrated within its walls. Financial indebtedness handicapped both parochial efforts. Rome's appointment of gentlemanly French scholar John Dubois (1764–1842) to preside over New York's Catholic affairs in 1826 undoubtedly pleased patrician Protestants. A biographer described Dubois as "respected by cultured non-Catholics . . . he had studied English with Patrick Henry, was friendly with President James Madison and the Randolphs of Virginia [and] . . . did not favor acrimonious religious debates." The scholarly pamphlet, the carefully crafted pastoral letter, and the methodically constructed sermon constituted his principal modes of discourse. The bishop lived simply, maintained a relatively spartan liturgical life, and scolded his flock for ostentatious displays at funerals and weddings. Pintard approvingly contrasted Dubois's modest $800 salary and living arrangements with those of Episcopal bishop John Henry Hobart (1775–1830), a Bible Society opponent, who "has a superb house & a salary of $3500 a year, as much I believe as nearly all the Roman Catholic clergymen together."[35]

Dramatic socioeconomic changes permanently altered the nature of American Catholicism in the twenty years following Dubois's appointment. Irish immigration accelerated rapidly in the late 1820s and early 1830s before the famine, and many chose New York City as their destination. By 1845, 34 percent of the city's population was foreign-born, and Irish Catholics accounted for the overwhelming majority of the newcomers. The Irish had few skills useful in an urban context, possessed meager economic resources, and thus concentrated in laboring jobs. Many historians have chronicled the relentless poverty, substandard tenement housing, irregular employment patterns, and high rates of mortality typical of antebellum immigrant life. The Roman Catholic parish occupied a central place in the Irish immigrant community, and the American church grew at an extraordinary and unprecedented rate. Be-

35. Dolan, *Immigrant Church*, pp. 11–13; Joseph McCadden and Helen McCadden, *Father Varela: Torch Bearer from Cuba* (New York: United States Catholic Historical Society, 1969), pp. 90–91; Richard Shaw, *John Dubois: Founding Father* (Yonkers: United States Catholic Historical Society, 1983); John Pintard to Eliza Pintard, January 15, 1828, in Barck, ed., *Letters*, 3:8; Charles G. Herbermann, "The Right Rev. John Dubois, D.D., Third Bishop of New York," in United States Catholic Historical Society, *Historical Records and Studies* (1899), 278–355.

tween 1826 and 1845, New York's Roman Catholics constructed fourteen new churches within the city limits. This expansion caused serious discomfort for both Bishop John Dubois and the city's Protestant elite.[36]

Patrician Federalists might coexist comfortably with a genteel, elite Anglo-American or French Catholic hierarchy, but they had little patience with the increasingly aggressive and nationalistic Irish clergy and foreign-born laity. By the early 1840s, Roman Catholicism appeared more menacing and threatening. Alien forces seemed in control of the city's working-class pulpits. Catholic clerics preached an aggressively separatist, militant message of ethnic exclusivity. The Irish missionary clergy denounced evangelical Protestantism in inflammatory tones, and the church's ecclesiastical hierarchy discouraged the reading of the King James Bible. Worst of all, the "papists" attracted parishioners, and their churches and institutions grew rapidly. Genteel American Protestants could not easily accept these foreign influences and this separatist ecclesiastical stance. They identified John Hughes (1797–1864) as a symbol of their discontent, claiming that New York's new bishop escalated the religious rhetoric and created the new divisions. In fact, the broader socioeconomic changes accompanying New York's transformation into an industrial metropolis and the evangelicals' unwillingness to accept the heterogeneity and pluralism of mid-nineteenth-century urban life were the primary problems.

John Pintard urbanely tolerated Bishop Dubois's genteel brand of Roman Catholicism; when he encountered a few Irishmen while strolling along Broadway following an Independence Day celebration in 1821, this cosmopolitan patrician reacted very differently. These poor Irish were truly alien, "the dregs & scum of creation." Gathering "round the whiskey with disgust & contempt," they

36. Robert Ernst, *Immigrant Life in New York City, 1825–1863* (Port Washington: Ira J. Friedman, 1949), remains the best study of antebellum New York immigrants. See also Dolan, *Immigrant Church;* Oscar Handlin, *Boston's Immigrants* (Cambridge: Harvard University Press, 1941); Clyde Griffen and Sally Griffen, *Natives and Newcomers: The Ordering of Opportunity in Mid-Nineteenth-Century Poughkeepsie* (Cambridge: Harvard University Press, 1978); Stephan Thernstrom, *The Other Bostonians: Poverty and Progress in an American Metropolis, 1880-1970* (Cambridge: Harvard University Press, 1973); Hasia R. Diner, *Erin's Daughters in America: Irish Immigrant Women in the Nineteenth Century* (Baltimore: Johns Hopkins University Press, 1983); and Kerby A. Miller, *Emigrants and Exiles: Ireland and the Irish Exodus to North America* (New York: Oxford University Press, 1985).

threatened uneasy middle-class pedestrians. On the Fourth of July, such a scene appeared especially menacing to a committed Federalist fearful of "mobocracy." In New York, "men unfit to associate with the menials of Civil Society" had secured "all the privileges of freeholders" and could be used by unscrupulous politicians "to answer party purposes." Politically, morally, and socially, the new arrivals from Ireland threatened evangelical conceptions of consensual order.[37]

America's antebellum Roman Catholic hierarchy viewed Irish immigration as a mixed blessing. Prefamine Irish Catholicism differed considerably from the French and English ecclesiastical traditions that had dominated Roman practice in the New World. Irregular attendance at mass, failure to fulfill sacramental obligations, infrequent communion and confession, and indifference to formal priestly authority existed throughout Ireland. Widespread complaints of clerical avarice, alcoholism, and sexual misconduct reflected the tensions between priests and parishioners. Irish popular devotional life owed much to pre-Christian rituals, magico-religious beliefs, Celtic folklore, and persistent faith in the power of ghosts, fairies, and healing. Ecclesiastical efforts to "reform" these practices and place Irish Catholicism in conformity with the decrees of the Council of Trent met with little success before the 1850s.[38]

Such folk traditions conflicted with episcopal authority, especially calls for devotional conformity from an aristocratic Frenchman like John Dubois. Conflicts with Irish priests marred his sixteen-year New York episcopate. "Trustee" controversies reflected further discord within the parishes, as priests and laymen battled over pew rents, cemetery management, clerical salaries, and building programs. The Catholic hierarchy grew concerned as the immigrant Irish laity affiliated with and established organizations outside the framework of church life. Labor organizations, political parties, and temperance unions often competed with neighborhood churches for parishioners' loyalties. In 1836, Irish New Yorkers established the Ancient Order of Hibernians, a secular

37. John Pintard to Eliza Pintard, July 5, 1821, in Barck, ed., *Letters*, 2:59.

38. On Irish Catholic devotional practices, see Lynn Lees, *Exiles of Erin* (Ithaca: Cornell University Press, 1979), pp. 164–212; David W. Miller, "Irish Catholicism and the Great Famine," *Journal of Social History* (Fall 1975), 81–98; and Emmet Larkin, "The Devotional Revolution in Ireland, 1850–75," *American Historical Review* (1972), 625–652.

fraternal organization that would create significant problems for the church hierarchy in future years. As lay Irish influences began transforming New York Catholicism, patrician bishops like John Dubois seemed increasingly irrelevant.[39]

John Joseph Hughes succeeded Dubois as bishop of New York in 1842. Born to a farming family in overpopulated and impoverished County Tyrone, Ireland, Hughes worked as a laborer before his ordination in 1826. Hughes faced two principal difficulties upon assuming charge of his new see. First, militant anti-Irish and anti-immigrant sentiments escalated dramatically during the 1830s. Nativist politics, tavern brawls, ethnic gang warfare, street violence, and a vitriolic anti-Catholic literature bordering on the pornographic heightened tensions. The rapid development and systematization of a centralized, Protestant-based common school system left a more enduring threat to Catholic culture. Second, Hughes needed to consolidate his episcopal authority within the Roman Catholic communion in the face of challenges from church trustees, competing lay organizations, and traditional Irish immigrant indifference to formal religious structures.

Ultimately, the bishop met the second challenge by aggressively confronting New York's evangelical Protestant leadership. His combative oratory, militant Roman Catholicism, virulent denunciation of American Protestantism, and personal attacks on prominent ministers such as Lyman Beecher contrasted dramatically with Dubois's approach and helped reshape New York's religious climate. Hughes attacked mixed marriages, the reading of the King James Bible in common schools, and unfavorable ethnic stereotypes in public school textbooks. His outspoken militance and refusal to suffer insults made the new bishop popular among immigrant working-class Irish Catholics and consolidated his ecclesiastical power. Catholicism assumed a new cultural significance for Irish peasants who abandoned their Gaelic language, their traditional agricultural regimen, and even their homeland in the face of growing commercialization and market pressures there. Hughes became their principal public champion. He served as a symbol, linking their religious devotionalism with strong na-

39. Dolan, *American Catholicism*, pp. 165–171; Shaw, *John Dubois*, pp. 135–164; Peter Guilday, "Trusteeism," in United States Catholic Historical Society, *Historical Records and Studies* (1929), 7–73; and Dolan, *Immigrant Church*, p. 89.

tionalistic feelings and providing a traditional cultural identity in the face of change.[40]

Hughes also effected an institutional revolution within the diocese. The number of Roman Catholic churches in the city doubled between 1842 and 1852. After failing to obtain public money for parochial schools in 1842, the bishop embarked on an aggressive building campaign designed to place an elementary school in every parish. Women religious, often from Ireland-based communities such as the Sisters of Mercy, staffed these schools, minimizing expense to the diocese. Hughes's commitment to build a separate Irish Catholic institutional network culminated in the establishment of numerous educational and social welfare organizations: St. John's College and Seminary [Fordham] (1841), Academy of the Sacred Heart for females (1841), St. Francis Xavier College on Fifteenth Street (1847), Manhattan College (1849), St. Vincent's Hospital (1849), House of Mercy to care for immigrant girls (1849), House of the Good Shepherd (1857), and New York Catholic Protectory (1863). Like Paul Cardinal Cullen in Ireland and Pius IX in the Vatican, Hughes contributed to a "devotional revolution" within the Catholic church that regularized sacramental life, romanized the liturgy, and placed formal institutions at the heart of Catholic worship.[41]

40. John R. G. Hassard, *Life of the Most Reverend John Hughes, D.D.* (New York, 1866); Henry J. Browne, "The Archdiocese of New York a Century Ago: A Memoir of Archbishop Hughes, 1838–1858," in United States Catholic Historical Society, *Historical Records and Studies* (1952), 129–190. For a more recent portrayal of Hughes's ecclesiastical style, see Vincent P. Lannie, *Public Money and Parochial Education: Bishop Hughes, Governor Seward, and the New York School Controversy* (Cleveland: Case Western Reserve University Press, 1968). Lannie views Hughes's militance as largely a reaction to Protestant nativist attacks. See also the discussion in Marvin Lazerson, "Understanding American Catholic Educational History," *History of Education Quarterly* (Fall 1977), 297–317, which broadens the issue and presents an argument concerning Hughes's need to consolidate from an internal, administrative perspective.

Miller, *Emigrants and Exiles,* pp. 234–250, discusses Roman Catholicism and nationalism and the cultural redefinition of Catholicism in Irish life.

41. Dolan, *Immigrant Church,* pp. 13, 99–140; Larkin, "Devotional Revolution." On the school controversy, see Lannie, *Public Money and Parochial Education;* Carl F. Kaestle, *The Evolution of an Urban School System: New York City, 1750–1850* (Cambridge: Harvard University Press, 1973), pp. 145–158; and Lazerson, "Understanding Catholic Educational History."

James Sanders, "Roman Catholics and the School Question in New York City: Some Suggestions for Research," in Diane Ravitch and Ronald K. Goodenow, eds., *Educating an Urban People: The New York City Experience* (New York: Teachers

The city's evangelical leaders refused to acknowledge that their own anti-Irish militance provoked Hughes's attacks and limited his options. Instead, they responded with new vigor. Protestant discontent fueled the rise of nativist politics in the 1840s. Bishop Hughes's aggressive stance helped elect Methodist publisher James Harper as mayor of New York in 1844. Tensions provoked violence and death. Philadelphia's Kensington and Southwark riots of 1844, for example, resulted from a dispute over Bible reading in public school classrooms. Within the Bible movement, the growth of Irish Catholicism precipitated a new confrontational public stance toward the Church of Rome and caused the managers to abandon their rhetorical commitment to universal Christian harmony.[42]

In 1839, one year after Hughes arrived in New York as coadjutor bishop and heir apparent to John Dubois, the board of managers invited Robert J. Breckinridge, pastor of the Second Presbyterian Church in Baltimore and a notorious nativist, to address the annual meeting. His topic, "A Plea for the Restoration of the Scriptures to the Schools," undoubtedly antagonized Catholic clerics who opposed this plan, and his denunciation of "the dogmas of popery" was one of the earliest public attacks on Romanism at an official ABS gathering. Further, Breckinridge's appearance seemed calculated to irritate Hughes personally. The future bishop had engaged Breckinridge's aristocratic brother John, a professor of pastoral theology at Princeton Seminary, in an acrimonious and well-publicized series of public debates while serving as a parish priest in Philadelphia. Breckinridge's remarks initiated an anti-Catholic rhetoric. By the early 1840s, stories concerning Roman Catholic clergymen who burned Bibles, resolutions claiming that "the Roman and other Eastern churches . . . have multiplied ministers, rit-

---

College Press, 1981), cautions that parochial schooling did not keep pace with public schooling in New York City between 1840 and 1865 and hypothesizes that Catholics had sufficient power by the 1850s to control ward schools. This would suggest, of course, that Hughes may not have been as successful as many historians have supposed and as I have argued.

42. Wilentz, *Chants Democratic*, pp. 315-324, and Bridges, *City in the Republic*, pp. 90–98, discuss New York nativism. Michael Feldberg, *The Philadelphia Riots of 1844: A Study of Ethnic Conflict* (Westport, Conn.: Greenwood Press, 1975); and David Montgomery, "The Shuttle and the Cross: Weavers and Artisans in the Kensington Riots of 1844," *Journal of Social History* (Summer 1972), 411–446, treat those riots. Ray Allen Billington, *The Protestant Crusade, 1800–1860: A Study of the Origins of American Nativism* (New York: Macmillan, 1938), remains a very useful treatment of antebellum nativism.

uals, and church edifices, but have dispensed, in great measure, with the *written* word," and assertions that "the sovereignty of the Pope impugns the supremacy of Christ" appeared regularly in the annual reports.[43]

In 1843, the issues crystallized at a special semiannual ABS meeting held in Cincinnati. John Cotton Smith (1765–1845), Bible Society president and former governor of Connecticut, set the tone. "The lurid atmosphere of Romanism," in Smith's view, had been brought to America by foreign emissaries. Worse still, "monuments of papal superstition" had arisen "in our principal cities and even on the soil first planted by the persecuted sires of New England." Gardiner Spring (1785–1873), the longtime pastor of Brick Presbyterian Church in New York, elaborated on this theme. As the principal speaker, he read a 103-page denunciation of the Church of Rome. Ridiculing the worship of saints, idolatrous statuary, the cult of the Virgin Mary, purgatory, prayers for the dead, and papal immorality, Spring lamented that "twenty years ago, few would have believed that a discussion of this subject would have been called for." By 1843, however, "even here, in a land consecrated to Protestantism," this traditional Presbyterian pastor encountered "men . . . among us, both among the clergy and the laity, who publicly endorse" papal errors. Christian diversity, social heterogeneity, and special interests now appeared to be permanent features of the American landscape, and the results did not please men seeking consensual harmony.[44]

A final clue to the changing nature of the American Bible Society's relationship with the objects of reform can be found in its first

43. For a summary of the Hughes-Breckinridge controversy, see James Hennesey, *American Catholics: A History of the Roman Catholic Community in the United States* (New York: Oxford University Press, 1981), p. 120. See "Sketch of Addresses Made at the Annual Meeting of the American Bible Society, New York, May, 1839," p. 10, Annual Meeting Papers, and ABS, *Twenty-seventh Annual Report* (1843), p. 174; Nothdurft, "The American Bible Society and Roman Catholicism," p. 22. On Breckinridge, see *Dictionary of American Biography*, 2:10–11.

44. John Cotton Smith, "Address to the Delegates appointed to attend a semiannual meeting of the Am. Bible Society to be held in the City of Cincinnati on the 1st Nov. 1843," Presidents' Papers, ABS Archives. For a biography of Smith, see William W. Andrews, *The Correspondence and Miscellanies of the Honorable John Cotton Smith* (New York: Harper & Brothers, 1847). Gardiner Spring, *A Dissertation on the Rule of Faith; Delivered at Cincinnati, Ohio, at the Annual Meeting of the American Bible Society and Published at Their Request* (New York: Leavitt, Trow, 1844), p. 103.

official history, published in 1849. Institutional histories frequently appear at moments of crisis in an organization's life. Reflections on past accomplishments and chronicles of ancient triumphs sometimes betray insecurities about present policies and future directions. Such compilations usually attempt to define and articulate coherent institutional ideologies in the face of change and uncertainty. William P. Strickland (1809–1884), an Ohio-based Bible agent, undertook the task of writing the ABS history in the late 1840s. As he sought to make sense of the Society's past, the Great Famine unleashed an unprecedented Irish exodus to North America. These new immigrants were even poorer, less skilled, and more likely to hail from Gaelic-speaking backwaters than their immediate predecessors. They brought with them a virulent hatred for Protestant England, and many embraced Irish-American Catholicism as a cultural expression.[45]

Strickland had served as the pastor of several Methodist churches in Cincinnati between 1833 and 1845. The year he arrived in that city, County Cork native John Baptist Purcell (1800–1883) had been consecrated as the diocese of Cincinnati's second Roman Catholic bishop. Although initially conciliatory toward the area's Protestant leaders, by the 1850s Purcell was the midwestern hierarchy's principal champion of parochial schools. Like Hughes, he constructed a widespread and elaborate institutional network in his see, building schools, orphanages, health care facilities, and savings and loan associations. As in New York, a separate and distinct religious life shielded Cincinnati's immigrant newcomers from the influence of native-born Protestant leaders. By the late 1840s, Cincinnati had emerged as America's midwestern center of immigrant Catholicism.[46]

Strickland claimed that his ABS institutional history, "like the enterprise it aims to promote," presented "no sectarian dogma," sought "to build up no party and sect," and deserved "a welcome in the family library of Christians of all denominations." On the same page, Strickland described "Romanism" as "the bitterest and

45. For a brief biography of Strickland, see Nolan B. Harmon, ed., *Encyclopedia of World Methodism* (Nashville: United Methodist Publishing House, 1974), pp. 2263–2264. On Irish famine immigration, Miller, *Emigrants and Exiles*, pp. 280–344, provides a persuasive reinterpretation.

46. John H. Lamott, *History of the Archdiocese of Cincinnati* (New York: Frederick Pustet, 1921), pp. 70–85, offers an introductory overview to Purcell's episcopate. See also Dolan's comments in *American Catholic Experience*, pp. 264–265.

most successful of all enemies of the Bible." Despite the church's institutional and devotional expansion in the late 1840s, the author claimed that Catholicism "is tottering to its fall." He also attacked "ecclesiastico-political demagogues, who . . . would expel the Bible from the schools of our land." Strickland identified the principal opponents of the Bible cause as "Roman Catholic priests" and decried "political demagogues . . . ready to coalesce with the Roman Catholic Church for the purpose of carrying any measure that Church might adopt." Clearly, the American Bible Society had narrowed both its mission and its definition of Christianity considerably between its founding in 1816 and the publication of Strickland's text in 1849.[47]

Strickland's historical treatment confirmed an already apparent institutional shift. In his preface, the ABS's first historian observed that "we rejoice that this is a Protestant country, and we do not believe it will ever cease to be a Protestant country so long as the 'Word of the Lord has free course and is glorified.'" The very need to assert this claim belied the reality of mid-nineteenth-century urban life. Commercial and industrial capitalism had introduced new foreign elements into the American population and created new classes of laborers. Social authority fragmented in the heterogeneous world of the nineteenth century, as various groups claimed their democratic rights and participated in political life. America's polyglot population also constructed a complex array of overlapping, yet essentially distinct, private institutions. Protestant elites grimly realized that the lessons learned at Transfiguration parish on Mott Street and Fordham College in Manhattanville differed radically from the values promulgated by New York's Public School Society and New England's antebellum colleges. The American Bible Society found some men irreconcilably hostile to its ministrations, while others followed the cross in a manner they found disconcerting.[48]

By the early 1840s, the Society had reconciled itself to the new age by narrowing its functions and escalating its rhetoric. Mariners were the first group the ABS defined as "a separate class of men" in need of reform. Despite concerted and intensive efforts, the crusade to convert seamen accomplished little and they remained "un-

47. William P. Strickland, *History of the American Bible Society, from Its Organization to the Present Time* (New York: Harper & Brothers, 1849), pp. xxix, 21, 81.

48. Ibid., p. 82.

regenerate" by the evangelicals' standards. The ABS responded to this failure by quickly deemphasizing the ministry and largely confining its efforts to selling Scriptures to the American Seamen's Friend Society. Cooperative efforts with Roman Catholics also ended by the early 1840s when the managers refused to accept the pluralist implications of a permanent Irish cultural presence in New York City. John Hughes successfully linked the immigrants' nationalist feelings with the interests of the Catholic hierarchy and created a separate religious institutional network within the city. ABS leaders retreated into the dreary and divisive rhetoric of nativism. Other defeats in the 1830s forced the Society to narrow its sights even further.

5

The Limits of Consensus in a Christian Republic: Jacksonians, Baptists, Translators, and Abolitionists

Each May, antebellum America's evangelical leadership assembled in New York City for "Anniversary Week." This seven-day celebration of a militant and millennial Protestantism featured the annual meetings of the interdenominational benevolent societies and offered an important opportunity to present the Christian cause to the American public. Meticulous advance planning ensured that the carefully crafted speeches and resolutions would receive unanimous approbation and reflect the commonly held beliefs of the national evangelical community. On May 14, 1829, the American Bible Society announced a bold new plan at this yearly gathering: the Society would begin a campaign to place the Scriptures in every American household within two years. This unprecedented endeavor attracted widespread attention, captured the imagination of evangelical America, resulted in the formation of hundreds of auxiliaries, and stimulated the Society to expand its agency system and increase its productive capacities.[1]

1. Charles I. Foster, *An Errand of Mercy: The Evangelical United Front, 1790–1837* (Chapel Hill: University of North Carolina Press, 1960), discusses Anniversary Week on pp. 147–151. A typical Anniversary Week in 1842 featured the following round of annual celebrations: Sunday, May 8: New York Bible Society in the Broad-

THE BROADWAY TABERNACLE.
in Anniversary Week.

The Broadway Tabernacle in Anniversary Week, 1856, Snyder, Black & Sturn lithographers. America's evangelical leadership gathered in New York City each May to celebrate the birth dates of the great Protestant philanthropies. The Broadway Tabernacle, a nondenominational church located at Broadway and Catherine Lane between 1836 and 1857, hosted many of the festivities. The well-dressed crowd contained a significant number of women, but only men appeared on the platform. *Courtesy of the Eno Collection, Miriam and Ira D. Wallach Division of Art, Prints, and Photographs. The New York Public Library. Astor, Lenox and Tilden Foundations.*

At this same meeting, a Baptist preacher from Philadelphia presented the following resolution: "That the co-operation of different denominations of Christians, in the distribution of the Bible, without note or comment, has a happy tendency to allay party feeling, and to strengthen the cause of evangelical religion." These two

way Tabernacle, 7:30 P.M.; Monday, May 9: American Seamen's Friend Society in the Broadway Tabernacle, 7:30 P.M.; Tuesday, May 10: New York and American Sunday

themes—a call for universal dissemination of the Scriptures and an attack on "party feeling" as socially divisive—encapsulated the early philosophy of the Bible movement. The architects of antebellum America's evangelical empire hoped to build a Bible-based, Christian, consensual social order in the young republic. They hoped to begin a national religious reformation that would touch the heart and mind of every American and assure the rule of the righteous. Abandoning older, more deterministic notions, antebellum evangelicals believed that a nation of free people would reject extreme forms of rationalism and unbelief when confronted with the words of Matthew, Mark, Luke, and John. Biblical injunctions, enshrined in the seventeenth-century language of the King James Version, could provide the Divine blueprint necessary for reintegrating political, moral, social, and economic authority.[2]

Of course, antebellum Christians never achieved the unity or unanimity of purpose implicit in the ABS's core philosophy. Denominationalism remained a potent force in American religion throughout the nineteenth century. Within the Bible movement, the Congregational, Presbyterian, Episcopal, and Dutch Reformed churches provided much of the initial stimulus behind the founding and growth of the ABS. In 1816, thirty-five of the fifty-two ABS officers and managers whose church affiliations are known belonged to these four denominations. They dominated the board

---

School Union procession at 3:00 P.M. and meeting in the Broadway Tabernacle at 7:30 P.M., Foreign Evangelical Society, in the Mercer Street Church, 7:30 P.M., American Anti-Slavery Society, 10 A.M.; Wednesday, May 11: American Tract Society in the Broadway Tabernacle, 10:00 A.M., American Home Missionary Society in the Broadway Tabernacle, 7:30 P.M., New York Colonization Society in the Middle Dutch Church, 7:30 P.M.; Thursday, May 12: American Bible Society in the Broadway Tabernacle, 10:00 A.M., Exhibition of pupils of the New York Institution for the Deaf and Dumb in the Broadway Tabernacle, 4:30 P.M., American Education Society, 10:00 A.M.; Friday, May 13: American Board of Commissioners for Foreign Missions in the Broadway Tabernacle, 10:00 A.M., New York Academy of Sacred Music in the Broadway Tabernacle, 4:30 P.M. This schedule was printed in the *New York Baptist Register,* May 6, 1842.

For a summary of the campaign to place the Scriptures in every household, see David Paul Nord, "The Evangelical Origins of Mass Media in America, 1815–1835," *Journalism Monographs,* no. 88 (Columbia: University of South Carolina, 1984), pp. 18–21. See also Henry Otis Dwight, *The Centennial History of the American Bible Society* (New York: Macmillan, 1916), 1:83–91, and William P. Strickland, *History of the American Bible Society, from Its Organization to the Present Time* (New York: Harper & Brothers, 1849), pp. 114–116.

2. ABS, *Thirteenth Annual Report* (1829), p. 6.

throughout the nineteenth century, despite an increased Methodist influence in the 1850s. This religious mix partly reflected the Protestant population of New York City, but it marginalized some Christian groups and excluded others. Despite their growth among Germans and their considerable regional success in the Midwest, for example, Lutherans remained peripheral to the ABS and did not receive one board appointment over the course of the nineteenth century. Black Christians also remained outside the Society's governing structure. Though leaders of the African Methodist Episcopal church in Philadelphia established their own Auxiliary African Bible Society in 1816, they elected not to affiliate with the ABS.[3]

The Bible movement was a divisive influence in some seemingly supportive denominations. High church Episcopalians, led by New York's Bishop John Henry Hobart, eschewed cooperative ventures with other Christians and resisted affiliation with the American Bible Society. Hobart favored denominationally exclusive organizations such as the New-York Bible and Common Prayer Book Society (1809), which were controlled by the diocesan hierarchy and combined distribution of Bibles with the promotion of specifically Episcopalian doctrines. Hobart was committed to notions of apostolic succession and faithful sacramental observance and did not seek common cause with Christians who minimized the importance of the institutional administration of grace. A more "evangelical" party within New York Episcopalianism, led by John Pintard, Rufus King, William Jay, and Cave Jones, aligned with the ABS and openly defied Hobart's hostility toward pandenominational cooperation. A

3. Timothy L. Smith, *Revivalism and Social Reform: American Protestantism on the Eve of the Civil War* (Baltimore: Johns Hopkins University Press, 1980), stresses the importance of denominationalism in antebellum religion, and his discussion on pages 15–32 is a useful corrective to historians who have overemphasized the existence of a controlling "interlocking directorate" within the benevolent empire. John H. Zimmerman, "The American Bible Society and the Churches, 1816–1900," ABS Historical Essay 23 (1966), 1:20–21, contains information on the denominational affiliations of officers and board members. The percentage of Presbyterians, Episcopalians, Congregationalists, and Dutch Reformed among officers and board members whose religious affiliations are known was 67 percent in 1816, 74 percent in 1826, 81 percent in 1836, 78 percent in 1846, 81 percent in 1856, 67 percent in 1866, 63 percent in 1876, 55 percent in 1886, and 61 percent in 1896. The reluctance of the Auxiliary African Bible Society to affiliate with the ABS is intriguing, but the reasons remain a mystery. See Robert L. Cvornyek, "The Bible in Slavery and Freedom: The American Bible Society and the Afro-American Community, 1816–1960," ABS Historical Working Papers, 1990-2, ABS Archives, pp. 16–17.

protracted and acrimonious pamphlet war ensued. Similar tensions between Protestants seeking to maintain their distinctive theological tenets and those exhibiting a broadly cooperative evangelical spirit emerged within other denominations. Such disagreements helped fuel the New School/Old School schism within Presbyterianism during the 1830s, and they affected the Dutch Reformed, German Reformed, and Baptist communions as well.[4]

Despite this divisiveness, optimism pervaded the ABS's 1829 annual meeting. The Society's consensual vision, however, did not survive the 1830s. The fourth decade of the nineteenth century was an especially disruptive period in American history. Jacksonians, promoting party competition as a virtue and placing government in the hands of professional politicians, brought a new divisive rhetoric to public life. They described a world of designing combinations, powerful factions, and sinister conspiracies. Terms like "money power" and "speculative credit" crept into public discourse. Jacksonian condemnations of "artful intriguers," who used "special privileges" to achieve wealth and power at the expense of the "productive classes," seemed to work against notions of harmony and common interest. Andrew Jackson's war against the "Monster Bank" captured the imaginations of many Americans who feared the impersonality of an expanding market economy. Interregional trading patterns had created a national network of translocal, horizontally organized social institutions that challenged traditional notions of kinship and local community. Strangers and drifters, dislocated by economic change and seeking to build new lives in the growing urban centers, moved easily over the Jacksonian landscape and operated outside the tight web of family, church, and town. Unprecedented wealth became concentrated among a small number of bankers, manufacturers, brokers, and insurance men living in cities along the Atlantic seaboard, exciting the suspicions of local merchants and farmers in the smaller towns.[5]

4. The Bible Society controversy within Episcopalianism is covered best in Robert Bruce Mullin, *Episcopal Vision/American Reality: High Church Theology and Social Thought in Evangelical America* (New Haven: Yale University Press, 1986), pp. 50–59 and 106–108. On New School Presbyterians, see George Marsden, *The Evangelical Mind and the New School Presbyterian Experience* (New Haven: Yale University Press, 1970).

5. Marvin Meyers, *The Jacksonian Persuasion: Politics and Belief* (Stanford: Stanford University Press, 1957), pp. 16–32; Robert V. Remini, *Andrew Jackson and*

A business climate that rewarded speculation at the expense of hard work and productive labor concerned many Americans. Some Christians perceived equally disturbing signs within the walls of their churches. Local religious life traditionally exerted a stabilizing social influence within the nation's communities. Parishes ideally exercised careful moral oversight, reinforced communal obligations, and lovingly but firmly guided their communicants' lives from birth through death. New religious philanthropies and moral reform organizations seemed to operate in a very different manner. Their concerns often transcended community boundaries and removed some ecclesiastical and moral matters from any local context. Americans perusing the lists of boards of managers of Bible, tract, and Sunday school societies would find the names of men who not only promoted centralization and commercial expansion in the young republic but also sat on the governing boards of banks, transportation enterprises, and insurance companies in the eastern urban centers. For many pious Protestants, physically and culturally removed from metropolitan influences, organizations like the American Bible Society bore a greater resemblance to the Second Bank of the United States than to their local parish churches.[6]

Urban riots, popular disorders, and collective violence reached unprecedented levels during the 1830s, exposing new cultural and social tensions. Sectionally divisive issues like slavery entered the national political arena, and class-based electoral movements emerged in the urban centers. Politicians increasingly courted popular support by exploiting the language of class conflict al-

the Bank War (New York: Norton, 1967). Peter Dobkin Hall, *The Organization of American Culture, 1700–1900: Private Institutions, Elites, and the Origins of American Nationality* (New York: New York University Press, 1982), pp. 151–177, discusses the emergence of this national network. Popular anxieties concerning the speculative nature of the Jacksonian economy are discussed in Karen Halttunen, *Confidence Men and Painted Women: A Study of Middle-Class Culture in America, 1830–1870* (New Haven: Yale University Press, 1982); Allan Stanley Horlick, *Country Boys and Merchant Princes: The Social Control of Young Men in New York* (Lewisburg: Bucknell University Press, 1975); and Neil Harris, *Humbug: The Art of P. T. Barnum* (Boston: Little, Brown, 1973).

6. I am not suggesting that this ideal ever perfectly corresponded with reality but rather that the ideal had begun to change. See Donald M. Scott, *From Office to Profession: The New England Ministry, 1750–1850* (Philadelphia: University of Pennsylvania Press, 1978), pp. 36–51; Richard D. Birdsall, "The Second Great Awakening and the New England Social Order," *Church History* (September 1970), 345–364; and Donald Matthews, "The Second Great Awakening as an Organizing Process, 1780–1830: An Hypothesis," *American Quarterly* (Spring 1969), 23–43.

though actually promoting business and elite interests. Rhetorical appeals to harmony and consensus appeared not merely outmoded and reactive but a transparent effort at masking elite self-interest. Financial panic in 1837 paralyzed much of the nation's business, and as the decade ended, the democracy remained mired in its worst economic depression. Social division seemed to be a permanent feature of the American landscape. Moral and civic life were being transformed, which, to some, sabotaged the republican experiment.[7]

The American Bible Society could not and did not remain insulated from these broader socioeconomic developments. Beginning in the late 1820s, public criticism of the Society and other influential organizations in the "evangelical united front" escalated sharply. This criticism came from diverse social and geographic sources. ABS critics ridiculed the society's consensual rhetoric and described it as merely another "party," "faction," or self-interested "cabal" in a hopelessly fragmented, polymorphous society. Detractors also linked the ABS with wealth, opulence, nonproductive speculation, and urban luxury. "Corrupt" forces controlled the Society, according to this view, and its managers preached a gospel of ornamentation and show far removed from the simple, frugal Calvinist precepts that informed true biblical Protestantism. Finally, antebellum critics questioned the Society's ultimate purpose. As the ABS began employing larger numbers of traveling agents

7. Recent work in social history has pointed to the importance of the late 1820s and early 1830s in the formation of new class relationships and social divisions in American society. On violence, compare the overviews in Michael Feldberg, *The Turbulent Era: Riot and Disorder in Jacksonian America* (New York: Oxford University Press, 1980), and Paul A. Gilje, *The Road to Mobocracy: Popular Disorder in New York City, 1763–1834* (Chapel Hill: University of North Carolina Press, 1987), but also consult the more specialized studies of Leonard L. Richards, *Gentlemen of Property and Standing: Anti-Abolition Mobs in Jacksonian America* (New York: Oxford University Press, 1970); Carl E. Prince, "The Great 'Riot Year': Jacksonian Democracy and Patterns of Violence in 1834," *Journal of the Early Republic* (1985), 1–19; Theodore M. Hammett, "Two Mobs of Jacksonian Boston: Ideology and Interest," *Journal of American History* (March 1976), 845–868; and David Grimsted, "Rioting in Its Jacksonian Setting," *American Historical Review* (February–June 1972), 361–397. For class-based electoral movements, see Sean Wilentz, *Chants Democratic: New York City and the Rise of the American Working Class, 1788–1850* (New York: Oxford University Press, 1984), esp. pp. 145–296; Michael Wallace, "Changing Concepts of Party in the United States: New York, 1815–1828," *American Historical Review* (December 1968), 453–491; and David Montgomery, "The Working Classes of the Pre-Industrial American City, 1780–1830," *Labor History* (1968), 3–22.

and building a substantial headquarters staff in New York, some Christians wondered whether simple "disinterested benevolence" remained the Society's principal aim. Certainly some men appeared to possess more than a disinterested stake in perpetuating the Bible Society's institutional existence. A historian wishing to discern the scope and nature of these new criticisms must be sensitive to developments on the working-class streets of Jacksonian New York, in the clapboard Primitive Baptist meetinghouses of Boone's Lick, Kentucky, and at the ornately decorated pulpit of the First Baptist Church on Broome Street.

The first indication of trouble appeared in a polemical pamphlet that was circulated on the streets of New York in 1830. *An Expose of the Rise and Proceedings of the American Bible Society, during the Thirteen Years of Its Existence*, by "A Member," excoriated the managers, ridiculed their benevolent posture, and sought "to strip [them] of their gauze and tinsel, and hold them up to public view in their proper colours." The author of this thirty-two-page pamphlet is uknown, though his frequent references to the sad state of the book trade suggest that he may have been a disgruntled printer or bookseller, upset with the increasing monopolization of the lucrative religious book market by the large nondenominational agencies. By itself, the pamphlet offers little definitive insight into popular attitudes and perceptions concerning the Bible movement. But viewed as part of recent political and social developments in New York City and the nation, it documents the coalescence of a comprehensive Jacksonian critique of the benevolent empire and a reaction against the nation's great religious philanthropies.[8]

"That the good of the public is not a primary, or, in fact, even a *minor* consideration with the Managers of this Society, is established beyond contradiction," stated the anonymous pamphleteer. He rejected the board's contention that Bible work benefited all members of the community and discerned narrow, selfish, privatistic motives in the managers' words and deeds. The rhetoric of the pamphlet touches the central ideological issue of the Age of Jackson: the relationship between "wealth" and "power." The Society's "grand aim" was "to obtain political influence and pecuniary advantages over their fellow citizens, and privileges incompatible with our republican government." Bible Society advocates had be-

8. A Member, *An Expose of the Rise and Proceedings of the American Bible Society during the Thirteen Years of Its Existence* (New York: N.p., 1830), pp. iii–iv.

come "rich in this world's goods" and adopted a "supercilious and arrogant attitude" toward the poor and those "whom they consider as not being possessed of power to expose them in their ulterior designs." Rather than serving any public good, the evangelical clergy hoped to use organizations such as the ABS to consolidate "that power which they have long been seeking."[9]

The *Expose* reflected the emergence of new political styles, strategies, and perceptions in antebellum America. Andrew Jackson's success testified to the efficiency and viability of professional party politics and to the emergence of permanent party competition as a desirable social ideal. Jackson's denunciation of aristocratic elitism seemed to promise a more democratic culture. Professional politicians in an age of almost universal adult white male suffrage soon discovered the advantage of excoriating "privileged aristocracy" and paying homage to the "producing classes." By 1830, the nation's learned clergy had become popular targets for these new Jacksonian politicians.[10]

Throughout the 1820s evangelicals brought their moral reform agenda to the political arena, hoping to enforce social decorum through legislative enactment. Notions of "disinterested benevolence" and personal responsibility to combat sin intersected with socioeconomic motivations for a political assault on "irreligion." New York City's religious reformers tried unsuccessfully to prohibit ferries and steamboats from operating on Sundays, promote universal temperance, and forbid the sale of groceries on the Sabbath. Clergymen did obtain municipal permission to "obstruct the public streets, by placing chains across them, in front of their churches and places of worship," in an effort to prevent pleasure-seeking New Yorkers from "riding in gigs and other vehicles" instead of attending weekly services. Such efforts to monitor personal behavior and orchestrate leisure time tore at the very fabric of everyday life. Recreation became increasingly important. By the late 1820s, the "Ten Hour Movement" attracted artisans and wage earners, who drew new and rigid distinctions between labor time and leisure time. Chains across the public streets reminded work-

9. Ibid., pp. 17, 27, 32.
10. Wallace, "Changing Concepts of Party." Two older works—Meyers, *Jacksonian Persuasion,* and John William Ward, *Andrew Jackson: Symbol for an Age* (New York: Oxford University Press, 1953)—contain insightful discussions of Jacksonian rhetoric.

ing-class New Yorkers that impersonal forces were exerting greater control over every aspect of their daily existence.[11]

The issue that engendered the sharpest national debate and held the greatest long-term implications for this evangelical political offensive, however, concerned Sunday mail delivery. Lyman Beecher established the General Union for Promoting the Observance of the Christian Sabbath in 1828 and spearheaded an intense national campaign to halt postal service on Sunday. Beecher and his colleagues employed such modern techniques of mass persuasion as the printing press, the petition, the letter-writing campaign, and the political rally to promote their cause with Congress. In New York City, Lewis Tappan and other benevolent laymen organized ward committees, distributed literature, and coordinated the petition campaign through the evangelical network. Beecher and Tappan, who had been key in establishing the interdenominational national agencies, attempted to apply similar persuasive techniques and adapt parallel organizational structures to achieve political goals.[12]

All accounts agree that the Sunday mail campaign was a disaster for the evangelicals. The United States Senate's Post Office Committee condemned the Sabbatarians in 1829, commenting that "extensive religious combinations lay the foundation for dangerous innovations upon the spirit of the Constitution, and upon the religious rights of the citizens." The vitriolic response to their aggressive political campaign taught supporters of the benevolent empire that many Americans did not share their definition of morality or their commitment to Sabbatarianism, temperance, and religious reform. Rather than ending moral abuses, the postal campaign unleashed a powerful reaction and exposed the political vulnerability of the "evangelical united front."[13]

Jacksonian politicians effectively exploited popular resentment

11. A Member, *An Expose*, p. 28. On the evangelical offensive during the late 1820s, see John Barkley Jentz, "Artisans, Evangelicals and the City: A Social History of Abolition and Labor Reform in Jacksonian New York" (Ph.D. dissertation, City University of New York, 1977), esp. pp. 39–111; Wilentz, *Chants Democratic*, pp. 146–154; and Bertram Wyatt-Brown, "Prelude to Abolitionism: Sabbatarianism and the Rise of the Second Party System," *Journal of American History* (September 1971), 316–341.

12. Wyatt-Brown, "Prelude to Abolitionism," and Jentz, "Artisans, Evangelicals and the City," pp. 66–111, analyze the mail campaign in detail.

13. United States Senate Post Office Committee, quoted in Jentz, "Artisans, Evangelicals and the City," p. 95.

of eastern, educated, middle-class churchgoers, claiming that a "Party of Church and State" threatened to destroy American liberty and subvert free institutions. Anticlericalism "reached a zenith" in the early 1830s, according to the historian Bertram Wyatt-Brown, and evangelical militance fueled popular resentment of Protestant America's religious leadership. The language of political discourse changed dramatically between 1816 and 1828, and the erosion of the consensual ideal meant that evangelical calls for social unity sounded reactive and antidemocratic. Egalitarian rhetoric escalated in Jacksonian New York with each passing year, as increasingly well-defined social groups challenged elite notions of a unified public culture. Ultimately, evangelicals could not successfully foster hegemony in a diverse, pluralist society. Religious reformers, professing to represent a widespread and clearly defined "public interest," were described by the professional politicians who managed the nation's public affairs as a "party," a "cabal," and a "faction."[14]

Not only was the evangelical alliance perceived as a special interest seeking power, but its scale and organization seemed to represent a concentration of money power. The *Expose of the Rise and Proceedings of the American Bible Society* was explicit on this point: "Money was the main thing needed, and money was collected from all parts, and from almost every individual in easy circumstances." The author chided ABS managers for possessing vast quantities of "Bank Stock, Insurance Stock, and Funded Debts," while simultaneously expressing a shallow and superficial concern for the welfare of the poor. The great philanthropies had transformed "almost every pulpit in our churches" into "a stall for the sale of their books" and made "clerical bookstores of our temples of worship." Pious young men, hoping to serve Christ, "have become travelling peddlers and hawkers, forcing their entrance into families which they had never before seen," and aggressively marketing "the books issued by this 'National Institution.'"[15]

Popular fears and agitation concerning the powers of the great philanthropies were not confined to New York City. As Bible Society agents traveled throughout the southern and western states in 1829

14. Wyatt-Brown, "Prelude to Abolitionism," p. 334; Wilentz, *Chants Democratic,* pp. 145–156; Wallace, "Changing Concepts of Party." See also the discussion in Paul E. Johnson, *A Shopkeeper's Millennium: Society and Revivals in Rochester, New York, 1815–1837* (New York: Hill and Wang, 1978), pp. 128–135.

15. A Member, *An Expose,* pp. 9, 11, 13.

and 1830 seeking to complete the general Scripture supply of the United States, they found, in the words of Tennessee Bible laborer William Eagleton, unanticipated "prejudices against the Bible Cause." Suspicion and skepticism greeted Bible agents in the small hamlets and isolated farmsteads of rural America. Eagleton attributed his difficulties with Tennessee natives to "the almost impregnable *encasement* of sturdy ignorance" among the area's residents, but letters from agents throughout the countryside revealed strikingly similar criticisms. As Eagleton observed from the vantage point of Newport, Tennessee, "some again have a strange fear, that this plan of circulating the Scriptures is a speculating trick."[16]

Throughout the frontier and in the nation's rural backwaters, ABS representatives repeatedly heard the national benevolence described in nearly identical language. Agent Samuel D. Blythe, writing from Woodford County, Kentucky, found that "the simple people of the church" believed that organizations such as the American Bible Society were *"money making schemes"* and that "money is the sole object." Herbert C. Thompson reported that the Ohio Baptist State Convention was investigating charges in 1829 that "the Society is a Speculating Institution." Louisiana residents had become convinced "that your object is to get their money," according to August Bayley, and that state proved resistant to the formation of local auxiliaries. Many Illinois Baptists, warned George Stacey, were "violently opposed to the Bible, T[emperance]. and M[issionary]. Societies thinking them to be *money making schemes* and that some few individuals are getting rich by them." Morris County, New Jersey, farmers, in the words of one auxiliary society officer, seemed "weak enough to believe that an agency is really a money-making concern to the man who engages in it." Lieutenant Governor William Kinney of Illinois "has declaimed much against the bible cause, told the people what vast property [Bible Society general agent John Nitchie] owned who is getting all the people's money ... [and] makes it a point in his 'Stump Speeches' to cry down all bible and charitable institutions." Jacksonian politicians, seeking votes and support in the hinterlands, had discovered that attacking "monopoly religion," no less than "monopoly banks" and "monopoly charters," elicited a passionate and positive public response.[17]

16. William Eagleton to John C. Brigham, June 17, 1829, Corresponding Secretary's Papers, ABS Archives.

17. Samuel D. Blythe to John C. Brigham, February 18, 1828; Herbert C. Thompson to John C. Brigham, July 29, 1829; August Bayley to John C. Brigham, December

Traveling Bible agents increasingly realized that the nation's yeoman farmers, local craftsmen, and small producers identified religious philanthropies with the capital-intensive, speculative, and seemingly nonproductive organizations reshaping the American economy. A central image of the Jacksonian mythology was the hardworking, manly, frugal, independent agrarian and artisan, juxtaposed against the luxurious, effeminate, opulent, parasitic entrepreneur. National philanthropies, financed and patronized by wealthy East Coast capitalists, appeared the private preserve of the rich and well-born. Before long, men would call into question the productivity and, indeed, the masculinity, of the Protestant clergy who served these institutions and urban elites. As early as 1830, many small producers would agree with the author of the *Expose*, who contrasted "the cry of distress ... among the hard-working part of our community" with the "vast sums of money" given to "the drones of the hive to build for themselves altars and high places."[18]

Bible Society administrators might dismiss such criticism as uninformed secular hostility and jealous political reaction. Combating Paineite infidelity and "party" hostility was not a new problem for them. As agents' reports reached New York City from remote corners of the nation in 1829 and 1830, however, it became distressingly apparent that not all Christians were joining the crusade to place the Holy Book in every American household. Some devoutly religious Protestants left their Bible-reading classes with unsettling theories about the concept of organized benevolence. Others questioned the Society's commitment to circulate the Scriptures "without note or comment" and charged that ABS policies served to advance narrow sectarian interests rather than promote universal biblical truth. As the managers painfully realized, the most serious

---

25, 1830; George Stacey to John C. Brigham, September 28, 1830; D. H. Johnson to John C. Brigham, September 8, 1829; and John Mason Peck to John C. Brigham, June 14, 1829, ibid.

18. A Member, *An Expose*, p. 32. On the development of this "producer ethic" in nineteenth-century America, see Howard B. Rock, *Artisans of the New Republic: The Tradesmen of New York City in the Age of Jefferson* (New York: New York University Press, 1979), pp. 301–329; Wilentz, *Chants Democratic*, pp. 157–171; Alan Dawley, *Class and Community: The Industrial Revolution in Lynn* (Cambridge: Harvard University Press, 1976), pp. 64–66; and Graham Russell Hodges, *New York City Cartmen, 1667–1850* (New York: New York University Press, 1986). On the eighteenth-century genesis of this ideology, see Eric Foner, *Tom Paine and Revolutionary America* (New York: Oxford University Press, 1976), esp. pp. 100–103.

challenges and devastating critiques came from the most dynamic and successful Protestant denomination in antebellum America.

Baptists were among the earliest and most vociferous supporters of the mission cause. Groups of local churches began forming cooperative associations in the 1780s, and by the first decade of the nineteenth century several Baptist missionary societies existed to "promote the knowledge of evangelical truth in the new settlements of the United States." New Englanders led the movement, but missionary fervor attracted considerable backing in New York, Philadelphia, and Charleston as well. Self-supporting farmer-preachers proved particularly effective in organizing congregations in the frontier South and West, and by 1814, the Baptist Board of Foreign Missions was spreading the practice of total immersion throughout the world. Early missionaries such as Adoniram Judson became denominational folk heroes.[19]

Many Baptists maintained a theological distinctiveness and denominational zeal that prevented cooperation with other Christians. They believed that only through communal and voluntary baptism by total immersion in water might one be accepted into the ranks of regenerated believers. Organized revivalism interfered with the work of the Holy Spirit and the freedom of individuals to approach God. Baptists traditionally adopted an extreme congregational form of church governance and prided themselves on their plain method of church worship. They shunned formal ministerial training, theological seminaries, and a paid clergy, leaving ordination to individual churches. As Sydney Ahlstrom has observed, Baptist preachers sprang from the common people of the small towns and countryside, "and they spoke to these people with simplicity and power, without pretense or condescension." The commitment to missions, however, brought new men and new ecclesiastical structures into the denomination. Disinterested benevolence subtly revolutionized the Baptist communion, pushing aside older men who adhered to a stricter, purer form of Calvinism. The life of John Mason Peck (1789–1857), a Bible agent and one of the most prominent proponents of Baptist missionary activity,

19. Charles L. Chaney, *The Birth of Missions in America* (South Pasadena: William Carey Library, 1976), pp. 157–158, 163, 170–172, provides an overview of Baptist participation in the mission movement. For a more sophisticated analysis, consult Joan Jacobs Brumberg, *Mission for Life: The Judson Family and American Evangelical Culture* (New York: New York University Press, 1984), pp. 1–144.

provides a starting point for examining the extraordinary denominational ferment and controversy that resulted.[20]

Peck had been born into a Congregational household in Litchfield, Connecticut, and, as his friend and Baptist biographer Rufus Babcock observed, "for eighteen years he was reared in the simplicity, frugality, and industry becoming a child of the Puritans." His father labored in "humble circumstances," and John Mason Peck's early life followed the seasonal routine of farm work in the summer and attendance at district schools in the winter. In 1807, he experienced conversion and soon married Sally Paine. By 1811, Peck moved from Connecticut to the dense wilderness of Greene County, New York, where his wife's family resided and where he continued subsistence farming. At New Durham, New York, John and Sally Peck decided that Baptist views more closely coincided with their religious leanings, and they joined the local church. Loose denominational affiliations characterized this period of American religious history, and men like Peck frequently shuttled between the evangelical churches, adding to the diverse, fluid, heterogeneous nature of the Protestant polities.[21]

In 1813, Peck decided to join the ministry. He preached regularly in Baptist churches throughout the region, received ordination from the New Durham congregation, and taught school to support his growing family. Although Peck wished to consecrate his entire life to saving souls, traditional Baptist practice required him to pursue some secular pursuit to earn his competence. He soon found that he lacked sufficient time either for studying the Scriptures or for exciting a missionary spirit among upstate New Yorkers. Peck heeded a call from a Baptist church at Amenia, Dutchess County, New York, in 1814, and supported himself solely through Gospel preaching and lecturing for nearly two years. By 1815, however, his

20. Sydney E. Ahlstrom, *A Religious History of the American People* (New Haven: Yale University Press, 1972), pp. 441–444. See also Timothy L. Smith, *Revivalism and Social Reform: American Protestantism on the Eve of the Civil War* (Baltimore: Johns Hopkins University Press, 1980), pp. 20–25. The most comprehensive denominational history remains William W. Sweet, ed., *Religion on the American Frontier: The Baptists*, vol. 1 (New York: Henry Holt, 1931). A more recent overview is William Henry Brackney, *The Baptists* (New York: Greenwood Press, 1988). The principal source for Peck is Rufus Babcock, *Forty Years of Pioneer Life: Memoir of John Mason Peck, D.D.*, reprinted with an introduction by Paul M. Harrison (Carbondale: Southern Illinois University Press, 1965).

21. Babcock, *Forty Years*, p. 13. On changing denominational affiliations, see Brumberg, *Mission for Life*, pp. 4–7.

parsimonious parishioners exhibited a lamentable "dilatoriness in furnishing [Peck] the stipulated support," and the twenty-six-year-old preacher decided to move on.[22]

Peck's experiences taught him that committed missionaries could not rely on the common folk in rural Baptist congregations to provide them with satisfactory support. With renewed zeal, he turned to organizations that transcended the boundaries of individual parishes. In 1816, Peck received a grant from an education society in New York to study under William Staughton in Philadelphia. One year later, the Triennial Baptist Missionary Convention provided funds for him to undertake a missionary tour in Missouri. For the remainder of his life, Peck received many commissions and salaries from Bible, tract, Sunday school, and missionary societies to evangelize throughout Missouri and Illinois. The American Bible Society employed him on four separate occasions between 1822 and 1830. The combined income provided a living wage. He operated independent of any congregation, yet his humble origins enabled him to speak the common language of frontier Baptists.[23]

An American sociologist analyzing Peck's career in 1965 remarked that he seemed less interested in theology than "in the infinitely organizational procedures and political conduct that was necessary to initiate and support these [frontier missionary] endeavors, and he participated in the institutional roles requisite for the maintenance of these societies." Peck promoted the formation of an extraordinary number and range of Baptist institutions, and his organizational accomplishments reveal his commitment to system: he cofounded the Baptist Home Mission Society; established Shurtleff College, the first institution of higher learning in the Illinois Territory; organized the Baptist Theological Seminary at Rock Spring, Illinois; edited four Baptist journals; served as secretary of the Baptist Publication Society; and authored numerous volumes, including a life of Daniel Boone for Jared Sparks's *Library of American Biography*. Peck actively encouraged temperance societies, Sunday school unions, and Bible societies, advocated open and tolerant discussion among all denominations, and played a major role

22. Babcock, *Forty Years*, p. 45.
23. On Peck's affiliation with the American Bible Society, see Minutes of Meetings of the Agency Committee, March 5, 1824, August 1825, June 7, 1827, March 20, 1828, October 1829, and May 3, 1830, ABS Archives. Peck's lengthy correspondence with John C. Brigham, Corresponding Secretary's Papers, ABS Archives, provides additional insight into his work, life, and personality.

in adapting the organizational structures developed by Presbyterians and Congregationalists to Baptist needs. He quickly learned, however, that not all Baptists welcomed these innovations. While stirring up revivals in Ste. Genevieve, Missouri, in 1819, Peck encountered two traveling Baptist preachers from Boone's Lick, Kentucky. The modern missionary soon found that "a set of crude and erroneous notions had been stereotyped in their minds, in Kentucky," concerning the Gospel and its teachings. Arguing that "missions, Sunday-schools, Bible societies, and such-like facilities were all men's contrivances, to take God's work out of his own hands," these preachers avoided organized benevolence and channeled their ecclesiastical energies in other directions. Peck and other Baptist promoters of missions would soon find that such men did not arrive at their opinions in isolation and that antimission feeling was not confined to small settlements along the Ohio River.[24]

Beginning in the late 1820s and increasingly during the next decade, religious observers commented on the strength, vitality, and growth of a group variously described as "Anti-Mission," "Old School," "Hard-Shell," "Primitive," and "Two-Seed-in-the Spirit" Baptists. Concentrated in the pinelands of the Carolinas, Alabama, and Georgia, the mountains of Kentucky and Tennessee, and economically isolated backwaters in upstate New York and the Midwest, Primitive Baptists discontinued correspondence with their mission-oriented brethren, withdrew from established Baptist associations, and aggressively promoted their own harsh brand of predestinarian theology. By 1844, the Primitives' numbers had grown so large that the American Baptist Publication and Sunday School Society was forced to include information concerning this schismatic group in the annual *Almanac and Baptist Register.* The "Regulars" estimated that over 31 percent of the associations and nearly 20 percent of all Baptist churches had aligned with the Primitives. *Almanac* editors also acknowledged that "probably some other associations would prefer to be placed with this class," but because "they furnish us, in but a few instances, the Minutes of their association," their numbers were unknown.[25]

24. Babcock, *Forty Years,* pp. xvii, 106–107.
25. Historians have only recently begun taking antebellum popular religious movements seriously. The most comprehensive and sweeping treatment of the phenomenon is Nathan O. Hatch, *The Democratization of American Christianity* (New Haven: Yale University Press, 1989). Principal sources on the Primitive Baptists include Bertram Wyatt-Brown, "The Antimission Movement in the Jacksonian South,"

Gilbert Beebe (1800–1881), a Norwich, Connecticut, native and itinerant preacher who led a Primitive Baptist schism at his parish in New Vernon, New York, in 1832, succinctly summarized the Old School's principal tenets: "no Mission Boards for converting the heathen, or for evangelizing the world; no Sunday Schools as nurseries to the church; no schools of any kind for teaching theology and divinity, or for preparing young men for the ministry." Hard-Shells rejected elaborate church edifices, instrumental music during the service, women preachers, "Secret Societies, Christmas Trees, Cake-Walks, and various other things tolerated and practiced by Arminian churches [and] condemned in plain terms in the New Testament." Their simple services included communal public expressions of self-abnegation and humiliation. Primitives worshiped in clapboard meetinghouses, ordained candidates for the ministry by the laying on of hands, demanded public professions of faith, and practiced foot-washing rituals. They recognized no authority higher than the congregation and promoted a broad equality of male communicants, attacking pomp, show, and pretension at every opportunity.[26]

Most critically, they argued against organized benevolence and scorned the great interdenominational societies that were reshaping antebellum religious life and removing ecclesiastical matters from the watchful eye of the local community. In their hymns, poetry, newspapers, and exhortations, the Hard-Shells ridiculed and attacked both their mission-oriented Baptist brethren and modern religion in general. The theological seminary, described by Beebe as "a work-shop of the Devil [where] he keeps his library, or Tool-chest, and Manufactures his Magicians," was a principal source of irritation to the Primitives. Beebe and his followers particularly disliked the American Bible Society, which they attacked in the language of Jacksonian Democracy. The ABS, according to the

Journal of Southern History (November 1970), 501–529; Reden Herbert Pittman, *Biographical History of Primitive or Old School Baptist Ministers of the United States* (Anderson, Ind.: Herald Publishing Company, 1870); "Primitive Baptists," *Encyclopedia of Southern Baptists* (Nashville: Broadman Press, 1958), pp. 1114–1115; "Primitive or Old School Baptists," in William Cathcart, ed., *The Baptist Encyclopaedia* (Philadelphia: Louis H. Evarts, 1883), pp. 77–78; Harry L. Poe, "The History of the Anti-Missionary Baptists" *Chronicle* (April 1939), 51–64. The statistics and quotation are from *The Almanac and Baptist Register, with Astronomical Calculations for the Year of Our Lord and Saviour Jesus Christ 1844* (Philadelphia: American Baptist Publication and Sunday School Society, 1844), p. 31, and (1845), p. 29.

26. Pittman, *Biographical History,* pp. 30, 382.

Primitives, constituted "a monstrous combination [whose] vast combination of worldly power and influence lodged in the hands of a *few*, renders it a dangerous engine against the liberties, both civil and religious, of our country." The Black Rock, Maryland, association attacked the pomp, ceremony, and show that accompanied "Anniversary Week" in New York as "a great religious parade . . . a theatre for the orator who is ambitious of preferment." Like the urban author of the *Expose*, Primitive Baptists criticized the ABS managers' financial statements, membership policies, and distribution arrangements.[27]

The observations of the Hard-Shells differed little from those of nonevangelical Jacksonian critics. Regular references to large-scale benevolent institutions "picking the pockets of the ignorant and unsuspecting" and using the Holy Book as an object of "speculation," while missionaries obtained "flocks and herds, farms and incomes, all under the color of religion," typified the reaction against the increasing inequalities and large-scale organizations dominating antebellum economic life. The Primitive challenge, however, constituted a special threat. Such attacks did not emanate from self-serving Deist politicians or Paine-influenced artisans in need of reform but from professing believers claiming to receive their inspiration from the Holy Scriptures. As such, they threatened the very notion of a common, consensual Christianity and suggested that factors such as wealth, class, organizational power, and cultural style divided Americans along lines that had little to do with the sincerity of their commitment to Jesus Christ.[28]

Some lay Baptists had aligned themselves with the American Bible Society and occupied seats on its board of managers. Socially, they were worlds apart from the Primitive Baptists and from such men as John Mason Peck, who relied on the national philanthropies for their competence. Leonard Bleecker (1755–1844), for example, was a member of the board between 1816 and 1836. A signer of the original agreement establishing the New York Stock Exchange in 1817, Bleecker served on the city's Chamber of Commerce for fifty years. His wide-ranging benevolent activities in-

27. "Popular Institutions," *Signs of the Times* 1 (February 13, 1833), and "Address to the Particular Baptist Churches of the Old School in the United States," *Signs of the Times* 1 (July 3, 1833).

28. "Report of the Committee of the Pocatalico Baptist Association, held with the Falls of Cole Church in Kanawha County, Virginia, on the 20th, 21st, and 22nd days of August, 1836," *Signs of the Times* 5 (January 13, 1837).

cluded active participation in numerous educational, missionary, and reform movements. Bleecker promoted Baptist foreign missions and theological training and helped establish such public institutions as the New York City Dispensary, New York State Prison, and New York Public School Society. He exemplified an urban, cosmopolitan, patrician approach to religious reform and operated comfortably in the social and business milieu of such New Yorkers as John Pintard.[29]

William Colgate (1783–1857) represented a different generation on the ABS board of managers, but despite his Baptist background he rarely troubled himself with the issues raised by such concerned Christians as Gilbert Beebe. Born in Kent, England, Colgate emigrated with his parents to Maryland at age twelve. His father failed as a commercial farmer and eventually lost his land owing to a title defect. By the time William Colgate found his way to New York City in 1804, his parents were eking out a meager subsistence livelihood in rural Delaware County, New York. Perhaps the family's agricultural experiences convinced young William that the future lay in the city; in any event, he quickly found employment with the largest tallow chandlery in the metropolis, became business manager of the firm, and within two years established his own laundry and toilet soap manufactory. A technological innovator, he helped transform the American soap industry, and in 1847 he opened one of the largest soap manufacturing plants in the United States at Jersey City. Colgate's innovative lines of toiletries, soaps, and shaving creams catered to the vanities, luxuriousness, and pomposity of the increasingly wealthy urban upper middle class. Frugality and simplicity had little place in his worldview, and such primitive virtues constituted a direct threat to his pocketbook as well. Old School Baptists knew him primarily as a heavy contributor to the hated Hamilton Literary and Theological Seminary (established in 1817). By the time this institution had become Madison University in 1846, Colgate and his sons had donated five-eighths of the property. Through his participation in and contributions to missionary, theological, and benevolent causes, Colgate sought to bring the Baptists into the mainstream of nineteenth-century religion and philan-

---

29. On Bleecker, see Jerome B. Holgade, *American Geneaology: Being a History of Some of the Early Settlers of North America and Their Descendants* (Albany: Joel Munsell, 1848).

thropy and into the urban capitalist world that had helped him overcome his father's economic failures.[30]

Baptist ministers who affiliated with the American Bible Society differed even more radically from their Primitive brethren. Beginning in the 1820s, the managers recognized the political desirability of reserving an unpaid secretarial position for a prominent Baptist preacher. Their choices for this post revealed the wide social gulf separating the Society's supporters from the common folk who attended Baptist services outside the urban centers. Charles G. Sommers (1793–1868) served as ABS secretary between 1825 and 1833. Born in London, he spent his youth preparing for commercial life. Sommers came to the United States in 1808 after spending several years attending school in Denmark. He found employment in John Jacob Astor's American Fur Company, experienced conversion around 1820, and decided to devote the remainder of his life to Christ. Sommers studied for the ministry in Philadelphia under the supervision of William Staughton, the learned doctor of divinity who introduced John Mason Peck and many other mission-minded Baptists to religious careers. Sommers spent the remainder of his life in urban parishes, serving as pastor of South Baptist Church in New York for over thirty years. His will provides an indication of his personal wealth and ecclesiastical commitments: he donated $5,000 to the American Baptist Home Mission Society, $5,000 to the American and Foreign Bible Society, and $10,000 to Madison University.[31]

Spencer H. Cone (1785–1855) succeeded Sommers as ABS secretary in 1833, and his career surpassed his predecessor's in worldly attainment and urbane sophistication. Cone spent his formative years in Princeton, New Jersey. He attended the College of New Jersey for two years before beginning a brief career as a teacher of Latin in a private academy in 1799. The following year he became master of a school at Burlington and went on to a wide range of secular studies and employments. Between 1800 and 1814, Cone

30. For Colgate, see William Wallace Everts, *William Colgate: The Christian Layman* (Philadelphia: American Baptist Publication Society, 1881); "William Colgate," *Dictionary of American Biography*, 20 vols., 8 supplements (New York: Charles Scribner's Sons, 1927–36), 4:299; "Colgate, William," *Appleton's Cyclopaedia of American Biography*, ed. James Grant Wilson and John Fiske (New York: D. Appleton, 1898–1931), 13:159.

31. On Sommers, see *New York Baptist Annual for 1870* (New York: James French, 1870), p. 21.

taught school in Philadelphia, studied for the Pennsylvania bar, traveled widely as a popular professional actor, joined an artillery company, obtained employment as bookkeeper and treasurer of a local newspaper, and purchased and edited the *Baltimore Whig*. Following his Baptist conversion in 1814, he procured a license to preach and soon became chaplain to the United States House of Representatives. A seven-year pastorate in Alexandria, Virginia, ensued, and in 1823 Cone moved to New York, where he would minister for the remainder of his life to the wealthy communicants of Oliver Street Baptist Church (1823–1841) and First Baptist Church on Broome Street (1841–1855). Cone always surrounded himself with the accoutrements of wealth and urbanity, and the style of worship at First Baptist was extraordinarily lavish and opulent by conventional Baptist standards. Even the generally sympathetic *New York Baptist Register* observed in 1842 that Cone's Gothic, symmetrical, and elegant First Baptist Church, "ornamented with a magnificent window of huge dimensions," broke sharply with denominational tradition and was "out of the ordinary fashion of Baptist architecture."[32]

Bleecker, Colgate, Sommers, and Cone clearly inhabited a social world closer in style and temperament to that of John Pintard, Anson G. Phelps, and Gardiner Spring than to that of many of their colleagues in the Baptist communion. Yet by 1837, all four Baptists had rejected the American Bible Society and three of them were instrumental in founding a direct denomination-based competitor. Eventually, they would publicly challenge the Society's policies and impugn the managers' integrity. The immediate issue involved a seemingly obscure and innocuous dispute concerning a complex translations problem. Broader questions of power and authority soon emerged, however, and produced an institutional schism. The result permanently doomed the Society's chances of forging even a narrow, class-based Christian consensus in nineteenth-century America.

Bible translating constituted a minor ecclesiastical industry between 1820 and 1860. The foreign mission movement stimulated churchmen to prepare biblical texts in strange tongues and, in some cases, to commit oral traditions to writing for the first time.

32. [Edward Winfield Cone], *Some Account of the Life of Spencer Houghton Cone: A Baptist Preacher in America* (New York: Livermore & Rudd, 1856); "Spencer Cone," *Dictionary of American Biography*, 4:342; *New York Baptist Register*, June 3, 1842.

In addition, an unprecedented number of new English-language versions appeared in bookstores between the third and sixth decades of the nineteenth century. Only one new American revision of the King James Bible had appeared between 1650 and 1820. By contrast, American translators and scholars constructed fourteen major new English-language works in the next four decades. Some, like Joseph Smith, grounded their writings in the authority of Divine revelation. Others carefully consulted ancient texts not available to the King James translators in 1611. Cumulatively, whether based on revelation, scholarship, or sectarian interest, these new Bibles challenged the authority of a "common version" and hinted that different classes of Americans might benefit from different versions of the sacred Scriptures.[33]

Noah Webster (1758–1843), the noted lexicographer and an orthodox New England Congregationalist, published his version of the Bible in 1833. Observing that "the language of the Bible has no inconsiderable influence in forming and preserving our own national language," he considered his revision "not merely a matter of expedience, but of moral duty." Webster understood language, and he realized that the traditional King James Version contained serious limitations which decreased its utility for the average nineteenth-century reader. "A version of the scriptures for popular use," he declared, "should consist of words expressing the sense which is most common, in popular usage." Accordingly, Webster modified obscure passages, standardized the grammar, and eliminated "some quaint and vulgar phrases" in an effort to make the document more accessible.[34]

Webster also understood authority. As a former Federalist, he knew well that "in this country there is no legislative power which claims to have the right to prescribe what version of the scriptures shall be used in the churches, or by the people." Modifying the sacred Scriptures posed serious dangers. He urged all denominations to "use the same version" and expressed his hope that "in all public discourses, treatises and controversies, the passages cited as au-

33. Harold P. Scanlin, "Bible Translation by American Individuals," in Ernst Frerichs, ed., *The Bible and Bibles in America* (Atlanta: Scholars Press, 1987). See also Margaret T. Hills, ed., *The English Bible in America* (New York: American Bible Society and New York Public Library, 1962).

34. Noah Webster, *The Holy Bible, Containing the Old and New Testaments, in the Common Version, with Amendments of the Language* (New Haven: Durrie & Peck, 1833), pp. iii, iv, v.

thorities should be uniform." Webster attempted to walk a fine line. He wished to address the needs of modern readers who could not relate to the seventeenth-century language of the Holy Bible, but he also recognized the dangers of undermining biblical authority by tinkering with the Word of God and transforming the sacred text into a mere expression of mortal man's sectarian doctrines. Other, less cautious men, whom Webster, Spencer Cone, and the American Bible Society all considered dangerous, pursued a very different course.[35]

Alexander Campbell (1788–1866) published his version of the sacred Scriptures in 1826. A native of Antrim County, Ireland, Campbell had studied at the University of Glasgow, rejected his Scotch-Presbyterian and French Huguenot heritage, and established a local and fiercely independent congregation in Brush Run, Pennsylvania, in 1811. Campbell's core doctrinal beliefs involved the need for all followers to interpret the Scriptures for themselves and to re-create a more primitive form of piety based on New Testament precepts. Campbell and his followers formed a separate denomination—the Disciples of Christ. The Disciples rejected all religious beliefs not directly sanctioned by the Bible, advocated an extremely congregational form of church polity, and called for a return to simplicity and informality in Divine worship. They expanded rapidly in the 1830s and 1840s after uniting with Barton Stone's Christian movement and claimed nearly 120,000 adherents by the middle of the nineteenth century.

Campbell's movement occurred during a period of extraordinary religious ferment. Religious sects, communitarian experiments, and pietistic movements proliferated between 1820 and 1850. Adventists, Universalists, Swedenborgians, Spiritualists, Mormons, Rappites, Hutterites, and a diverse group of smaller popular sects all rejected mainline denominational thought and sought a more intense, simpler, communal, and ultimately more democratic form of religious experience. Biblical fundamentalism remained central for many of these sects, and, much to the chagrin of the American Bible Society, they frequently offered not only new interpretations but new forms of Scripture as well.[36]

35. Ibid., pp. iv, v.
36. "Alexander Campbell," *Dictionary of American Biography*, 3:447–448. Ernest Garrison Winfred and Alfred T. DeGroot, *The Disciples of Christ: A History* (St. Louis: Bethany Press, 1948), is the standard denominational treatment. Cecil K. Thomas, *Alexander Campbell and His New Version* (St. Louis: Bethany Press, 1958),

"A living language," argued Alexander Campbell in the preface to his *Sacred Writings of the Apostles and Evangelists of Jesus Christ, Commonly Styled the New Testament,* "is constantly changing." Words, "like the fashions and customs in apparel," become "awkward and obsolete" and sometimes "convey ideas not only different from, but contrary to, their first signification." Such misinterpretation, in Campbell's view, had perverted the original words of the King James Version. Some well-meaning Christians had become "so wedded to the common version that the very defects of it have become sacred" in their minds. Campbell proposed to throw "a new light and lustre on many passages" and correct the errors of biased English translators who "did, on many occasions, give a wrong turn to words and sentences bearing upon their favorite dogmas."[37]

Campbell denied any sectarian motives, but his choice of language reinforced many of his own scriptural convictions. He substituted the word "congregation" for "church," for example, believing that the latter term had become too closely identified with expensive ecclesiastical edifices and denominational hierarchies. The most controversial feature of the new translation, however, concerned Campbell's use of the words "immerse" and "immersion" to denote "baptism." Campbell, in line with orthodox Baptist teachings, maintained that baptism could occur only by an individual's complete immersion in water. Immersionists claimed scriptural authority for their beliefs, arguing that previous translators had mistakenly transliterated the Greek *baptizo* into *baptize* and thus perverted the Creator's intentions. Non-Baptist denominations rejected this view, and the popularity of Campbell's New Testament, the appearance of numerous similar works in antebellum America, and the labors of missionary Baptist translators in preparing "immersion versions" for the heathen abroad heightened the debate. The technological innovations in printing that precipitated the founding of the ABS and fostered the growth of an evan-

---

discusses Campbell's Bible. On these sectarian movements generally, see Hatch, *Democratization of American Christianity.*

37. George Campbell, James Macknight, and Philip Doddridge, *The Sacred Writings of the Apostles and Evangelists of Jesus Christ, Commonly Styled the New Testament* (Bethany, Va.: Alexander Campbell, 1828), pp. iii, vi, x. Alexander Campbell wrote the preface and compiled the appendix, but the text was principally the work of George Campbell, Macknight, and Doddridge, who had published a London edition of their New Testament in 1818.

gelical mass media could also be employed by smaller and somewhat suspect denominations to disseminate their own distinctive beliefs and tenets.[38]

The American Bible Society, confronted with new, popular, readable versions, moved to assert its authority over scriptural translation in the 1830s. In 1836, the managers appointed the Reverend George Bush (1796–1859), chair of the Oriental Languages Department at New York University, to edit all their publications and preserve "the purity of the sacred text in all versions and editions which they may issue." They formed a select committee on versions to counsel Bush and made that group a standing committee of the board four years later. A few years earlier, the ABS had initiated a formal program of monetary grants to overseas missionaries to encourage the preparation of "accurate" translations, ensuring their conformity with Bible Society regulations and the "common version." The managers further considered placing their own agents in foreign lands, partially to oversee and supervise translation work and thereby promote textual orthodoxy.[39]

The tighter control over translation work resulted in a schism that destroyed the fragile evangelical coalition. In 1835, Baptist missionaries in Calcutta requested funds to publish a second edition of their revised New Testament in Bengali. The British and Foreign Bible Society had rejected their application because the revision differed from the King James Version and the missionaries translated *baptizo* as *immersion*. Debate dragged on in ABS board meetings for several months until, in November 1835, the managers voted thirty to fourteen, largely along denominational lines, to reject the request. In the future, the board would "encourage only such versions as conform in the principles of their translation to the Common English Version, at least so far that all the religious

---

38. Thomas, *Alexander Campbell,* esp. pp. 26–43. See also the discussion in Scanlin, "Bible Translation."

39. American Bible Society, *Twentieth Annual Report* (1836); Minutes of Meetings of the Board of Managers, July 7, 1836, and March 19, 1840; Minutes of Meetings of the Committee on Publication and Finance, February 3, 1836, and March 4, 1836, ABS Archives. On Bush, see Woodbury M. Fernald, *Memoirs and Reminiscences of the Late Prof. George Bush: Being, for the Most Part, Voluntary Contributions from Different Friends, Who Have Kindly Consented to This Memorial of His Worth* (Boston: Otis Clapp, 1860). Bush, ironically, eventually withdrew from the Presbyterian faith, aligned himself with the New Jerusalem Church, and became a prominent advocate of Swedenborgianism.

denominations represented in this Society, can consistently use and circulate said versions in their several schools and communities."[40]

The Baptist Board of Foreign Missions, observing that the Society had supported the work of the Calcutta translators for several years, expressed outrage at the ABS's lack of commitment to non-sectarianism. Cone, Bleecker, Colgate, and other Baptists on the board resigned in protest and established a rival organization, the American and Foreign Bible Society (AFBS). Acrimonious public debate between the two Bible concerns followed, and the ABS spent considerable time and money publicly denouncing the new group and attempting to frustrate its efforts to obtain a corporate charter in Albany. Baptists had always constituted a small minority of board members, contributed less than other denominations to the Bible cause, and contained a large, dissenting faction of Primitives and Hard-Shells who excoriated the ABS at every opportunity. For the ABS to sacrifice its ties with this group so as to assert greater control over Bible translation and distribution seemed a justifiable and reasonable corporate strategy.[41]

Baptists on the board appeared to have no choice but to end their affiliation with the ABS. For years they had been under attack from many communicants for abandoning basic denominational tenets and sacrificing orthodox beliefs to accumulate personal fortunes and minister to wealthy easterners. Men such as Cone and Sommers could not afford to alienate their coreligionists by condemning "immersion versions." To retain political influence and power within the Baptist communion they had to sever relations with Presbygational colleagues who shared their commitment to mis-

40. A large polemical literature documents this controversy. The most useful overviews are William H. Wyckoff, *The American Bible Society and the Baptists* (New York: John R. Bigelow, 1842); American Bible Society Board of Managers, *Bible Translations: A Brief Statement as to the Principles and Practices of the American Bible Society in Relation to Versions of the Scriptures Patronized by It, Together with a Reply to Certain Complaints against the Course Pursued* (New York: American Bible Society, 1841); and Margaret T. Hills, "Text and Translation: Principles and Problems, 1831–1860," ABS Historical Essay 16, Part III-A (1964), pp. 8–71, ABS Archives; Minutes of Meeting of the Board of Managers, November 19, 1835, ABS Archives.

41. *Proceedings of the Bible Convention, Which Met in Philadelphia, April 26, 27, 28, and 29, 1837, Together with the Report of the Board of Managers of the American and Foreign Bible Society, Embracing the Period of Its Provisional Organization* (New York: John Gray, 1837). Subsequent annual reports give a good indication of the nature and structure of the AFBS.

sions, highly centralized organizations, and national philanthropies. Cone and his friends rejected none of these modernizing impulses. The American and Foreign Bible Society's institutional structure directly paralleled that of the ABS. A board of managers decided organizational policy from its New York headquarters, agents and auxiliaries solicited funds and supplied local Baptists with the Scriptures, a state charter allowed the institution to acquire property and legacies, and grants supported mission work overseas. Despite complaints and condemnations from some Primitives, the AFBS became a source of Baptist cohesiveness, joining the Board of Foreign Missions, Publication Society, and Board of Home Missions in the pantheon of separate national denominational institutions. Cone eventually published his own "immersion version" in 1850, offering Baptists an officially sanctioned English New Testament for home use.[42]

Denominational controversies seriously divided Christians during the 1830s, but no issue exposed the limits of Christian consensus more than the slavery question. Radical abolitionism emerged as a potent force during the early 1830s, and the Bible became an important instrument in the antislavery assault on the "peculiar institution." Slaveholders long had used biblical theory to justify the subjugation of black slaves to white masters, basing their arguments on "the curse of Ham" and similar passages. Christian abolitionists promoted a very different understanding of Scripture, arguing that the spirit of the Bible prohibited human bondage and that mere association with slaveholders was sinful. Beginning in the 1830s, radical abolitionists began a national crusade to purge the Christian churches of slaveholders and marshal an evangelical united front against slavery.[43]

42. Spencer H. Cone and William H. Wyckoff, eds., *The Commonly Received Version of the New Testament . . . with Several Hundred Emendations* (New Orleans: Duncan, Hurlbutt, 1850). Cone's revision precipitated a schism within the American and Foreign Bible Society. Cone and several disaffected Baptists formed the American Bible Union when confronted with the AFBS's reluctance to sanction their revision of the Scriptures. See *Discussion on Revision of the Holy Oracles, and upon the Objects, Aims, Motives, the Constitution, Organization, Facilities, and Capacities of the American Bible Union, for Revision* (Louisville: Morton and Griswold, 1856).

43. A huge secondary literature covers abolitionism and Christianity. See John R. McKivigan, *The War against Proslavery Religion: Abolitionism and the Northern Churches, 1830–1865* (Ithaca: Cornell University Press, 1984); Lawrence J. Friedman, *Gregarious Saints: Self and Community in American Abolitionism, 1830–1870* (New York: Cambridge University Press, 1982); and James B. Stewart, *Holy War-*

Tensions crystallized during the early 1830s. The Nat Turner revolt and Jamaica slave rebellions of 1831, growing southern militancy exemplified by South Carolina's nullification crisis in 1832, and the formation of statewide antislavery societies in Massachusetts, Vermont, New Hampshire, New York, Pennsylvania, and Ohio reflected the escalating violence and growing divisions. In 1833, immediate abolitionists gathered in New York City to establish the American Anti-Slavery Society (AASS), thus bringing a new level of organization and institutional sophistication to their campaign. New York City quickly became the center of organized antislavery agitation despite its mercantile connections with the South and the racial tensions that characterized its working-class subculture.[44]

Immediate abolitionists wanted to enlist the great Christian philanthropies in the antislavery crusade. The AASS held its first meeting during Anniversary Week in 1834, thus consciously and publicly linking its cause with the evangelicals gathered in New York. On May 7, the AASS appointed a special committee to petition the American Bible Society, offering a $5,000 contribution if the ABS agreed to appropriate $20,000 "for the purpose of supplying every family of colored persons (regarding every five persons as constituting a family) in the United States, not already supplied, with a copy of the Bible, within two years from the fourth of July next." The petitioners included many prominent Christian names associated with antebellum antislaveryism: Cyrus Pitt Grosvenor, Arnold Buffern, Lewis Tappan, Theodore S. Wright, Simon Jocelyn, Beriah Green, Samuel J. May, and E. M. P. Wells.[45]

Few prominent abolitionists played significant roles within the American Bible Society. Of nearly six hundred individuals who served as officers of the four major abolition societies between 1833 and 1864, only five—Leonard Bleecker, George B. Cheever, Samuel Hanson Cox, Joshua Leavitt, and Arthur Tappan—were ever members of the ABS board of managers. Cheever did not be-

---

riors: The Abolitionists and American Slavery (New York: Hill and Wang, 1976). For a good summary of biblical justifications for, and opposition to, slavery, see James Brewer Stewart, "Abolitionists, the Bible, and the Challenge of Slavery," in Ernest R. Sandeen, ed., *The Bible and Social Reform* (Philadelphia: Fortress Press, 1982).

44. Stewart, "Abolitionists, the Bible, and the Challenge of Slavery," ably summarizes these developments.

45. "Proposition of the American Anti Slavery Soc. to raise and pay to the Amer. Bible Soc. $5000 of $20,000 to be appropriated to supply cold. persons in the U.S. in 2 years," May 7, 1834, Corresponding Secretary's Papers, ABS Archives.

come active in the Bible movement until 1846, and his interest was confined largely to translation matters. Leavitt contributed some money to the ABS, but his service to the board did not begin until after the Civil War, when he was in his seventies. Cox concluded his term on the board in 1832 before his active involvement with the antislavery crusade, and Bleecker was approaching his seventy-ninth birthday when the AASS presented its petition. The only solid link between the Antislavery Society and the Bible Society appeared to be Arthur Tappan.[46]

A native of Northampton, a successful silk merchant and capitalist innovator, and a supporter of myriad reform causes in New York City, Arthur Tappan was an early advocate of the Bible cause. Lewis Tappan recalled that his brother "took a deep interest" in the ABS's success during the late 1820s and was instrumental in financing the Society's 1829 plan to place a Bible in every American household within two years. By the time of the AASS petition, however, Arthur Tappan's interest in the Bible Society appeared to be waning. He regularly attended board meetings from his election in May 1828 through the early months of 1830 but attended only one of sixty-one meetings between September 1830 and May 1834. Tappan signed the AASS petition, but his absence from Bible Society activities eroded his power on the board. The abolitionist wing of antebellum antislaveryism counted virtually no influential advocates within the Bible movement.[47]

46. This analysis was compiled by comparing the list "Religious Affiliations of the Officers of the Four National Abolition Societies, 1833–1864," in McKivigan, *War against Proslavery Religion* with the biographies of ABS managers in Margaret R. Townsend, "Biographical Data on the Managers of the American Bible Society, 1816–1966," ABS Historical Essay 102-C (1968) (3 vols.), ABS Archives. This essay and the Biographical Files in the ABS Archives also contain data on Bleecker, Cheever, Cox, and Leavitt. William Jay, who was an active abolitionist and instrumental in the founding of the ABS, never served on the board of managers. He was elected an honorary vice-president in 1843, but he was not actively involved with the ABS at the time of the abolitionist controversy and apparently made no effort to influence its policies.

47. Lewis Tappan, *The Life of Arthur Tappan* (New York: Hurd and Houghton, 1870), pp. 74–75. Lewis Tappan's hagiographic biography is a good source, but the classic interpretive work on the Tappans is the superlative study by Bertram Wyatt-Brown, *Lewis Tappan and the Evangelical War against Slavery* (Cleveland: Case Western Reserve University Press, 1969). The data on Tappan's attendance were compiled from Board of Managers Minutes, ABS Archives. Tappan attended five of nine meetings in 1828, ten of eighteen in 1829, six of fourteen in 1830, none of thirteen in 1831, one of twenty-five in 1832, none of eighteen in 1833, and none of eight

The spirit and temperament of most American Bible Society board members was more amenable to the American Colonization Society. The ABS's two presidents during the period of the antislavery crusade, John Cotton Smith (1831–1845) and Theodore Frelinghuysen (1846–1862), advocated moderate, colonizationist positions. They provided the Society with its symbolic leadership and left the public with little doubt concerning the organization's sympathies. Influential lay managers, including William H. Aspinwall, Pelatiah Perit, and Richard T. Haines, had important commercial connections with southerners and opposed any "radical" agitation that might divide the nation. They were among the leading financial backers of the colonization movement. Other ministerial members of the ABS board such as Alexander Proudfit served the American and New York colonization societies in various administrative capacities. Abolitionists could expect little sympathy and support from the American Bible Society's leadership.[48]

The Society sought to maintain its fragile national coalition by navigating around the antislavery issue. The board thanked the Antislavery Society for its donation but reminded the abolitionists that "the direct labor of distributing" Bibles and "the responsibility of selecting the proper families and individuals . . . who are to receive them" should "be left wholly to the wisdom and piety of those who compose" local Bible Society auxiliaries. By affirming their commitment to local control, the managers avoided taking a position on the most serious moral issue dividing antebellum Americans. They placed the responsibility for distributing Bibles to slaves squarely in the hands of southern auxiliaries and silently acquiesced to local influences. When a major "Bibles for Slaves" program emerged later in the antebellum period, it was sponsored by the American Missionary Association, not the American Bible Society. Not surprisingly, the managers' approach alienated the aboli-

---

in 1834. He was not reelected to the ABS board in May 1834, though it is unclear whether his lack of attendance or his activities with the American Anti-Slavery Society was the primary reason.

48. Robert L. Cvornyek, "The Bible in Slavery and Freedom: The American Bible Society and the Afro-American Community, 1816–1890," ABS Historical Essay, American Bible Society Working Papers, 1900-2, pp. 4–7, traces the colonizationist ties of the ABS managers. See also Clifford S. Griffin, "The Abolitionists and the Benevolent Societies, 1831–1861," *Journal of Negro History* (July 1959), esp. 197–201.

tionists, who viewed the ABS as a "proslavery" organization until the Civil War introduced a new dynamic.[49]

The managers considered alienating the abolitionists a risk worth taking. By petitioning the American Bible Society and holding their own meeting during Anniversary Week, the abolitionists had transformed this celebration of Christian unity into a divisive affair. Anniversary Week in 1834 concluded with a scuffle at Chatham Street Chapel, where the Tappans invited a black carpenter who had recently returned from Liberia to denounce the colonizationists and expose the depressing state of affairs in that African nation. The ensuing uproar presaged more serious rioting in New York City in July, when antiabolitionist mobs burned down Arthur Tappan's house, sacked the Chatham Street Chapel, and directed most of their rage at New York City's growing African-American community. The American Bible Society, adhering strictly to its policy of avoidance, remained far removed from the fray. When rioting threatened New York's moral order in 1834, the Society had nothing to say.[50]

By 1840, the Society's original hope of ending faction and party feeling through Christian commitment had failed. New classes, new sects, and even new Bibles presented a depressingly complex challenge to men who believed in a unified consensual social order and hoped to solve all social problems by presenting their countrymen with the Word of God. The men who founded the American Bible Society no longer managed its day-to-day affairs, however. They had died relatively early in its institutional life, and their replacements judged the organization by very different standards. Placing the philanthropy on a sound administrative footing meant pursuing a cautious and conservative course. Ensuring institutional persistence and growth forced the managers to compromise the earlier commitment to inclusivity and to sidestep moral dilem-

49. Minutes of Meeting of the Committee on Distribution of the Board of Managers of the American Bible Society, June 4, 1834, ABS Archives. John R. McKivigan, "The Gospel Will Burst the Bonds of the Slave: The Abolitionists' Bibles for Slaves Campaign," *Negro History Bulletin* (July–September 1982), 62–64, 67, discusses the campaign by the American Missionary Association.

50. On the riots of 1834, see Paul A. Gilje, *The Road to Mobocracy: Popular Disorder in New York City, 1763–1864* (Chapel Hill: University of North Carolina Press, 1987), pp. 162–169; Wyatt-Brown, *Lewis Tappan and the Evangelical War against Slavery,* pp. 115–120; Richards, *Gentlemen of Property and Standing,* pp. 150–155; and Linda Kerber, "Abolitionists and Amalgamators: The New York City Race Riots of 1834," *New York History* (1967), 28–39.

mas. The American Bible Society remained successful and survived the conflicts of the 1830s, but the definition of success had changed and the stakes had narrowed considerably. A new religious philanthropy emerged from the struggles of the 1830s, and it sought more limited goals and espoused more corporate objectives.

6

"Motives of Both Duty and Expediency": Entering the Foreign Field, 1831–1844

The American Bible Society began moving in a new direction during the 1830s. The managers, conscious of the clear divisions within American society and lamenting their inability to forge a national consensus, elected to expand overseas. Foreign distribution and translation work began slowly, almost hesitantly. Initially, the board appeared divided over the issue and reluctant to commit significant resources abroad. Different elements suggested divergent approaches to aiding the "perishing heathen." Gradually, however, the Society's managers and administrators decided to link their institution's interests with the great Christian crusade to convert the world. Though dimly aware of its profound implications, they developed a brilliant strategy for institutional survival.

Missionary work provided an important outlet for the Society's energies in the 1830s, allowing it to assume a more critical position within the global Protestant crusade. Developments within the Society's first foreign agency—the Levant—elucidate many of the socioeconomic changes, internal tensions, and confusions over purpose that ultimately transformed the ABS from a traditional missionary moral reform agency to a modern national nonprofit corporate bureaucracy. As the managers correctly observed in

1831, "motives of both duty and expediency" informed their efforts.[1]

The motives of duty appeared straightforward enough. Article II of the American Bible Society's 1816 constitution clearly stipulated that the new organization would, "according to its ability, extend its influence to other countries, whether Christian, Mohammedan, or Pagan." During its first fifteen years, the Society responded to occasional requests from pious merchants, American consuls, and Protestant denominational missionary organizations. Still, between 1816 and 1830 the ABS appropriated less than $5,300 for foreign Bible work, although its total expenditures approached $900,000. Only 7,800 of 585,000 complete Bibles and less than 7 percent of all New Testaments, Gospels, and Epistles were circulated overseas during this period. The Society's principal focus remained domestic, and pleas for foreign aid drifted in on an irregular basis.[2]

In 1831, the ABS's board of managers received the usual ad hoc appeals for funding. Throughout that year, several denominational organizations and individual missionaries requested financial assistance. The American Board of Commissioners for Foreign Missions (ABCFM) needed money to publish Scriptures in the Mahratta language and also wished to prepare a Hawaiian edition. The Baptist General Convention required additional support for Adoniram Judson's translation work in Burma. The Reverend Eleazer Williams, working with the Mohawk Indians, sought funds to publish the Epistles of St. John in Mohawk. Further, the New Jersey Bible Society offered to raise money for Scripture work in the Sandwich Islands and called upon the ABS to develop a New Testament in modern Greek. The board decided to develop a formal policy concerning mission work abroad and appointed

1. "Report Presented by the Committee for Foreign Distribution," Minutes of Meeting of the American Bible Society Board of Managers, November 10, 1831, ABS Archives.

2. "Constitution & By-Laws," in ABS, *First Annual Report (1817)*. The Letter Book, Secretary for Foreign Correspondence Papers, 1816–1832, illustrates the types of requests received. See also George Fife Angus to Divie Bethune, October 1, 1821, and Rev. Israel Putnam to ABS, October 4, 1825, Secretary for Foreign Correspondence Papers; Rufus Anderson to John Nitchie, January 18, 1825, General Agent's Papers, ABS Archives, for other examples. See also J. Orin Oliphant, "The Parvin-Brigham Mission to Spanish America, 1823–1826," *Church History* (1945), 85–103. Rebecca Bromley, "Distribution Abroad, 1831–1860," ABS Historical Essay 15, Part III (1964), also discusses early distribution. The statistics were compiled in the "Report Presented by the Committee for Foreign Distribution."

a four-member committee on foreign distribution in October 1831 to consider these specific requests and formulate a more general statement.[3]

This committee's composition reflected the divergent outlooks within the Society and offered a clue to changing attitudes that would emerge more clearly later in the decade. James Milnor (1773–1845) was the only active clergyman on the committee. One of the Society's founders, he had served as its secretary for foreign correspondence since 1820. As the full-time rector of the prestigious St. George's Episcopal Church in Manhattan, Milnor could devote only a limited amount of energy to the Bible cause. He served on a voluntary, unpaid basis, performing largely ceremonial duties. He corresponded with foreign dignitaries about the Society's work and represented the ABS at meetings of other benevolent organizations, but his letterbook contains just a handful of items documenting overseas work. Observing in 1823 that the ABS "would not be justified, considering the lamentable want of the Scriptures among ourselves, in going into any extensive operations abroad," Milnor adopted a passive approach to his responsibilities.[4]

The remaining committee members were intimately connected with New York City's mercantile economy. Zechariah Lewis and Anson G. Phelps (1781–1853) migrated to the metropolis from small towns in the Connecticut River Valley. Richard Townley Haines spent his formative years in a New Jersey backwater. Lewis studied theology and received a license to preach but elected to channel his energies into more secular pursuits. In 1803, he began editing the *New York Commercial Advertiser* and *New York Spectator,* and he spent the remainder of his laboring life in publishing. By 1820, Lewis fused his evangelical commitments with his publishing interests when he assumed charge of the *American Missionary Register.* He exploited the opportunities of the new business information economy centered in New York City to secure his fortune. By 1825, he was able to retire from active business and devote

3. "Report Presented by the Committee for Foreign Distribution," Minutes of Meeting of the American Bible Society Board of Managers, November 10, 1831, ABS Archives.

4. James B. Milnor to Rev. Doctor Carey and his Associates in Serampore, January 20, 1823, Letter Book, Secretary for Foreign Correspondence Papers, ABS Archives. The volume of outgoing correspondence from Milnor and his predecessor, John Mitchell Mason, covering the period 1816–1832, contains just twenty-four pages.

all his time to the tract, missionary, and Bible societies that he helped establish and finance. Haines founded the successful New York City dry goods firm that provided Frederick S. Winston with his introduction to business life. Phelps pioneered in organizing the New York–Charleston packet, built a large warehousing business, and eventually earned fame as a major importer of precious metals. All three committee members owed their fortunes to the economic boom following the War of 1812, and each was prominent in New York City's globally conscious mercantile community.[5]

The committee's final report, issued on November 10, 1831, recommended expanding the Society's commitment to overseas distribution and reflected the sharp Yankee business sense that Lewis, Haines, and Phelps brought to their tasks. The "motive . . . of expediency" lay at the heart of their efforts to enter the foreign field in 1831. The committee report repeatedly referred to the wishes of the "Christian public" and the Society's responsibility to "be molded into a consonance with public feeling and expectation." Arguing that an unprecedented "zeal for Foreign Missions is felt by Christians of almost every religious name," the men of business who authored this document urged the ABS to recognize its "duty to our highly important trust" and respond to this public outcry. A consideration of the broader Protestant philanthropic marketplace illuminates the committee's sense of urgency.[6]

Since the founding of the ABCFM in 1810, foreign missions had excited the imagination of American Christians. Other denominations soon rivaled the Congregationalists in founding their own societies, and by the early 1820s these agencies had established stations throughout the Near East, Far East, Africa, and South America. The missionaries wrote prolifically, publishing their memoirs, contributing innumerable articles to the religious press, and creating a distinctive formulaic literature. By the early 1830s, the evangelical press had evolved into a very big business. Reli-

5. "Lewis, Zechariah," in *Appleton's Cyclopaedia of American Biography*, ed. James Grant Wilson and John Fiske, 12 vols. (New York: D. Appleton, 1898–1931), 3:708; "Haines, Richard Townley," in *Appleton's Cyclopaedia*, 3:28; Harold U. Faulkner, "Anson Greene Phelps," *Dictionary of American Biography*, 20 vols., 8 supplements (New York: Charles Scribner's Sons, 1927–36), vol. 7, pt. 2, pp. 525–526; Robert G. Albion, *The Rise of New York Port, 1815–1860* (New York: Charles Scribner's Sons, 1939), discusses the rise of the merchant princes and the contribution of foreign commerce to the port's prosperity. .

6. "Report Presented by the Committee for Foreign Distribution," Minutes of Meeting of the Board of Managers, November 10, 1831, ABS Archives.

gious gift books, denominational newspapers, tracts, biographical volumes, and travel accounts of missionary adventures in foreign lands all found their way into Christian homes. Reading audiences thrilled to accounts of exotic cultures, narrow escapes, physical abuse, unspeakable customs, heathen degradation, pagan rituals, sinister ecclesiasts, and dangerous exploits. Merely contributing money to the foreign cause offered Protestants the chance to participate, albeit vicariously, in an exciting adventure.[7]

By the 1830s, all Protestant philanthropies were competing aggressively in the benevolent marketplace for funds and donations. The ABS's committee on foreign distribution realized that participation in the "glamorous" foreign field would enhance the prospects of obtaining donations. Indeed, aggressive and effective fundraising appeared necessary merely to maintain financial solvency. While the Jacksonian economy concentrated larger amounts of capital in individual hands, the growing number of outlets for Christian philanthropy pressured directors of the voluntary associations to find new ways of generating interest in their enterprises. Historians have too often ignored this aspect of antebellum philanthropy, assuming instead that the Bible, tract, Sunday school, foreign mission, and educational societies functioned as individual components of a centrally coordinated, evangelically inspired benevolent empire. Noting the overlapping membership on these societies' governing boards, scholars have concluded that their managers constituted an interlocking directorate and have as-

7. On the founding and growth of the ABCFM, see Clifton Jackson Phillips, *Protestant America and the Pagan World: The First Half Century of the American Board of Commissioners for Foreign Missions, 1810–1860* (Cambridge: Harvard East Asian Monographs 32, 1969); Charles L. Chaney, *The Birth of Missions in America* (Pasadena: William Carey Library, 1976); William E. Strong, *The Story of the American Board: An Account of the First One Hundred Years of the American Board of Commissioners for Foreign Missions* (Boston: Pilgrim Press, 1910); and Rufus Anderson, *Memorial Volume of the First Fifty Years of the American Board of Commissioners for Foreign Missions* (Boston: ABCFM, 1862).

More general treatments are found in Joan Jacobs Brumberg, *Mission for Life: The Judson Family and American Evangelical Culture* (New York: New York University Press, 1984); Martin Marty, *Righteous Empire: The Protestant Experience in America* (New York: Dial Press, 1970); and Robert T. Handy, *A Christian America: Protestant Hopes and Historical Realities* (New York: Oxford University Press, 1971).

On evangelicals and publishing, see Brumberg, *Mission for Life*, pp. 62–78, and David Paul Nord, "The Evangelical Origins of Mass Media in America, 1815–1835," *Journalism Monographs*, no. 88 (Columbia: University of South Carolina, 1984).

sumed that they moved harmoniously toward the single goal of creating a Christian America.[8]

The men who administered the daily concerns of the great philanthropies and whose positions depended on their financial solvency knew better. John C. Brigham, the American Bible Society's corresponding secretary between 1826 and 1862, recognized the need for innovative fund-raising techniques. In 1829, his agents attributed their difficulties in securing donations to competition from other reform organizations. William Eagleton in Tennessee noted that contributions were "less by reason of the applications that have been recently made in behalf of the Tract Society & the Sunday School Union" and the people's perceptions that "these Presbyterians come too often." George B. Davis, in upstate New York, stressed the necessity of "visiting counties and getting pledges as earley as possable before [competing] agents had past through the several districts." Daniel Gould, writing from Nantucket, Massachusetts, complained that "this region is *full* of Agents of benevolent Societies. Dr. Edwards is to plead the temperance cause at Medford tomorrow. An Agent of the Coloniz[ation] So[ciety] is to present his object their on Tuesday next. And I hope to exhibit the B[ible]. Cause on the following Sat." Such reports underscored the need to remain conscious of the public's interests when structuring fund-raising appeals.[9]

The boards of managers of the American Bible Society, American Tract Society, American Education Society, and American Sunday School Union cooperated on many levels and provided some coordination and coherence to the institutions' activities. Their growing paid staff and agents, however, lived in the competitive and individuated economy of early nineteenth-century America. Home office administrators and roving Bible men recognized that

8. This view informs Clifford S. Griffin, *Their Brothers' Keepers: Moral Stewardship in the United States, 1800–1865* (New Brunswick: Rutgers University Press, 1960); Charles I. Foster, *An Errand of Mercy: The Evangelical United Front, 1790–1837* (Chapel Hill: University of North Carolina Press, 1960); John R. Bodo, *The Protestant Clergy and Public Issues, 1812–1848* (Princeton: Princeton University Press, 1954); Charles C. Cole, *The Social Ideas of the Northern Evangelists, 1826–1860* (New York: Columbia University Press, 1954); and Paul Boyer, *Urban Masses and Moral Order in America* (Cambridge: Harvard University Press, 1978).

9. William Eagleton to Brigham, October 22, 1829, Nashville, West Tennessee; George B. Davis to Brigham, August 17, 1829, Colosse, New York; Daniel Gould to Brigham, August 27, 1829, Nantucket, Massachusetts, Corresponding Secretary's Papers, ABS Archives.

the steady, methodical administrative work performed by the Bible Society offered little of the excitement and passion of other missionary labors. And though the ABS enjoyed a full treasury in 1831, problems were looming on the horizon.

The two-year campaign to supply every family in the United States with a Bible was ending when the committee on foreign distribution began its work. The publicity this effort generated revived many auxiliary societies and stimulated widespread support, but the ABS feared "the apathy which followed the season of high excitement and great exertion." As soon as this campaign ended in 1832, the managers' fears appeared justified. Issues of Bibles decreased nearly 70 percent. The amount of money remitted by auxiliaries for Bibles, which totaled $64,089 in 1829, decreased to $33,178 by 1832. Many auxiliaries stopped ordering, and "many of the destitute imbibed the sentiment that in this great enterprise books could be obtained without compensation." Perhaps a new appeal explicitly directed toward overseas work, argued the committee on foreign distribution, might "revive that spirit which only now slumbers, because the motives to exertion seem to have ceased." An increased effort to aid foreign missionaries could "excite emotions of gratitude, and fresh efforts for our cause" among the public "in this interval of obvious apathy in many places."[10]

Entering the foreign field offered other advantages. The committee recognized that aiding the missionary societies would make them "united in the support of the American Bible Society, the almoners of its bounty to distant lands." It would establish the Society as a patron of other evangelical efforts, thereby creating a unique function for it in the missionary community and maximizing its influence within individual denominations. Further, in the mood of ferment of the late 1820s and early 1830s public criticism of the Society escalated, some Jacksonian politicians described it as a monstrous monopoly, and strict predestinarian Protestants viewed it with suspicion. Efforts at reforming mariners had been disappointing, and American Catholicism began to assume a more hostile and Gaelic look. Perhaps a crusade directed at

10. Comments on the two-year campaign appear in ABS, *Seventeenth Annual Report* (1833). Statistics were compiled from "Treasurer's Account," *Fourteenth Annual Report* (1830), and "Treasurer's Account," *Seventeenth Annual Report* (1833). "Report Presented by the Committee for Foreign Distribution," Minutes of Meeting of the Board of Managers, November 10, 1831, ABS Archives.

reforming heathens abroad could again unite Christian Americans and restore a consensual vision to mission work.[11]

Finally, an exciting new crusade might counteract recent New York State legislation directed against charitable corporations. The triumph of Jacksonianism in 1828 dramatically altered the political climate. The state legislature enacted laws limiting the amount of property an endowed institution could hold and restricting the proportion of a decedent's estate that could be left for charitable purposes. A more broadly based appeal on behalf of the "heathen" might interest new donors in the Bible cause and free the Society from reliance on a small number of large contributors. Recognizing all of these factors, the committee recommended the full funding of all proposals before the managers and exhorted the ABS to new efforts for the cause of missions.[12]

The full board enthusiastically received this committee report, and during the next several months the ABS approached the Christian public through circulars, public meetings, the exhortations of its agents, and appeals in the *Bible Society Record*. It voted grants to various missionary organizations for translation and distribution projects, taking special care to scatter the funds among several denominations and avoid too close identification with the Congregational- and Presbyterian-based ABCFM. In May 1832, the managers reminded their supporters of the great demand for Scriptures overseas that would require "numerous and large contributions for the coming year." If philanthropists failed to meet their obligations, the board warned, "the dying heathen . . . must be told to wait and wait until American Christians have time to make collections."[13]

By 1833, the managers decided on an even more dramatic gesture. At the annual meeting, at which the ABS always emphasized and brought its special concerns before the public, the board voted to attempt "the supply of the Bible, within a definite period, to all

11. "Report Presented by the Committee for Foreign Distribution," Minutes of Meeting of the Board of Managers, November 10, 1831, ABS Archives.

12. Peter Dobkin Hall, *The Organization of American Culture, 1700–1900: Private Institutions, Elites, and the Origins of American Nationality* (New York: New York University Press, 1982), p. 120. See also Ronald E. Seavoy, *The Origins of the American Business Corporation, 1784–1855: Broadening the Concept of Public Service during Industrialization* (Westport, Conn.: Greenwood Press, 1982).

13. Minutes of Meetings of the Board of Managers, December 20, 1832, January 3, April 4, 1833; *Monthly Extracts from the Correspondence of the American Bible Society,* December 1831, February, April, May, September 1832; Minutes of Meeting of the Committee on Agencies, April 5, 1832, ABS Archives.

the inhabitants of the earth accessible to Bible Agents, and who may be willing to receive, and able to read, that sacred book." This commitment, according to the annual report for that year, "awakened a degree of emotion which it would be impossible to describe." The addresses supporting it "were characterized by eloquence and religious fervor." Recalling this event thirty years later, one board member felt "there was probably more of real, hopeful, and visible unity among the working Protestant forces of this country at that time than ever before or since."[14]

The financial response to these appeals confirmed the success of the managers' new strategy. Annual income increased by 17 percent from $85,000 to over $100,000 between 1833 and 1835; funds designated for foreign lands rose from 15 to 31 percent of the Society's cash on hand. A broader financial base and increased donations appeared to be desirable goals. In fact, the "motive of expediency" prompting the new appeals had very potent transforming implications. It contributed to the developments that were altering the American Bible Society's traditional domestic moral reform focus and changing the organization into a more structured and national corporate concern.[15]

The broadened responsibilities, financial base, and activities caused by entering the foreign field placed new constraints on the board. The managers would serve as evangelical interest brokers among the Protestant sects, dispensing aid to Baptists and Methodists as well as Congregationalists and Presbyterians. Bible Society decision makers needed to consider the potential impact of any proposal on all of these groups. Further, the wishes of the "Christian public" helped determine the nature of programs and emphases. Just as Jacksonian politicians structured their rhetoric to court the "common man" in the public arena, so the Bible Society officers crafted their appeals with one eye on the concerns of the philanthropic laity. Subtly, almost imperceptibly, the ABS began to forfeit its role as moral steward and reforming force. Novel and broad con-

14. ABS, *Eighteenth Annual Report* (1834); *Resolutions of the American Bible Society and an Address to the Christian Public, on the Subject of Supplying the Whole World with the Sacred Scriptures; within a Definite Period* (New York: D. Fanshaw, 1833); William Adams, *Life and Services of Rev. John C. Brigham, D.D., Late Corresponding Secretary of the American Bible Society* (New York: American Bible Society, 1863).

15. Statistics are taken from "Treasurer's Account," ABS, *Seventeenth Annual Report* (1833); and "Treasurer's Account," *Nineteenth Annual Report* (1835).

siderations of expediency increasingly influenced institutional policy and decision making.

These changes not only transformed the relation of the ABS to
its Christian public, they also altered the Society's dealings with
missionaries in the foreign field. Perhaps the most revealing way
to grasp these shifts is by examining the changing understanding,
even ideal, of the ABS fieldworker. The first foreign agent was appointed in 1836 during a time of institutional transition and confusion. Juxtaposing his personal goals and aspirations against the
new institutional strategies of the ABS clarifies some of the problems. He conceived his mission in traditional evangelical terms,
but as new men began exerting influence on the board in the late
1830s, the managers adopted a more modern, bureaucratic view of
his enterprise.

By 1836, the American Bible Society recognized that its foreign
appeals had not realized their full potential. Supplying grants to
missionaries and denominational boards promoted the general
cause of Christianity and increased the ABS's visibility in Protestant circles, but the denominational agencies remained more
closely identified with the foreign field. A more systematic approach to overseas work would be required to capture the attention
of the Christian public. Only by sending its own agents abroad, for
the express purpose of furthering Bible work, would the Society
achieve the recognition it sought.[16]

16. The board of managers established an agency in South America at the November 7, 1833, meeting. The managers contracted with a Newburyport, Massachusetts, educator, Isaac Watts Wheelwright, to travel throughout Spanish America and
"make strenuous efforts ... to effect distribution by sale, at whole or part price
among booksellers, Schools, and Individuals." Wheelwright traveled throughout
Chile, Peru, and Ecuador between 1834 and 1836 but enjoyed limited success. He
attributed his difficulties to hostility from the Roman Catholic clergy, government
interference, and the fact that the British and Foreign Bible Society had been distributing Scriptures without cost, thereby creating an excessive supply of Bibles. By
1836, he had received an offer from Ecuadorian president Vincente Rocafuerte to
establish a system of Lancasterian schools in that country, and his connection with
the Bible Society ended. See Wheelwright to Brigham, April 14, 24, July 8, August
25, September 22, 26, October 12, November 6, 10, December 1, 4, 18, 1834, March
12, April 9, 24, May 5, 11, June 23, August 10, 18, October 22, November 27, 1835,
January 1, June 29, 1836, Corresponding Secretary's Papers, ABS Archives.

The ABS's approach in the Levant, which involved stationing an agent in a particular place, broadening his responsibilities, and assuming that his position would
be of longer duration, constituted a significant change from the transient, tempo-

Bible Society officers identified the Levant region as a potentially fertile field for evangelical work. Bible and missionary activity had been under way in the Near East for some time. British evangelicals typically pioneered in these labors. England's Church Missionary Society had established stations at Constantinople (1819) and Smyrna (1830) and began operating a printing press at Malta in 1822. The British and Foreign Bible Society also entered this field early, appointing a representative in 1820 to oversee distribution and translation efforts in the Levant. In 1822, the BFBS had prepared an Armenian-Turkish translation of the New Testament, in cooperation with the Russian Bible Society.[17]

American Protestant missionaries also maintained a substantial presence in the Near East. In 1819, Pliny Fisk and Levi Parsons embarked for the Mediterranean under the aegis of the ABCFM, preaching and distributing literature throughout Syria, Palestine, and Egypt. By the 1830s, the ABCFM was established in the Near East, and its agents had founded schools and seminaries throughout Greece, Armenia, and Syria. ABCFM missionaries wrote prolifically, and several volumes appeared in the 1830s to interpret the area's religion, culture, and society for an American audience. The Levant was a powerful emotional reference point for Christians throughout the world. Exporting American Protestantism to the "Bible Lands," where the stories of the Old Testament actually took place, generated intense excitement.[18]

---

rary nature of Wheelwright's assignment and marked the real beginning of serious overseas work.

17. Julius Richter, *A History of Protestant Missions in the Near East* (New York: Fleming H. Revell, 1910). In January 1835, Brigham asked missionaries in Constantinople, Bombay, and China "what they should think of our sending a Bible Agent" (Letter Book, Corresponding Secretary's Papers, ABS Archives). See also Minutes of Meetings of the Committee on Agencies, May 3, 17, 1836, ABS Archives.

18. Accounts of early American missionary efforts in the Levant can be found in Robert L. Daniel, *American Philanthropy in the Near East, 1820–1960* (Athens: Ohio University Press, 1960), pp. 1–40; James A. Field, *America and the Mediterranean World, 1776–1882* (Princeton: Princeton University Press, 1969), pp. 68–103; Richter, *History of Protestant Missions;* Phillips, *Protestant America and the Pagan World,* pp. 133–140; and Joseph L. Grabill, *Protestant Diplomacy and the Near East: Missionary Influence on American Policy, 1810–1927* (Minneapolis: University of Minnesota Press, 1971), pp. 1–10.

Published contemporary accounts by Near Eastern missionaries include Eli Smith and Henry G. O. Dwight, *Missionary Researches in Armenia; Including a Journey through Asia Minor, and into Georgia and Persia, with a Visit to the Nestorian*

The Levant region intrigued the commercially minded managers who governed the American Bible Society for other reasons as well. In the mid-1830s, the area possessed relatively insignificant commercial links with the United States. Many ABS managers, like the Aspinwalls, participated in far-flung overseas trading ventures in Russia, the Far East, and South America. New markets attracted their attention, and the Levant offered a rich storehouse of exotic and luxurious goods. John Quincy Adams, an ABS vice-president, attempted to negotiate a trade treaty with the Levant region while he served as secretary of state in 1820. Adams selected Luther Bradish (1783–1863), a New York attorney and active member of the ABS board of managers, to explore the region and gather information concerning its commercial possibilities. Bradish spent six years traveling throughout Turkey, and although the treaty effort failed he returned to New York with a strong sense of the Levant's potential for American merchants. Perhaps American missionaries might serve as a vanguard, exploring the region, providing data concerning its topographical features and mysterious population, and establishing international links with Western-oriented businessmen and traders.[19]

The mid-1830s seemed an especially favorable time to begin Bible work in the Near East for other reasons as well. The Greek war for independence, which many Americans enthusiastically supported, freed Greece from Turkey in 1829 and seemingly opened up another receptive nation for the Gospel message. A large and influential group of Armenian merchants and bankers at Constantinople also welcomed Western culture, believing that contact with Protestant missionaries would help their countrymen. From the Bible Society's perspective, the fact that the ABCFM already operated in the region heightened its attractiveness. The Society maintained especially close ties with this Congregational-Presbyterian organi-

---

and *Chaldean Christians of Oormiah and Salmas* (London: George Wightman, 1834); Pliny Fisk, *Memoir of the Rev. Pliny Fisk,* ed. Alvan Bond (Boston: Crocker & Brewster, 1828); Levi Parsons, *Memoir of Rev. Levi Parsons,* comp. Daniel O. Morton (Poultney, Vt.: Smith & Shute, 1824); and Rufus Anderson, *Observations upon the Pelopennesus and Greek Islands, Made in 1829* (Boston: ABCFM, 1830).

19. "Luther Bradish," *The National Cyclopaedia of American Biography* (New York: James T. White, 1897), 3:463.

zation, which helped ensure that the new agent would find a warm reception among the missionary community.[20]

Engaging a satisfactory individual to represent the Society in this new venture required careful background work. Writing to Professor Moses Stuart at Andover Theological Seminary, corresponding secretary John Brigham summarized the prerequisites for a prospective agent: "We want a man of good scholarship, pious, prudent, energetic, and who likes the missionary work. He will be with the missions & must sympathize with them. He must help translate, read proofs, see to printing, distribution, travel some. He must be the A.B.S. in miniature. He must be a *mission* man."[21]

Brigham, in effect, advertised for a "man of character." Although a few specific administrative qualifications and a general missionary commitment appeared necessary for a successful Bible agent, Brigham relied on more general evangelical virtues when selecting a reliable employee. The success of his search depended on the national evangelical institutional network that the founders of the American Bible Society helped establish. New England's small colleges and seminaries, many of which were founded by evangelicals in the early decades of the nineteenth century, were integral to this network and served as the principal character-forming institutions in antebellum America. Their graduates internalized the standards of behavior and methods of self-control necessary for social and economic success, and their alumni functioned as the corps of trustworthy, dependable evangelicals who administered the nation's benevolent enterprises.[22]

20. On the Americans and the Greek war for independence, see Paul Constantine Pappas, *The United States and the Greek War for Independence, 1821–1828* (Boulder: East European Monographs, 1985); and Daniel, *American Philanthropy in the Near East*, pp. 1–16. Richter, *History of Protestant Missions*, discusses Armenian bankers. James A. Field, "Near East Notes and Far East Queries," in John K. Fairbank, *The Missionary Enterprise in China and America* (Cambridge: Harvard University Press, 1974), pp. 23–55, discusses the increasing predominance of the Near East in ABCFM work.

21. John C. Brigham to Moses Stuart, June 11, 1836, Letter Book, Corresponding Secretary's Papers, ABS Archives.

22. For an analysis of the concept of "character" in antebellum America, see Paul H. Mattingly, *The Classless Profession* (New York: New York University Press, 1975), pp. xii–xiii, 44–50; Joseph Kett, *Rites of Passage: Adolescence in America, 1790 to the Present* (New York: Basic Books, 1977), pp. 104–108; Hall, *Organization of American Culture*, pp. 89–94.

The American Bible Society's managers and administrators naturally corresponded with contacts, colleagues, and fellow graduates at these colleges when checking an aspiring agent's credentials or seeking someone to fill a vacancy. By the 1830s, the directors of religious benevolencies, educational institutions, and other privately supported corporations had formed a translocal elite, exchanging ideas through the expanding religious press, meetings of presbyteries and synods, alumni associations, and voluntary organizations. They staffed their agencies with reliable young men of character who presented credentials from the proper institutions and bore letters of introduction from recognizable members of the "evangelical united front." So it is not surprising that, after an extensive correspondence, John C. Brigham (Williams College, 1819) selected a tutor at his alma mater to serve as the Bible Society's first agent for the eastern Mediterranean.

Simeon Howard Calhoun was born in Boston on August 15, 1804, the sixth of nine children of Andrew and Martha Chamberlain Calhoun. His early life, however, was influenced more by rural New England's quiet countryside than the bustle of State Street. By 1814, Andrew Calhoun abandoned his mercantile pursuits and Simeon spent the remainder of his childhood on farms in Rindge, New Hampshire, and Canajoharie, New York. Like many other rural New Englanders of his generation, young Calhoun found neither economic incentives nor personal gratification on the farm. His father's acreage could not support nine children, and by 1821 Simeon Calhoun was following a well-worn path away from economic dependency and country living. Teaching in a district school, editing a local newspaper, and active in Jacksonian politics, the young man gradually accumulated sufficient capital to achieve financial independence. In 1827, Calhoun entered the junior class at Williams College, contemplating a career in law or politics.[23]

23. Biographical information on Simeon H. Calhoun has been culled from John H. Hewitt, *Williams College and Foreign Missions* (Boston: Pilgrim Press, 1914), pp. 162–169; Mrs. James S. Dennis, "Rev. Simeon Howard Calhoun," in H. C. Haydn, ed., *American Heroes on Mission Fields: Brief Missionary Biographies* (New York: American Tract Society, n.d.); Wendell Prime, ed., *Samuel Irenaeus Prime: Autobiography and Memorials* (New York: Anson D. F. Randolph, 1888), pp. 167–170; and Henry Harris Jessup, *Fifty-three Years in Syria* (New York: Fleming H. Revell, 1910), pp. 97–104. The issue of marginal New England youths is treated in David F. Allmendinger, *Paupers and Scholars: The Transformation of Student Life in Nineteenth Century New England* (New York: St. Martin's Press, 1975), pp. 1–11; and Kett, *Rites of Passage*, pp. 14–36, 93–102.

Williams, established in 1793, was one of several New England colleges founded in the late eighteenth and early nineteenth centuries close to New England's hill towns and rural poor. Drawing on marginal agricultural regions of western Massachusetts, eastern New York, and southern New Hampshire, Williams attracted a poorer, older student body than the more established collegiate institutions. It also occupied a special place in Protestant mission lore. In 1806, a significant revival occurred there, and a group of students soon coalesced around young Samuel J. Mills. Forming the Society of Brethren, they dedicated themselves to overseas missions, eventually carried their enthusiasm to Andover Theological Seminary, and ultimately stimulated the formation of the American Board of Commissioners for Foreign Missions.[24]

Calhoun—twenty-three years old, from marginal origins, yet with a broad range of worldly experiences—appeared indistinguishable from many of his hill country classmates. He had little interest in mission fervor. In fact, like many of the older and poorer students entering New England colleges, he became a disruptive force on the rural campus. Samuel I. Prime, a classmate and future Bible Society life director, recalled that Calhoun "encouraged grossly wicked conversation, and the whole influence of his association with me was deleterious, destructive of religious life, and suggestive of infidelity." Baiting his strait-laced evangelical professors, introducing students to Voltaire, advocating the election of General Jackson, and attracting "a gay, wild, wicked set of young men" to his social circle, Calhoun deservedly earned the enmity of college administrators.[25]

Unfortunately for the faculty, he also proved one of the most promising students in the Class of 1829. He graduated with Phi Beta Kappa rank, spoke on Clinton and Canning at the commencement, and even delivered the salutatory oration in Latin. An enthusiastic supporter of the Greek war for independence, Calhoun prepared a

24. Allmendinger, *Paupers and Scholars*, p. 11. On Williams College, see Calvin Durfee, *A History of Williams College* (Boston: A. Williams, 1860); Richard Austin Rice and Leverett Wilson Spring, *Williams College, Williamstown, Mass.: Historical Sketch and Views* (Boston: G. H. Ellis, 1904); and Frederick Rudolph, *Mark Hopkins and the Log: Williams College, 1836–1872* (New Haven: Yale University Press, 1956). Chaney, *Birth of Missions*, p. 191; and Gardiner Spring, *Memoirs of the Rev. Samuel J. Mills* (London: Printed for Francis Westley, 1820), treat Mills's role in mission hagiography.

25. Allmendinger, *Paupers and Scholars*, pp. 81–110; Prime, *Prime*, pp. 167–168.

Fourth of July oration on this subject, which was published that same year. Following commencement, he journeyed to Springfield and began studying law with his brother, who was serving a term as president of the Massachusetts Senate. While preparing for his new career, the prospective lawyer also accepted a position as principal of Springfield High School.[26]

Traditional missionary biography dates Calhoun's conversion to the death of his mother in 1830. This common literary convention generally served to satisfy Christian readers' taste for tales of pious womanhood, but some change evidently did occur in Simeon's life that year. By 1833, he had abandoned his law practice, resigned his position at the school, and returned to Williams to study under Mark Hopkins and Edward Dorr Griffin. For Calhoun, conversion and evangelical commitment meant renouncing his past and eschewing worldly activity. He turned his back on secular pursuits, retreated from the realm of politics, and sought to help other young men find spiritual solace through his teaching. The college quickly retained this now reliable and pious scholar as a tutor on the faculty, and he was serving in that capacity when Brigham engaged him for work at the Bible Society.[27]

The thirty-two-year-old tutor's evangelical credentials were impeccable. Hopkins and Griffin provided unqualified endorsements. Perhaps the most revealing recommendation came from David Dudley Field (1781–1867), the pastor at Stockbridge, Massachusetts. Field enthusiastically supported Calhoun's fitness for the foreign agency in a lengthy letter to Brigham which summarized the necessary qualifications for a Bible man and defined the traits required for successful missionary labor.

First, Field stressed "a good constitution," noting that Calhoun "walks considerable distances—chops wood" and "would be willing if called to it like Paul to make tents—gather sticks to make fire, & the like." Having established Calhoun's physical suitability, the pastor analyzed the tutor's mental faculties. Calling him "a thorough scholar," Field emphasized his "good common sense," and "strong vigorous mind." The prospective agent was thus endorsed not for theological brilliance or extraordinary scholarship but for his moderate intellectual attainments and ability to balance theo-

26. Hewitt, *Williams College and Foreign Missions,* p. 162; Prime, *Prime,* pp. 167–168; Simeon H. Calhoun, *An Oration Delivered July 4, 1829, before the Faculty and Students of Williams College* (Williamstown: Ridley Bannister, 1829).
27. Dennis, "Calhoun," pp. 7–8.

retical learning with worldly knowledge. Calhoun's most impressive credential was his "unusual talent in gaining the love & esteem of others & of swaying their minds." These revivalistic virtues might prove especially useful in converting the heathen and bridging cultural gaps. Finally, Calhoun was portrayed as possessing the temperate, moderate, reliable personality necessary for evangelical success. He was "bold, not rash—decided, not violent—persevering, not obstinate."[28]

Field's endorsement is significant for the issues it ignored as well as the information it provided. Much of the Bible agent's work involved translating and evaluating biblical texts. Nowhere does Field refer to Calhoun's linguistic capabilities or familiarity with the many and confusing languages of the Levant. The agent would administer a budget and distribute funds thousands of miles from the watchful eyes of the board of managers, yet no attention was given to his financial acumen or administrative skills. Calhoun would labor with a handful of American and British Protestants in a foreign land populated primarily by Moslems, Orthodox churchgoers, and Jews. Except for his romantic identification with the Greek revolution, little evidence points to his knowledge or understanding of these cultures.

Rather, the values Field extolled and the Bible Society endorsed were general evangelical virtues, believed universally applicable to any endeavor: piety, bodily vigor, sound but practical scholarly attainment, persuasiveness, reliability, moderate habits. The Bible agent needed no specific training, nor was he required to master any unique body of knowledge. Committed to the cause, he need only be a member in good standing of the national evangelical community. Indeed, when Brigham announced Calhoun's appointment to ABCFM missionary Daniel Temple on June 27, 1836, he summarized the agent's qualifications in a single sentence: "He is a man of high character."[29]

Their recent controversy over translation with the Baptist Board of Foreign Missions caused the managers to stipulate that the agent "shall be of the same religious denomination as that to which the missionaries on the ground belong." The ABS did not mandate his ordination, but Calhoun obtained a license to preach from the

---

28. David D. Field to John C. Brigham, June 20, 1836, Levant Correspondence, Corresponding Secretary's Papers, ABS Archives.

29. John C. Brigham to Daniel Temple, June 27, 1836, Letter Book, ibid.

Berkshire Association in June 1836 and was received into the Springfield Presbytery shortly before leaving for Smyrna. He received little additional guidance. His written instructions simply stated that he "will no doubt promote & aid many parts of miss[ionary] labour yet must be mainly devoted to translating, procuring paper, binding books, corresponding with miss[ionarie]s & visiting remote Stations." He was appointed for "no definite period of time," and his field was defined vaguely as the "Eastern Mediterranean." Almost as an afterthought, Brigham suggested that "he had better study Hebrew." The committee on agencies authorized Calhoun to make grants of Scriptures to American missionaries throughout the Levant but required him to "obtain the sanction of the [grants] by two, at least, of the Missionaries resident at Smyrna." Any "considerable expenditure" would require the consent of the board of managers.[30]

In many respects, Calhoun proved an effective representative of the Society, and his agency appeared to be successful. He wrote prolifically, and his descriptions of life in the Levant appeared in the *New York Observer, Missionary Herald,* and several other widely read evangelical journals, as well as in the ABS's monthly organ. This publicity permanently identified the Society as an active participant in the missionary crusade and brought its name before the philanthropic and benevolent Christian public.

Calhoun worked well with his Protestant colleagues throughout the region. The British and Foreign Bible Society wondered why its American brethren needed to station a representative at Smyrna. They already supplied Scriptures to the American missionaries in Turkey, Greece, Syria, and other Mediterranean countries and committed considerable funds to translation work. BFBS agent Benjamin Barker observed that he viewed Bible societies as having been instituted "for the Honor & Glory of God, & for the snatching of souls from eternal damnation." He feared that Americans might perceive them as mere "national institutions, to require in those who labor in them that they should endeavor to draw forth worldly

---

30. "Foreign Agent," *Extracts from the Correspondence of the American Bible Society,* October 30, 1836; Hewitt, *Williams College and Foreign Missions,* p. 164; John C. Brigham to Simeon H. Calhoun, July 13, 1836, Corresponding Secretary's Papers; Minutes of Meeting of the Committee on Agencies, September 20, 1836; Minutes of Meeting of the Board of Managers, July 7, 1836, ABS Archives.

applause in their respective countries, to the detriment of perishing souls."[31]

Calhoun quickly assured Barker that he considered himself a
member of an international Christianizing force and that his Society sought to work with the British to support evangelical goals.
Characterizing his mission as primarily exploratory, Calhoun reaf-
firmed that the ABS did not intend to establish Bible depots or sales-
rooms in areas already occupied by the British. By February 1837,
Barker reported back to England that "I was, in every respect,
much pleased with [Calhoun] & I hope we shall be able so to arrange matters as to be of mutual service to one another without
interfering with each other's work." Indeed, the ABS became one
of the British society's best customers in the Levant, purchasing
over eighteen thousand copies of the Scriptures in the eight years
of Calhoun's tenure.[32]

The experiment in the Levant appeared reasonably successful from a quantitative standpoint. The ABS either purchased,
received, or printed over seventy-eight thousand volumes between
1836 and 1844 and distributed Scriptures in Hebrew, Hebrew-Spanish, Arabic, Syriac, Persian, Turkish, Armeno-Turkish, Graeco-
Turkish, ancient and modern Armenian, ancient and modern
Greek, German, Italian, French, and English. The Society also
played a major role both in helping William Schauffler prepare
his Hebrew-Spanish Bible and in publishing William Goodell's
Armeno-Turkish version in 1841.[33]

Calhoun judged his agency by other criteria, however, and reality did not always satisfy his expectations. Rather than defining his
mission as that of a translator, proofreader, or administrator, he
viewed himself as an agent for reforming the Orthodox churches
and Christianizing the heathen. He traveled widely, seeking to
carry on a direct, personal ministry among the people of Greece,
Turkey, and Syria. Like his ABCFM colleagues, he quickly de-

31. Benjamin Barker to A. Brandram, February 4, 1837, British and Foreign Bible
Society Archives, Cambridge University, Cambridge, England.

32. Ibid.; Simeon H. Calhoun to John C. Brigham, August 22, 1844, Levant Correspondence, Corresponding Secretary's Papers, ABS Archives.

33. Simeon H. Calhoun to John C. Brigham, August 22, 1844, Levant Correspondence, Corresponding Secretary's Papers, ABS Archives; Margaret T. Hills, "Text
and Translation, Languages of the Near East," ABS Historical Essay 16, Part IV-F
(1966).

spaired of working with the Moslems and Jews and concentrated most of his efforts among Armenians and Greeks.

Calhoun penned a letter to the members of the Society of Inquiry at Williams College shortly after his arrival, hinting at his growing disillusionment with the people he encountered. "There are two classes, and but two really, of men in this world," he reminded the students. "One class consists of those who are regenerated by the Holy Ghost, and have been adopted into the family of God. The rest of our race, whether they be Turks, or Pagans, or Jews, or *speculative believers,* form the other class ... all enemies of God." In September 1837 he noted that "in no part of the world has Satan a firmer hold on the hearts of men than here." Apologizing for not preparing any material for the Society's *Extracts,* Calhoun said the cause of his negligence was that "there are very few christians or pious inquirers in the Levant" and suggested that "if Christians can be induced to pray, we shall then have something to write."[34]

Calhoun shared with other missionaries a low regard for the inhabitants of the Near East. William Goodell, for example, on a visit to the United States in 1853, rejoiced at returning "after having for so many years seen scarcely a face which was not more or less distorted by arrogance or cringing servility, by intolerance, bigotry, selfishness, or unjust suffering." Villainizing the heathen and excoriating the Eastern churches for their formalism were consistent themes in evangelical literature. Most missionaries saw the Bible as the one hope for removing the degradation they chronicled and creating universal Christianity. The Gospel was at the center of their efforts, and they strove to bring the Word of God to every land. Many developed extraordinary linguistic skills, learning new languages, compiling dictionaries and orthographies, and ultimately preparing new translations of the Scriptures in foreign tongues. Goodell viewed the Holy Book as the Sword of the Spirit "with two edges to cut into the very heart of superstition, bigotry, intolerance, and wickedness." The evangelicals' sense of personal mission demanded that they spread the Good Word to others and work for universal salvation.[35]

34. Simeon H. Calhoun to the Society of Inquiry, January 24, 1837, Williamsiana Collection, Williams College. Simeon H. Calhoun to John C. Brigham, September 1, 22, 1837, Levant Correspondence, Corresponding Secretary's Papers, ABS Archives.

35. William Goodell, *The Old and the New; or, the Changes of Thirty Years in the East, with Some Allusions to Oriental Customs as Elucidating Scripture* (New York: M. W. Dodd, 1853), pp. 3, 122.

Was Bible work the most effective way to save the heathen? As Calhoun's agency progressed, he began having doubts. In New England and New York, where literacy among the free white population appeared extraordinarily widespread, circulating Bibles and tracts might touch moral sensibilities. The Ottoman Empire presented a very different challenge and perhaps required very different solutions. Writing from Smyrna in 1837, Calhoun complained that "the door seems to be closed against the distribution of any Greek translation in Asia Minor." Pondering the Divine implications, he concluded that "it may be that [God] intends that the Gospel be *preached,* and that less dependence be placed on schools." Perhaps, "if the attention of the people could be roused by the preaching of repentance and faith," the Holy Ghost would intervene and "the united priesthood could not prevent the circulation of the Scriptures."[36]

Returning to this theme in subsequent correspondence, Calhoun reiterated that Christian educational efforts seemed futile "until the gospel is first faithfully preached, and a spirit of inquiry excited among the people." Rather than simply circulate the Scriptures, he called on missionaries to "take emphatically their lives in their hands, and go forward in the strength of the Lord Jesus and preach repentance toward God, and faith in the Lord Jesus Christ." The Society's first agent practiced this direct, personal, oral ministry in his travels through Turkey, Greece, Syria, and Egypt. This work carried him far from the tasks of translating, printing, and proofreading that the board of managers believed to be the legitimate purview of a Bible agent.[37]

Calhoun recognized his departure from his initial instructions and sought to redefine his responsibilities and mission. In September 1837, he wrote to Brigham arguing that translation work required highly specialized skills: "a knowledge of the structure and idiom of the language to which few, as I humbly think, ever attain, or can attain without many years spent in very favorable circumstances." If an agent seriously devoted himself to this work, he could never perform the time-consuming labor of distributing the Scriptures, coordinating the supply among missionaries, and overseeing printing and publication. Calhoun concluded that the Society must either send a second agent with sole responsibility for

36. Simeon H. Calhoun to John C. Brigham, January 18, 1837, Levant Correspondence, Corresponding Secretary's Papers, ABS Archives.

37. Ibid., January 24, 1837.

translating or, preferably, continue to support the work of qualified men in the field through grants. Freed of the burden of translating, the agent might assume another important role. "Will it not be better," Calhoun asked, "for the agent of the A.B.S. to be, to all intents and purposes, a missionary himself?" Rather than devoting his time to routine administrative work and difficult translations, he could serve the cause "by the supply of such information as he will be able to gather up in journeying, preaching, & distributing the Word of God."[38]

The board of managers took a different perspective. If Calhoun was just another missionary, preaching the Gospel and saving souls for Christ, why should the Bible Society support him? The ABS, after all, viewed its role in the Near East as unique. It supported other missionary efforts through its translation, Scripture production, and Bible distribution work. Involving its representative in direct evangelization might expose the Society to the charge of sectarianism. Further, the Society's substantial contributors might begin to use new criteria for judging its effectiveness. As matters now stood, the managers could point to the number of new translations and the number of Scriptures distributed as tangible results of their efforts. Calhoun complained that "we have been, and are yet looking altogether too much to the numbers put out, to the funds raised &c &c, and too little to God." The practical men of affairs who set Bible Society policy understood that all of the missionary work in the Levant had thus far yielded few actual converts or the establishment of Protestant churches. In the competition for funds in the philanthropic marketplace, the managers sought to preserve the ABS's unique role and distance it somewhat from the marginal successes or even outright failures of the mission societies.[39]

Protecting the Society's financial interests now assumed even greater importance. The Panic of 1837 ushered in the most serious depression in American history, and contributions to philanthropic causes declined dramatically. Between 1836 and 1837 the amount the Society collected for foreign distribution decreased from $13,789.19 to $6,205.09. The following year was worse, and later ABS work in the Near East was characterized by diminishing resources and increasing financial constraints.[40]

38. Ibid., September 21, 1837.
39. Ibid., September 1, 1837.
40. ABS, *Twenty-first Annual Report* (1837).

Calhoun initially reacted to the depression by commenting that "pride and fulness of bread usually bring with them some testimony of the displeasure of God" and suggesting that "the churches must pray and give more, if they would be rich." As the situation worsened and it became obvious that the churches would not give more, Calhoun insisted that if American Christians "would but reflect a little upon the condition of a nation which has no Bible, a sufficiency of funds would be forthcoming." By 1840, the Society had recalled Calhoun to America and the board debated the future of Bible work in the Levant. Calhoun toured Massachusetts in an attempt to raise funds for the work abroad but was largely unsuccessful. Joseph Hyde, the ABS's assistant treasurer, doubted "whether Mr. Calhoun has exactly the qualifications for stirring appeals in raising funds. I am somewhat doubtful as to the expediency of his undertaking even to do, what ought to be done in Boston [by the ABCFM]." Hyde's comments reflected the new belief that fundraising was a specialized task, removed from missionary and purely religious labor. By 1841, donations to the Society increased moderately, and the managers decided to reappoint Calhoun to the Levant. Increasingly, decisions concerning where and when to place agents depended more on financial exigency than on the demonstrated needs of a particular area.[41]

The Society's unstable finances made the managers reluctant to commit substantial resources to the Near East, and they urged Calhoun to seek other employment in the area. They hoped to fund his labors part-time so as to maintain a presence in the region, but the same monetary problems that plagued the ABS's fund-raising efforts also handicapped the denominational missionary organizations. Calhoun and the ABCFM workers continually urged the Society to upgrade its Mediterranean operations, but the managers voted instead in November 1842 to cut the agent's salary from $700 to $400 and regretfully informed him that they could "give no assurance of his agency being continued, beyond the expiration of the present year."[42]

41. Simeon H. Calhoun to John C. Brigham, June 24, 1837, and January 17, 1840, Levant Correspondence, Corresponding Secretary's Papers; and Joseph Hyde to John C. Brigham, October 15, 1840, Corresponding Secretary's Papers, ABS Archives.

42. Turkey Mission to John C. Brigham, April 22, 1842; Simeon H. Calhoun to John C. Brigham, May 9, 1842; Simeon H. Calhoun to John C. Brigham, January 30, 1843, Levant Correspondence, Corresponding Secretary's Papers; Minutes of Meeting of the Board of Managers, February 2, 1843, ABS Archives.

In 1843, the ABCFM finally agreed to hire Calhoun as a missionary in Syria. He left the Bible Society's employ in 1844 to begin a long and distinguished career with both the ABCFM and the Presbyterian Board of Foreign Missions. He assumed charge of an educational institution at Abeih, atop Mount Lebanon, and directed this training school and seminary until his death in 1876. Calhoun's teaching gifts, missionary impulse, and desire to work directly with natives found an outlet in the work of the denominational missionary agencies; his dedication earned him the admiration of fellow missionaries and the nickname "Cedar of Lebanon." Calhoun remained on good terms with the Bible Society, corresponded regularly with its officers, and even addressed the annual meeting on a visit to the United States shortly before his death. Eight years' experience with the ABS convinced this "man of character," however, that his missionary talents and impulse might be put to better use elsewhere.[43]

Between the presentation of the committee on foreign distribution's report in November 1831 and Calhoun's resignation in 1844, the ABS's governing board moved toward defining a new international role for the Bible Society. Committed to Christianizing the heathen and mindful of the economic realities of American life, the early managers initially perceived no conflict between the forces of God and Mammon. Calhoun's agency demonstrated that true missionary enthusiasm did not always blend well with sound fiscal and administrative policy. The managers did not yet perceive the full implications of this lesson. The ABS reopened its Levant agency in 1854, but the problems that plagued Calhoun's tenure remained unresolved. When the Society finally reconciled the tensions between pure missionary work and its own increasingly bureaucratic orientation later in the nineteenth century, its transformation into a fundamentally new and different type of institution, one far removed from the vision of its founders, was complete.

43. Dennis, "Calhoun," pp. 14–38; Jessup, *Fifty-three Years in Syria,* pp. 98–104; *Bible Society Record,* August 17, 1876, January 18, 1877.

7

Making Agents Accountable: Bureaucratization and the Agency System, 1845–1865

In the early 1850s, the managers began demanding new things from their foreign and domestic field representatives. The Bible Society produced written manuals outlining agents' responsibilities, regularized internal reporting arrangements, and created a well-defined communications system for regulating the flow of information between the field and the home office. Insurance executives, corporate attorneys, and investment bankers now wielded the power on the board, and they hoped to bring the precision of the actuarial table and the rationality of the organization chart to Bible affairs. As administrative models, the new managers relied on the railroads, the most complex and sophisticated business concerns of the age and the only other enterprises heavily dependent on nonlocal capital resources. Structural innovation naturally generated institutional debate and resistance. Older board members, used to operating informally, endorsed a more personal and "missionary" definition of Bible labor. But events of recent years—the languishing auxiliaries, failure to convert Roman Catholics and mariners, denominational and political schisms in the 1830s—convinced most managers that to be solvent, the Society, paradoxically, must distance itself from the objects of reform. Centralized, highly capitalized, efficiently coordinated organizations could withstand temporary setbacks and failures.[1]

The managers applied this business lesson to benevolence and in the process created a new institution: the national nonprofit corporate bureaucracy. They succeeded because they were able to engage a new breed of employee: the career-oriented professional agent. Agents increasingly found it profitable to play by the board's impersonal rules. Administrative work emerged as their full-time occupation, and they traded a bit of their independence and missionary zeal for the fixed monetary salary and the security of the written contract. Some agents and auxiliaries certainly challenged centralization. Dissenters on the board attempted to reverse the course of events. Change did not occur in a linear, straightforward manner, and the issues surrounding institutionalization provoked internal debate into the 1860s. Still, when the Society's officers moved into their new Bible House in 1853, certain assumptions seemed clear. The American Bible Society had narrowed its mission from Christianizing the world to producing the Scriptures and coordinating their distribution. It appeared to be a purely corporate task, measurable by purely corporate standards.

In 1853, the Society's committee on agencies produced a twenty-four-page volume of instructions intended to initiate new Bible agents to their work. This perceived need for written procedures and guidelines signaled a significant change in the managers' approach to their employees. Line-and-staff relations could no longer proceed informally. The ABS now employed thirty-seven agents, and their salaries totaled over $32,000. After 1848, agents received permission to engage their own Bible distributors and colporteurs. Agents were directly responsible for nearly $100,000 in annual donations and sales of Scriptures, and the auxiliaries they supervised contributed another $125,000 to the home office. Each agent was responsible for a specific region, usually a state or United States territory. When vacancies occurred, the managers moved quickly and decisively to fill them. The informal, haphazard nature of the

1. Brief overviews of some of the concepts addressed in this chapter can be found in Reinhard Bendix's "Bureaucracy" and Peter M. Blau's "Organizations and Theories" in *International Encyclopedia of the Social Sciences* (New York: Macmillan, 1968), 2:206–217, 11:297–304.

system dissolved in the 1830s and 1840s, when the monetary stakes increased.[2]

The language of the instructions booklet reflected this new commitment to centralization and systematization. "The Managers," observed the committee on agencies, "are trying to establish a more permanent system of Agencies than they have hitherto had." They hoped to "have the whole country divided into districts," each with "a good Agent." Good agents exhibited sound, reliable administrative virtues. They wrote to the corresponding secretary monthly, maintained accurate journals of receipts and expenditures, kept copies of all correspondence, and carefully canvassed their territories. Good agents supervised the auxiliaries but also solicited private donations and encouraged pastors to aid the cause through congregational collections. The committee urged its representatives to live conspicuously frugal lives, boarding with Christian families to reduce expenditures, and avoid any impression of extravagant salaries. Most critically, the good agent avoided "all metaphysical, sectional, ecclesiastical, or political topics, which divide the opinions of even many good men," seeking instead always to engender "harmony, forbearance, and kindness." As a representative of the Bible Society, a minister forfeited his right to discourse on the great moral issues of the day. His loyalty was to the institution, and he was expected to repress his personal opinions while on company time. He thus represented the organization in a way that his predecessors in the 1820s might have found disconcerting. Agents did receive greater incentives for their troubles. The same year the committee on agencies published its instructions, the managers also created a new class of employee. Four "Agents and Superintendents" now appeared on the payroll, with salaries of $1,200 plus expenses, a significant advance over the $800 normally allotted for agents' salaries and an indication of possible mobility within the institution.[3]

The managers welcomed the new manual but pushed for further reforms. In 1854, the agencies committee was charged with preparing a detailed report outlining the number and location of agen-

2. Report of the Sub-Committee, Minutes of Meeting of the Committee on Agencies, March 1, 1855, ABS Archives.

3. American Bible Society Committee on Agencies, *Instructions of the Committee on Agencies* (New York: American Bible Society Press, 1853), pp. 11–12, 15; Minutes of Meeting of the Committee on Agencies, March 17, 1853, ABS Archives.

cies and analyzing the distribution and collection statistics for each region. The managers also desired recommendations "to reduce the whole Expense of Agencies, if possible, or to Classify those Expenses more accurately among the accounts to which they belong." The board never before had required detailed breakdowns of receipts and expenditures. As the system expanded and the managers sought to keep individual agents for longer periods of service, some impartial standard of accountability appeared necessary.[4]

During the 1850s, managers frequently questioned the efficiency of the Society's inner workings. A corporate culture constructed on such devices as the Produce Exchange (formed in 1850), the Mercantile Agency (founded in 1841) and the telegraph ("What hath God wrought?" was transmitted in 1844) viewed the personal exhortation and the oral plea with increasing skepticism. Conducting business through a voluntary network of auxiliary societies appeared a quaint and reactive approach, more appropriate for a society based on well-defined local elites. A capital-intensive corporate age required new strategies. American jurisprudence encouraged the growth of charitable trusts and large-scale benevolence following the United States Supreme Court's ruling in the Girard Will case in 1844. By upholding Stephen Girard's posthumous grants, the Court established a permissive public policy toward private philanthropy and limited heirs' rights to contest legacies. This ruling did not affect more restrictive regulations in New York, but the Bible Society took full advantage of its political contacts to modernize its administrative structure within the state's legal framework. Throughout the 1840s, the ABS gradually revolutionized its operations: it secured incorporation from the New York State legislature in 1841, pursued a new and aggressive policy concerning legacies and annuities after 1848, and amended its charter so that it might "purchase, take hold and convey or lease certain real estate" in 1852.[5]

4. Minutes of Meeting of the Board of Managers, June 1854, ABS Archives.
5. On changes in the corporate world, see especially Alfred D. Chandler, Jr., *The Visible Hand: The Managerial Revolution in American Business* (Cambridge: Harvard University Press, 1977), and Thomas C. Cochran, "The Business Revolution," *American Historical Review* (December 1974), 1449–1466. Evangelical Protestants played a prominent role in many of the developments cited by Chandler and Cochran: for example, Samuel F. B. Morse invented the telegraph and Lewis Tappan played an instrumental role in creating the credit system. See Gregory Singleton, "Protestant Voluntary Organizations and the Shaping of Victorian America," in Daniel Walker Howe, ed., *Victorian America* (Philadelphia: University of Pennsylvania

Printing House Square, 1866, Endicott & Company lithographers. By the time the ABS moved uptown, lower Manhattan presented a very different appearance, as this print illustrating a parade only two blocks from the site of the original Nassau Street Bible House suggests. Larger corporate concerns replaced small commercial establishments, and occasionally unruly crowds created a new type of street culture. *Courtesy of the Eno Collection, Miriam and Ira D. Wallach Division of Art, Prints and Photographs. The New York Public Library. Astor, Lenox and Tilden Foundations.*

As they considered various methods to finance the new Bible House in 1852, the managers decided "that the amount proposed cannot be raised in the ordinary way or by any hired Agency." Rather, the money might be secured "by the different members of the Board associating together, or associating their Pastors with

Press, 1976); and Bertram Wyatt-Brown, *Lewis Tappan and the Evangelical War against Slavery* (Cleveland: Case Western Reserve University Press, 1969).

Concerning the legal questions surrounding legacies and charitable trusts, see Howard S. Miller, *The Legal Foundations of American Philanthropy, 1776–1844* (Madison: State Historical Society of Wisconsin, 1961); Sandford Hunt, *Laws Relating to Religious Corporations* (New York: Nelson & Phillips, 1876); Austin W. Scott, "Charitable Trusts in New York," *New York University Law Review* (April 1951),

them and calling upon prominent individuals of known wealth & liberality." Twenty prominent New Yorkers, many of them linked directly with the new world of investment banking and brokerage, contributed nearly $30,000. The names of William B. Astor, James Muncaster Brown, Anson G. Phelps, William E. Dodge, James Lenox, Edward J. Woolsey, and William H. Aspinwall appeared on the building fund donor list. Money, wealth, financial institutions, and corporate power were concentrated in the great metropolis. Soliciting subscriptions and peddling Bibles in Kentucky and Tennessee might stimulate a few conversions, but were they an effective use of resources or good business?[6]

When the agencies committee received the board's mandate to review expenditures in 1854, it reacted with caution. Older men with traditional views still influenced committee proceedings, and not all evangelicals were anxious to judge their work by the new business standards. William Forrest (1791–1865), a member of the Church of Christ who spent his entire career conducting a training institution for young men in Manhattan, chaired the agencies committee. His report to the full board in March 1855 contained a strong defense of the existing system. "The Agent is a Missionary," he explained, and his work "in exploring the destitution of the Country, and in seeing the individuals & families, and whole communities" supplied with Scriptures deserved equal rank with his fund-raising acumen. By placing the Word of the Lord "into their *hands,* he is often the means, under God, of putting it into their *hearts."* His work "bears directly upon the salvation of men—upon their personal holiness and benevolent activities." Success should not always be measured by immediate results. Not all objects of reform contributed to the Bible cause, but the influence of the Good Book helped men do "good to other interests, and shows itself in increased benevolent action towards other and more kindred institutions." Forrest thus articulated an older conception of Bible work:

251–265; and Peter Dobkin Hall, *The Organization of American Culture, 1700–1900: Private Institutions, Elites, and the Origins of American Nationality* (New York: New York University Press, 1982), pp. 114–124.

On the Bible Society's internal efforts to change its structures, see ABS, *Twenty-fifth Annual Report* (1841); Minutes of Meeting of the Board of Managers, March 2, 1848, and May 6, 1852, ABS Archives.

6. Minutes of Meeting of the Committee on Agencies, November 3, 1852, ABS Archives; "Final Report of the Building Committee," reprinted in ABS, *Thirty-eighth Annual Report* (1854).

the agent as missionary, revivalist, and soldier in the greater cause of Christ and religious benevolence. He reserved harsh words for those who applied different standards. "To measure such work by the dollars and cents which are derived from it, or to estimate it by the amount which it costs, is like counting the price of the ointment, when poured upon the head of the Saviour—like an attempt to bring within the computation of a business transaction the worth of truth, or the gain of Godliness."[7]

In the same report, the committee undermined its plea to place God before Mammon. Ultimately, Forrest and his colleagues provided the board with the breakdown it requested and even heralded the results. An in-depth analysis revealed "how intimately this system is Connected with the prosperity of this Society." When the board "materially diminished the action of its Agencies," the committee found "a corresponding diminution in the amount of its receipts." Increased expenditures on agencies produced "a corresponding increase in the amount of receipts." The committee used this crude economic analysis to justify the agency system. It accepted receipts and expenditures as valid gauges of success and failure. The intangible factors not subject to quantitative measurement receded to the background. Improving the system meant simply spending more money: paying agents better, creating smaller districts, and providing sufficient inducements to lure men from pastoral labor. Forrest's more telling critique remained buried beneath statistics and balance sheets.[8]

The board received and studied this information but still wished to tighten its control over the agents. By 1858, the ratio of expenditures to receipts in the agency department rose and the managers expressed alarm. In July of that year, Archibald Russell (1811–1871) pressed for new measures. Russell had been born in Edinburgh, Scotland, and trained in the law, but he made his greatest mark in the new science of statistics and was one of the founders of the American Geographical and Statistical Society. His *Principles of Statistical Inquiry* gained him widespread recognition, and he was instrumental in revising the schedules for the 1850 census. As president of the Five Points House of Industry and presiding officer of a savings institution for the poor, he knew the value of a well-

7. Minutes of Meeting of the Committee on Agencies, March 1, 1855, ABS Archives.
8. Ibid.

managed benevolent enterprise. Russell began his active association with the board of managers in 1843 (eight years after Forrest), and his concerns reflected the anxieties of recently appointed businessmen. He asked the agencies committee to consider three resolutions. First, Russell wished to introduce "a tabulated Schedule to be filled [out] by each Agent, weekly, and transmitted to the Bible House, monthly." The printed schedule would include "all the information relative to the acts of the Agents and result of their labors that may be easily stated in this form." Second, he suggested that when an agent's commission came up for renewal, an "abstract of the last year of the tabulated reports which have been forwarded from time to time" be carefully examined and presented to the full board. Finally, Russell proposed "abolishing all Sub-Agencies and making each Agent report to the Bible House." These measures significantly reduced agents' autonomy, provided new instruments for gauging their effectiveness, and revolutionized institutional record keeping.[9]

The agencies committee, still chaired by Forrest, responded in February 1859. Members especially objected to changing the standard reporting format. Traditionally, each agent presented his monthly account "in a narrative form." The older report included "most of the particulars enumerated in the schedule proposed to be adopted," but it also offered much more. The agent attempted to "weave the whole into a narrative, which affords an opportunity of introducing anything interesting in the way of incident, anecdote, remarks or conversations coming under their notice or to their knowledge." This narrative helped committee members keep abreast of the agent's personal progress and evaluate the general state of the Bible cause in a specific district. It was "decidedly preferable to giving a dry tabulated statement."[10]

The full board disagreed. Its members had no time to sift through long stories and anecdotes. Business concerns and service on benevolent boards took up more time in 1859 than in 1816. The revolutions in transportation and communication that allowed

9. "Russell, Archibald," *Appleton's Cyclopaedia of American Biography,* ed. James Grant Wilson and John Fiske (New York: D. Appleton, 1898), 41:432; Margo J. Anderson, *The American Census: A Social History* (New Haven: Yale University Press, 1988), pp. 36–37; *New York Times,* April 21, 1871; Minutes of Meeting of the Board of Managers, July 1, 1858, ABS Archives.

10. Minutes of Meeting of the Committee on Agencies, February 2, 1859, ABS Archives.

businessmen to accumulate great fortunes also tremendously increased the daily volume of business transactions. New York's rising capitalists spent long hours in the office and found little time for the cultural and intellectual interests that occupied the Federalist gentry. The separation of work and residence caused further pressure. Managers commuted to Wall Street and Pearl Street from uptown residences, rode the cars to Astor Place late in the day to look after ABS affairs, and then returned home. The new capitalist lifestyle created a constant struggle against the clock, and time assumed a new significance.

Using time economically demanded a new form of communication. The managers sought brief summaries, statistical breakdowns, and easily assimilable factual data. Sacrificing complexity for simplicity, they wished to reduce information to its most basic level—a single number if possible. The destruction of the narrative report accomplished this goal. Along with the credit rating and the stock-turn ratio, the tabulated statement heralded the birth of a new age. It concealed as much as it offered. Despite the agencies committee's protest, Russell's recommendations became official policy. The narrative report belonged to the past.[11]

The managers also required greater accountability from the growing and scattered field staff. Board members could not personally monitor each agent. They met too infrequently and were burdened with too many other tasks for such painstaking labor. The corresponding secretaries might handle simple personnel decisions, but the board required a general managerial overview. Similar problems plagued the railroads, and in the 1850s unprecedented structural innovation occurred in transportation industries. The same issues that concerned the ABS managers—checks on employee responsibility, better reporting schemes, prompt detection of dereliction of duty—also occupied the new national rail lines. The board of managers, which included the president of the Delaware, Lackawanna and Western, the corporate attorney for the Chicago, Rock Island and Pacific, and the founder of the New York and Erie, adapted the language and administrative principles of the consolidated transportation companies to the cause of benevolence.

11. Arthur H. Cole, "The Tempo of Mercantile Life in Colonial America," *Business History Review* (Autumn 1959), 277–299; Chandler, *Visible Hand*, pp. 207–215; Cochran, "Business Revolution"; Alan Trachtenberg, *The Incorporation of America: Culture and Society in the Gilded Age* (New York: Hill and Wang, 1982), pp. 47–48.

They established the position of general agent at Bible House and hired career salaried administrators to fill vacancies in the accounting area. Although the treasurer remained a part-time, unpaid position, the managers engaged full-time assistants to work in this department. A clear distinction developed between the work of the corresponding secretaries and the treasurer. Corresponding secretaries once routinely processed donations and answered all inquiries from agents; now, financial responsibility was centralized in the treasurer's office, with the board retaining tight control over money matters. The corresponding secretaries handled day-to-day operational problems, solicited narrative reports for the *Bible Society Record,* and, significantly, processed requests for free donations of books. All "pecuniary remittances, and letters in relation to the accounts of Agents, Auxiliary and other Societies and persons, and legacies" went directly to the treasurer's office. Increasingly, the business aspect of Bible operations became administratively divorced from the benevolent.[12]

In 1864, the agencies committee revised and updated its *Instructions to Agents.* The new manual was twice as large as its 1853 predecessor, an indication of the many rules and regulations now applicable to agents. It included sample financial reports, statistical reports, and annual reports. Each monthly statement required twenty-six separate entries. Agents specified the "No. of Bible Sermons and Addresses delivered," but the managers exhibited minimal interest in the sermons' content. Agents counted up the "No. of Pastors, Officers of Bible Societies, and Bible Patrons visited," but bore no obligation to describe the resulting conversations. The last column in each report adequately measured their success: "Total Receipts from Sales and Donations." The 1864 report also contained an important statement not included in the 1853 volume. Under the heading "Pecuniary Transactions," the managers informed their field representatives that "this Society expects its Agents to be systematic, prompt, and exact. They can never be successful labourers in the Bible field unless they are *conscientious* and *thorough business men.*" The word "missionary" did not appear

12. Chandler, *Visible Hand,* pp. 95–109. The three managers alluded to in the text were George D. Phelps, Charles E. Tracy, and Eleazer Lord. See American Bible Society Board of Managers, *Instructions to Agents of the American Bible Society with Miscellaneous Items of Information* (New York: American Bible Society Press, 1864), p. 44.

in the volume. The board had effected its own managerial revolution.[13]

Hiring "good agents" who accepted tighter regulations and conducted business according to the new policies became a critical consideration. Informal arrangements, sporadic efforts, and brief agencies could not coexist with the more systematic, centralized approach adopted by the managers. Accordingly, by the late 1840s, the secretaries began looking for new men and evaluating their suitability by different criteria. Evidence of "good character," orthodox theological training, and a burning desire to spread the Gospel no longer sufficed. Between 1845 and 1850, the American Bible Society hired fifty-five new agents. Biographical data reveal that these men differed considerably in background, training, and career patterns from the agents hired during the 1820s. A detailed analysis of their life histories. charts important changes in Bible work and, more broadly, in American Protestantism.[14]

Denominational affiliation is one of the most striking differences. Over half (twenty-seven of fifty-two) of the Bible agents hired in the late 1840s belonged to the Methodist church, as op-

13. American Bible Society Board of Managers, *Instructions to Agents*, p. 13.

14. For information on the sources consulted to accumulate these biographies, see Chapter 3, note 17, above. The fifty-five agents analyzed in the subsequent discussion are Henry W. Adams (1818–1881); William Anderson (1803–1859); John A. Baughman (1802–1868); S. F. Blackman (dates unknown); Harvey Blodgett (1801–1850); Richard Bond (1800–1853); Frederick Buel (?–1873); Daniel Butler (1808–1893); Alanson Baldwin Chittenden (1797–1853); George Clark (1822–1850); Thomas Cochran (1800–1849); Thomas K. Coleman (dates unknown); William H. Corkhill (dates unknown); Daniel Deruelle (1796–1858); Charles Devol (1809–1894); Hozier J. Durbin (1812–1851); Aaron Foster (1794–1870); John S. Galloway (1806–1862); John Goodenough (ca. 1817–1850); John Harrell (1805–1876); Edward Hollister (1796–1870); Jacob S. Hughes (1816–1853); James Jamison (1802–1880); C. P. Jones (dates unknown); Amasa Lord (dates unknown); Dallas D. Lore (1815–1875); Thomas Lounsbury (1789–1867); Joseph Mahon (1805–1884); Benjamin Miller (dates unknown); Francis T. Mitchell (1821–1902); Christopher D. Oliver (1819–1892); William J. Parks (1799–1873); Hamilton Wilcox Pierson (1817–1888); John Poisal (1807–1882); John B. Richardson (1804–1885); Moses Coleman Searle (1797–1865); George Sheldon (of New Jersey) (1813–1881); E. W. Smith (dates unknown); Stephen Sanford Smith (1797–1871); John Storrs (1802–1854); James Stratton (1810–1884); William Peter Strickland (1809–1884); Thomas Stringfield (1796–1858); Mortimer Strong (dates unknown); L. S. Sweezey (dates unknown); John Thompson (1800–1878); Manley Tooker (1799–1871); Samuel L. Tuttle (1815–1866); Hugh A. C. Walker (1809–1886); Phanuel W. Warriner (1799–1879); James V. Watson (1814–1856); George West (1815–1882); Calvin Wolcott (dates unknown); Aaron Wood (1802–1887); and John Kimball Young (1802–1875).

posed to only two of forty during the 1820s. Several factors contributed to this shift. By 1855, Baptists and Methodists accounted for nearly 70 percent of America's Protestant communicants. Their preachers, exhorters, and ministers came from country villages and small towns, and both denominations were extraordinarily successful in the rural South and along the western frontier. The circuit rider and the farmer-preacher became important religious symbols, and Baptists and Methodists proudly contrasted their "plain-style" revivalists with the seminary-trained, salaried theologians staffing Congregational and Presbyterian pulpits. Benevolent agencies hoping to reach the "common folk" and the vast expanses of the continent still relatively isolated from metropolitan influences needed to court the leaders of these denominations.[15]

Following the Baptist schism of 1836, the American Bible Society could no longer draw upon that denomination's preachers to staff its rural agencies. Accordingly, the ABS struck an informal agreement with the Methodists. Beginning in 1840, the Bible Society reserved one of its secretaryships for a nationally prominent Methodist minister. Edmund Storer Janes (1807–1876), Noah Levings (1796–1849), Joseph Holdich (1804–1893), and Albert Sandford Hunt (1827–1898) successively served the ABS between 1840 and 1898, and each either retired or died while in the Society's employ. The Methodists, for their part, ceased printing Bibles at the Methodist Book Concern in New York and purchased all Scriptures from the ABS. Methodist bishops recommended and appointed suitable ministers to serve as agents, and the Society diligently consulted the hierarchy at every opportunity. Predominantly Methodist territories in the South and West received Methodist agents. Participation in the Society's governance ensured amicable relations, and Methodists soon supplanted "Presbygationalists" as the Bible cause's most consistent and vocal allies. Denominational considerations, the managers found, could prove useful.[16]

15. For a general survey of Protestant religion in antebellum America, see Timothy L. Smith, *Revivalism and Social Reform: American Protestantism on the Eve of the Civil War* (Baltimore: Johns Hopkins University Press, 1980). Chapter 1 provides a useful statistical overview of the major denominations. Sydney E. Ahlstrom, *A Religious History of the American People* (New Haven: Yale University Press, 1972), pp. 433–443, discusses the rise of the Methodists and Baptists.

16. The Methodists dissolved their own Bible Society in 1836, the year of the Baptist schism. See Nolan B. Harmon, ed., *The Encyclopedia of World Methodism*, 2 vols. (Nashville: United Methodist Publishing House, 1974), pp. 99–100; and ABS, *Twenty-first Annual Report* (1837). Growing cooperation with the Methodist church

By the time Methodist preachers began staffing Bible agencies in the 1840s, that church had undergone significant changes. Historians associate Methodism with the itinerant ministry, the camp meeting, and the informally educated preacher. Each of these had evolved over the nineteenth century so that in 1850 the church's internal structure resembled a modern bureaucracy more than it did the informal communion of 1800. Some Methodist leaders, including Bible Society manager Nathan Bangs, had long criticized the itinerant ministry and the circuit system for not effecting permanent conversions. Although older ministers trained in the Francis Asbury tradition resisted change, the early nineteenth-century church encouraged the staffing of permanent stations where preachers could discharge all pastoral duties. By 1844, according to the denomination's principal historian, "even the newer Conferences had some Station appointments and in the older and stronger Conferences many of the appointments in the larger cities and some of those in the towns were stations." Methodists divided the country into districts and created a well-defined hierarchy of bishops, presiding elders, station pastors, and circuit riders at different salaries. Bishops increasingly selected pastors for local churches, and the quarterly meeting assumed greater significance as a policy-making body. Graded distinctions appeared in the ministry, and it became possible to make a modern career wholly within the communion.[17]

Camp meetings and revivals were more formal, organized, centrally directed, and orchestrated by 1850. Participants at the great Cane Ridge, Kentucky, revivals in 1801 pitched their tents in

and frequent consultation with Methodist bishops concerning agency appointments are documented in the Minutes of Meetings of the Committee on Agencies, 1836–1850. Another indication of the increasingly close tie is the Society's selection of a nationally prominent Methodist, former Bible agent, and editor of the *Christian Advocate* to write and publish the first book-length history of the American Bible Society in 1849. See William P. Strickland, *History of the American Bible Society from Its Organization to the Present Time* (New York: Harper & Brothers, 1849).

17. Wade Crawford Barclay, *History of Methodist Missions*, 6 vols. (New York: Board of Missions and Church Extension Society of the Methodist Church, 1950), pt. 1, vol. 2, p. 301. See also Donald Matthews, "The Second Great Awakening as an Organizing Process, 1780–1830: An Hypothesis," *American Quarterly* (Spring 1969), 23–43; Ahlstrom, *Religious History of the American People*, pp. 433–437. For an interesting examination of one Methodist's career and an example of the new men entering the Methodist ministry, see Henry B. Ridgeway, *The Life of Edmund S. Janes, D.D., LL.D., Late Senior Bishop of the Methodist Episcopal Church* (New York: Phillips & Hunt, 1882).

groves to shelter themselves from the August heat. By midcentury, Methodist leaders purchased permanent campgrounds, erected cottages and two-story residences, and even designed great auditoriums. Orchestration, crowd manipulation, and institutionalization replaced spontaneity. Eventually, the camp meeting served primarily as a Christian summer seaside vacation resort. Choirs, pipe organs, and large-scale architecture simultaneously began appearing in parishes as the "plain style" gave way before new techniques of attracting and retaining the faithful. By 1850, the Methodist church owned more property than any other American denomination, and communicants increasingly demanded a style of worship acceptable to the wealthy.

Educational institutions also grew to train the ministry. Concord Biblical Institute in Boston (1847), Garrett Biblical Institute in Evanston, Illinois (1854), and Drew Theological Seminary in Madison, New Jersey (1867), attested to a new movement toward a learned and trained clergy. Formal courses in theology and church history replaced the informal circuit system through which young recruits acquired knowledge from older, seasoned, veteran preachers. Bishops assumed charge of education and provided stricter guidelines for aspiring ministers. In 1844, the bishops of the General Conference appointed a committee on course of study for the first time. Prescribed courses of reading became common in all annual conferences, and the time a licentiate spent in study increased to four years. "The Methodist Way" had changed since the first annual conference met in 1773, and the ministers who accepted American Bible Society appointments in the late 1840s and 1850s knew the value of meticulous organization and planning, modern techniques of mass communication, and efficiency in religious administration.[18]

Denomination was not the only distinguishing characteristic of mid-nineteenth-century Bible men. Agents' median age (forty-four) was thirteen years older than that of their predecessors in the 1820s. They tended to be men in middle age, at an advanced stage of their careers. Of the forty-five agents whose birth dates are known 47 percent were between the ages of forty-three and fifty-two. Only three agents had not reached their thirtieth birthday, and

18. Barclay, *History of Methodist Missions*, 2:327–331, 432–444, 3:40–49; Ahlstrom, *Religious History of the American People*, pp. 437–438; Charles A. Johnson, "The Frontier Camp Meeting: Contemporary and Historical Appraisals, 1805–1840," *Mississippi Valley Historical Review* (1950), 91–110.

none were under twenty-five. In the 1820s, one-third of the agents were under twenty-seven and many began their careers with the Bible Society. In fact, Bible men beginning their ABS affiliations in the 1840s had grown up with those who undertook agencies in the 1820s. They all came of age in the second decade of the nineteenth century, when the great revivals and call to missions inspired many to begin a personal crusade for Christ. Their difficulties in obtaining settled pastorates, boredom with the routine of local religious life, and exposure to the contentiousness increasingly dividing parishes and pastors convinced them that joining the American Bible Society constituted a wise career move.[19]

More and more, the ABS secretaries looked for agents who had served in similar capacities with other institutions. Nearly 58 percent worked as agents, academic administrators, editors of denominational journals, or traveling missionaries for other religious organizations. The Bible Society showed less interest in men carrying on traditional parish labors or those seeking a brief interlude from the demands of full-time church work. Conditions in the ministry helped this policy to succeed. As the ideal of the permanent pastorate for Presbyterians and Congregationalists eroded, benevolent agencies offered attractive and stable employment. Donald Scott has documented mid-nineteenth-century churches' increasing tendency to break pastoral engagements and the number of unemployed ministers laboring without charge in the latter stages of their careers. Benevolent labor offered both a way out and the promise of steady work.[20]

Ordination alone no longer determined suitability for Bible agencies. The committee on agencies observed in 1855 that "the introduction of the lay Element into these Agencies, has been followed with happy results. More of such laborers might add considerably to the interests of the Cause." The overwhelming majority of Bible agents secured ordination, but some did so only after successful secular careers. At least eight of forty-seven Bible agents for whom reasonably detailed career information exists worked in some nonreligious capacity. Others applied the administrative experience they gained working for benevolent enterprises to other pursuits. Henry W. Adams (1818–1881), for example, left religion

19. Donald Scott, *From Office to Profession: The New England Ministry, 1750–1850* (Philadelphia: University of Pennsylvania Press, 1978), pp. 52–75.
20. Ibid.

after holding agencies for Wesleyan University and the Bible Society and urban pastorates in Boston and Springfield. He eventually patented and developed improvements in mining and established the Adams Mining and Reduction Company. Although the sacred and the secular constituted well-defined spheres in mid-nineteenth-century America, men were beginning to find that the skills cultivated in one sphere might help them succeed in the other.[21]

The Society expected and received fairly permanent commitments from its agents. Only 11 percent remained with the ABS for less than one year, contrasted with 58 percent in the 1820s sample. Approximately 38 percent of the men beginning careers in the late 1840s completed more than five years with the ABS, and 16 percent worked in their fields for over a decade. The three-month agency became obsolete when secretaries began to expect year-long commitments. Managers began treating the agents as permanent employees. They frequently provided widows' and orphans' benefits for families of deceased laborers. Some agents experienced career mobility within the institution. District superintendencies, for example, offered the promise of more responsibility and an increased salary. Samuel Tuttle (1815–1866), who served as an agent between 1849 and 1853, eventually was made an assistant secretary in New York.

State Bible societies offered another avenue for future employment. The growth of the agency system in the 1820s and 1830s had stimulated activity among some auxiliaries. Many smaller and weaker county societies had dissolved or remained marginal. A few larger county and state organizations, however, responded to the excitement generated by traveling agents, participation in the international missionary movement, and the domestic crusades to place a Bible in every American household. Bible societies in Vermont, Massachusetts, Maryland, Pennsylvania, and Virginia now appointed their own agents and occasionally maintained their own office staff. Several ABS agents later found work there. In sum, the Bible Society offered attractive career opportunities, intrainstitutional mobility, and security. Ministers seeking to make their mark in American religious life no longer needed to settle in an isolated rural parish or trust to the uncertainty of itinerant mission work.

21. Minutes of Meeting of the Committee on Agencies, March 1, 1855, ABS Archives. On Adams, see Frank W. Nicholson, *Alumni Record of Wesleyan University* (New Haven: Tuttle, Morehouse & Taylor, 1911).

The American Bible Society provided an important affiliation and promised more. It sought and attracted a new type of employee. The transition from Alexander Moncreif Proudfit's world to that of Robert Baird appeared well under way.[22]

During this transitional period, conflict frequently erupted between the home office and its field representatives. Managers' expectations did not always coincide with the reality of organizing and successfully supervising an agency. A confusion of goals and aims sometimes resulted. Even agents who believed they conducted their business according to the board's modern administrative notions sometimes found themselves in opposition to specific rules and demands. The easiest way to understand these internal tensions is to examine a particular Bible agency. Amasa Lord's life and work in Illinois and Wisconsin cannot be described as typical. Within the institution, however, his story contains great significance.

In many respects, Amasa Lord personified the new agent-administrator. He wielded considerable influence within the Society. On occasion, he pushed the board even further than the managers appeared willing to venture. Lord's eventual failure and rebuke illustrate that significant elements within the Society still retained considerable trepidation and uncertainty concerning its future course. His career clearly crystallizes several issues: the shared belief that sound business principles should govern the Society's operations, the new definition of field representative work, and the problems that resulted when an agent's ambitions and career interests conflicted with the bureaucratic canons and procedures of an increasingly large and impersonal institution.

When Amasa Lord decided to apply for a vacant agency in Wisconsin and northern Illinois on May 4, 1846, he observed that "I am anxious to devote my *life* to the promotion of the cause in which I have labored for the last six years." Lord had been working in western New York in the service of the Cayuga, Orleans, Genessee, and Wyoming County Bible societies. The opening in the Midwest of-

22. This information was compiled from the biographies of the agents named in note 14 above. On Tuttle, see Viola Shaw and Barbara Parker, "An Intimate History of the Presbyterian Church of Madison, N.J. 1747 to 1862 from the Journal of Samuel L. Tuttle Pastor Dec. 1853 to April 1862" (1979–1980), manuscript in Rutgers University Special Collections. Annual Reports from the Vermont, Massachusetts, Virginia, Maryland, and Pennsylvania Bible societies shed light on the work of strong state auxiliaries during this period.

fered him an opportunity to affiliate with the American Bible Society, and he pursued the post, wishing to operate in a larger sphere and secure the advantages that the parent society offered its employees. Lord seemed little attached to place or locality and welcomed the chance to serve the ABS. The Bible Society offered him the position with remarkably little concern about his theological training, social background, and career outside the Bible cause.

For a reference, Corresponding Secretary John C. Brigham simply wrote to a pious businessman in Rochester, New York, who provided all the necessary information. Lord, according to George A. Henry, had been "remarkable for self denial & economy" and exhibited "unusual power of accomplishment in the practical business detail of distribution &c. . . . For real *efficiency* as a bible agent we have not known his equal & doubt not he would be useful anywhere." The last phrase was key to the endorsement: Lord's usefulness did not depend on attachment to a particular community. His business acumen, attention to detail, and practical bent assured success independent of any town or locality. This and Lord's own observations that his dealings in western New York increased subscriptions for Bible work to an average of $150 per week were the principal facts the home office needed to know. Seven years later, another corresponding secretary asked Lord whether he had been ordained. The Methodist agent responded that "I would say that I have license to preach but am not an ordained minister." The issue appeared irrelevant: both question and answer were contained in postscripts to letters dealing primarily with more pressing matters.[23]

Lord labored for the Bible Society from 1847 through 1868, and several significant themes recur throughout his lengthy correspondence with the secretaries. First, he continually advocated the establishment of one national uniform system for conducting Bible agencies, removing the responsibility for circulating Scriptures from the agents and narrowing their functions. Agents would solicit donations, serve as district coordinators for the auxiliaries, and supervise a network of local distributors, who would procure and circulate the Bibles needed to supply their regions. Lord defined his own job as "starting the machinery" and subsequently auditing

---

23. Amasa Lord to John C. Brigham, May 4, 1846; George A. Henry to Brigham, September 15, 1846; Amasa Lord to Joseph Holdich, December 15, 1853, Corresponding Secretary's Papers, ABS Archives.

the books of local depositories and auxiliaries on a regular basis. Each auxiliary society in a region would be assigned to hold its annual meeting on a particular day. The meetings would be "arranged to be held on successive days so that I could attend them all" and would begin a week of intensive fund-raising activity. The local agent, preferably a volunteer, would handle all routine administrative tasks after Lord left for another county. The ABS agent, responsible for maintaining all contact with the New York office, would closely monitor each society and local agent through correspondence and regular, standardized reports. Uniform implementation of this approach could, in Lord's words, be "so systematic" that "the machinery" would proceed "almost with the regularity of clockwork."[24]

Lord established this system in Wisconsin and northern Illinois and freely admitted that it changed the nature of his job. "My Agency," he observed in 1853, "is assuming more and more the nature of a Secretaryship." He relied increasingly on "the instrumentality of others" to "cultivate" it. His own time was occupied in "keeping up a constant correspondence with my fellow laborers— requiring 20 or 30 letters per week besides hosts of circulars." Lord found it necessary to occupy his time "in the preparation of circulars—subscription books—reports & suggestions and notices of our designs and operations for the press." Rather than expending energy by "spending the same amount of time in traveling," he discovered that such attention to administrative routine helped him "accomplish more" and paid off in larger subscriptions. His principal goal was to have "matters so arranged" that he might "be at home more attending to my correspondence and still keep the machinery moving over the whole field." The traveling agency had evolved into a purely administrative agency. Just as the board of managers wished to distance itself from the daily drudgery of the work and base its decisions on brief statistical reports, the ambitious agent chose to concentrate his talents on developing better forms, refining accounting procedures, and communicating through correspondence. Attention to administrative detail, not personal exertion in the field, paid off.[25]

Another theme that emerges from Amasa Lord's correspon-

24. Lord to Noah Levings, November 8, 30, 1848; Lord to John C. Brigham, May 4, 1846, August 2, 1850, December 3, 1851, and April 5, 1852, ibid.
25. Lord to John C. Brigham, June 7, July 4, 1853, ibid.

dence concerns the necessity of standardizing education for Bible agents. A uniform national system, in Lord's view, required well-trained men able to understand its intricacies and perfect its execution. Lord echoed the idea that Bible work was a unique and specialized task, which required the mastery of a specific body of knowledge and technique. He often referred to his years of service with western New York's county Bible societies as "a 7 years apprenticeship" and believed that agents for the parent Society should spend time learning his system with county auxiliaries. When engaging a county agent without previous experience, Lord took care "to spend some time with him until he has *learned the trade.*" Lord described the virtues of William A. Chambers, a thirty-six-year old Methodist minister from southeastern Illinois whom he proposed for an assistant agency: "His principal qualification for the field is his acquaintance with this system and his experience in the Agency." Previous training, Lord argued, "is just as necessary for an Agent as is training with a view to preaching or practicing Medicine to the Minister or Physician." This candidate's extensive service with a county Bible society in Ohio qualified him for the task much more than theological degrees or personal connections. "I regard it as a ruinous policy," Lord concluded, "to employ Agents merely because they can preach and are recommended by partial friends who have no adequate idea of the qualifications needed."[26]

Lord's thoughts concerning the education of Bible agents crystallized when the board appointed George Washington Elliott (1797–1885) to succeed him in Wisconsin in 1853. Lord had recently requested to be relieved from his responsibilities in Wisconsin and Minnesota so that he might devote more time to the cause in Illinois. He expected to participate in naming his successor, but the managers selected Elliott, a fifty-seven-year-old Congregationalist, instead. A New Hampshire native, he had pursued a traditional ministerial educational route through Phillips Academy, Dartmouth College, and Auburn Theological Seminary. After ordination by the Congregational Council of Lenox, New York, in 1826, he spent a quarter-century attending parishes in upstate New York and Illinois. Elliott had served as secretary for the Home Missions Board in Wisconsin between 1851 and 1853, and an earlier genera-

26. Lord to John C. Brigham, February 8, 1847; Lord to Noah Levings, June 30, 1848; Lord to Joseph Holdich, October 13, 16, 1855, ibid.

tion might have viewed his credentials as impeccable for missionary work. Despite the ABS's modernizing tendencies, the board still felt comfortable appointing a traditional Bible agent like Elliott in 1853.

In Lord's view, Elliott's educational and career accomplishments offered little promise for success in the Bible cause. Referring to the Wisconsin agency as "this complicated machinery," Lord chastised the board for choosing a man "who knows nothing about it." Reminding the managers that "the fact of a man's being a minister no more qualifies him to do it than the fact of a man's being a Merchant qualifies him to preach the gospel," Lord complained that Elliott "should have spent several months as a County Agt and become thoroughly acquainted with the business himself before superintending the labors of others."[27]

Lord pointed toward a system of well-structured apprenticeships, whereby a man would work himself up through the ranks of the county societies and eventually receive a more responsible position with the Bible Society—the career path he himself had taken, which he viewed as a model. His remarks also suggest the reaction of a practical man of business with little formal theological training and no advanced degree. When the managers appointed Lord in 1846, the Rochester businessman who recommended him remarked that "he is not polished or graceful in his manner & is not we think familiar with the conventional forms & usages of Society." Lord strove to overcome these disadvantages, but he ultimately viewed them as marginal qualities. He resented the appointment of men like Elliott, who advanced owing to superior social advantages and educational attainments but had no particular qualifications for the task at hand. By assigning a mystique to purely administrative work and claiming special prerogatives for it, he insulated himself from the challenge of better-educated and socially connected ministers. Lord eventually compiled and published his own small instructional manual for the use of county Bible agents. In a section called "Characteristics of a Good Agent," Lord paid homage to traditional evangelical virtues such as "Industry," "Piety," and "The Absence of Sectarian Spirit." His com-

27. On Elliott, see *General Biographical Catalogue of Auburn Theological Seminary, 1818–1918* (Auburn: Auburn Seminary Press, 1918). Lord to Joseph Holdich, December 15, 1853, Corresponding Secretary's Papers, ABS Archives.

ment under the subheading "Education" consisted of only one line: "Especially should the agent be a good penman and accountant."[28]

Lord's conduct of the agency contained several innovations. He consistently looked to expand his territory and eventually built up a substantial empire of county auxiliaries. Initially, he had been appointed agent for "parts of Wisconsin & Illinois" by the agencies committee. Shortly after arriving in Wisconsin, Lord prevailed upon Illinois agent Harvey Blodgett to cede several counties to him. Before the end of 1847, he received permission to extend his field over the entire state of Wisconsin. By April 1850, he had enlarged his original jurisdiction four times and secured administrative control over an area of forty-seven counties in three states, with a population of nearly half a million. The number of Bible societies increased from "about 40" to nearly 350 in less than five years. Lord had commissioned nearly twenty-five hundred local voluntary agents to monitor distribution throughout the region. When Blodgett died in 1850, Lord received permission to take charge of several additional counties in Illinois. Territorial expansion brought with it increased supervisory responsibility. He pressed the board almost immediately for assistant agents, and by 1855 he had hired four. These assistants, chosen by Lord and salaried by the American Bible Society, supervised and instructed fifteen or twenty county agents employed by the local auxiliaries but also under Lord's jurisdiction.[29]

Lord's hiring practices underscored his business philosophy concerning agencies. One applicant for a Minnesota agency received praise for his work as "a Merchant in the State of N.Y.—is a good businessman and a man of good address . . . a practical surveyor." Another appeared "well qualified for the Bible work. For some time before uniting with the [Methodist] Conference he was a clerk in a store in Beardstown Ill. and hence of course has some acquaintance with business." A third seemed suitable because he "has been a merchant and is now a Book keeper. Though he does not excel as a public speaker he is a good business man." Lord's assistants and county agents rose rapidly and assumed additional

28. George A. Henry to John C. Brigham, September 15, 1846, Corresponding Secretary's Papers, ABS Archives; Amasa Lord, *Suggestions to County Bible Agents* (N.p.: N.p., n.d.), p. 2.

29. Minutes of Meetings of the Committee on Agencies, January 6, December 22, 1847, March 28, 1849, July 26, 1850; Lord to John C. Brigham, April 1, 1850; Lord to Joseph Holdich, May 14, 1855, Corresponding Secretary's Papers, ABS Archives.

responsibility in the Bible cause. William A. Chambers worked his way up from an assistantship to the position of agent for northern Iowa. T. C. Hartshorn, a subagent for Illinois under Lord, became agent for eastern Ohio and western Virginia. Christopher C. Hoagland, a county agent, eventually directed the Society's operations in southern Iowa. Absalom Mosher, who served twelve years under Lord, received an appointment as agent for Nebraska and Colorado in 1866. Samuel Reynolds, another Lord protégé in Wisconsin, assumed charge of work in that state and Michigan from 1864 through 1876. Clearly, Amasa Lord had created a formidable network of assistants who dominated Bible affairs in the Midwest through the 1860s. He trained these men, and they internalized the businesslike system he created, applying its lessons to their own regions. Operating independently of the board but within the managers' general guidelines, Lord had achieved considerable power and influence within the institution.[30]

The managers' increasing preference for permanent, businesslike agents might lead one to expect that a man of Lord's temperament would enjoy a long and happy relationship with the ABS. He raised unprecedented sums in Illinois and Wisconsin, thoroughly canvassed and supplied the field, established hundreds of auxiliaries on a sound business basis, and developed an efficient network of like-minded agents to spread his system throughout the Midwest. Yet Lord's affiliation with the Bible Society ended in a stormy controversy resulting in his forced resignation. As early as 1856, Corresponding Secretary Joseph Holdich warned Lord that his comments and criticisms concerning ABS management offended some New York administrators and received a frosty reception from many managers. The agent curtly replied that "I am sorry to learn that it is deemed more important that an Agent should be harmless and inoffensive than industrious and efficient," and he continued making periodic suggestions designed to increase the Bible Society's efficiency.[31]

Lord regularly badgered the home office to extend his system throughout the United States, criticized the way the Society kept

30. Lord to Joseph Holdich, May 20, 1856, January 29, 1857, and April 10, 1856, Corresponding Secretary's Papers, ABS Archives. Minutes of Meetings of the Committee on Agencies, September 2, 1868, April 6, 1870, June 4, 1856, October 3, 1866, January 6, 1869, October 5, 1864, ABS Archives.

31. Lord to Joseph Holdich, June 12, 1856, Corresponding Secretary's Papers, ABS Archives.

its accounts, and advocated raising the price of Scriptures sold to auxiliaries to reflect real cost rather than simply manufacturing cost. He also irritated the secretaries by his continual requests for promotions and salary adjustments and his tendency to call himself "District Secretary" rather than his official title "Agent." Lord always offered his opinion concerning major board policies: he prodded the Society to denounce slavery and complained about the relative paucity of Methodists involved in institutional governance. His final effort to redirect board policy came in 1863, when he began a campaign to eliminate the 5 percent discount for auxiliaries and urged the managers to sell Bibles at a reasonable profit. As always, he cited efficiency, cost-effectiveness, and the need to bring Bible Society policy closer to market conditions. The board and secretaries, recognizing that such a move would damage the Society's claim to benevolence, bring it into closer competition with booksellers, cripple the auxiliaries, and serve as "a stimulus to speculation," rejected Lord's proposals.[32]

Lord persisted and pushed his point through unorthodox channels. He circulated his plan among colleagues in the Midwest and presented their favorable comments to the board. He stimulated auxiliaries to petition the managers in support of his ideas. Finally, he drafted a circular directly to the board, bypassing the secretaries and mailing information to the managers' home addresses. Lord had violated the accepted chain of command and failed to use proper bureaucratic channels. This serious transgression proved his undoing. William J. R. Taylor (1823–1891), corresponding secretary between 1862 and 1869, became incensed. In January 1864, he warned Lord that "any further agitation . . . will only do harm to the Cause; and our Agents must conform to the decision of the Board, without further disturbance of its principles & system of operation." Later that month Taylor complained about Lord's "discourtesy of manner" and failure to "put the customary 'dear sir' or 'sir' after my name" on correspondence. The secretary noted that "more than half the time your letters are simply subscribed without

32. Lord's continual suggestions and petulance can be discerned in the following letters: Lord to the Secretaries, November 6, 1854; Lord to Holdich, September 1, December 15, 1853, January 12, August 23, 29, 1854, May 22, October 16, 1855, June 12, August 12, 1856, May 4, 1858, Summer 1858, and November 17, 1859; Minutes of Meeting of the ABS Board of Managers, January 7, 1864; "Hints for Reply to Agent Lord's Circulars on Prices," 1863, Corresponding Secretary's Papers, ABS Archives.

any of the usual courtesies of correspondence." In August, the agent was informed that his "very unusual mode of reaching the Board by other than the customary channels of communication has roused considerable unpleasant feeling, and that persistence in the same course will certainly increase that feeling."[33]

Lord remained in the Society's employ for a few more years, but his effectiveness and his hopes to spread his system throughout the United States had ended. He found that successful management and administrative skills did not automatically guarantee power and influence in the new corporate structure. Proper manners, attention to bureaucratic regulations, and willingness to work within a well-defined structure constituted a different, and increasingly important, set of virtues. The soldier of Christ must also serve as a reliable footman in the cause of the company.

The board also learned some valuable lessons from dealing with Lord. Experienced, trained, "professional" agents might labor more efficiently, but they brought their own problems. As the pace of centralization and bureaucratization quickened, the managers could not afford to employ agent-administrators who outran institutional change. The board did not speak with one mind in the 1850s and 1860s, and the managers still preferred to appoint "safer" and more traditional men to many posts. When the managers selected Lord's replacement in 1869, they chose Edwin Graham Smith. A Vermont native, graduate of Union Theological Seminary, and Congregational pastor, Smith possessed no agency experience. He brought little innovation and few new ideas to his field in northern Illinois. But he followed the board's directives, faithfully executed its policies, and remained in the same job for thirty-three years.[34]

33. Lord to William J. R. Taylor, July 25, 1863; Amasa Lord, "Circular," Elgin, Ill., 1863; Lord to "the Managers of the American Bible Society," July 1863, Corresponding Secretary's Papers, ABS Archives; William J. R. Taylor to Amasa Lord, January 14, 26, 1864, August 7, 1863, Letter Book, Corresponding Secretary's Papers, ABS Archives.

34. On Lord's resignation, see Lord to "The Agency Committee of the American Bible Society," November 16, 1868, and T. Ralston Smith to William J. R. Taylor, December 3, 1868, Corresponding Secretary's Papers, ABS Archives. A biographical sketch of Edwin Graham Smith can be found in Charles Ripley Gillett, *Alumni Catalogue of the Union Theological Seminary in the City of New York, 1836–1926* (New York: Union Theological Seminary, 1926), p. 60.

8

Race, War, and Sectionalism: Reconstructing the Southern Agencies, 1850–1867

To survive on a national level, the American Bible Society was forced to make political and moral compromises. As the Society rationalized, bureaucratized, and centralized its operations, the managers and officers recognized the persistence of countervailing local forces. Race and slavery were divisive, explosive issues that threatened all national institutions in mid-nineteenth-century America. Sectional tensions deepened during the antebellum years, and organizations addressing the slavery question divided. Within the Christian community, Methodists (1844), Baptists (1845), New School Presbyterians (1857), Old School Presbyterians (1861), and Lutherans (1861) suffered schisms. The American Bible Society, seeking to preserve its national character, responded to the deepening crisis with a policy of studied avoidance. An essential paradox drove the board's policies. Only by tolerating and encouraging an extreme southern localism could the Society maintain its efficient and centralized national philanthropic operation. War split the Society, but the delicate balance between national survival and moral commitment had been altered permanently by 1861. The ABS's efforts to reconstruct its southern auxiliaries illustrated the logical conclusions.

Abolitionists, reformers, and even a few northern Bible agents periodically prodded the Society throughout the 1840s and 1850s to adopt a more aggressive policy concerning "Bibles for Slaves." The ABS, however, simply reinforced the stance it had taken in the early 1830s, placing the question in the hands of its local southern auxiliaries. The Society regularly reprinted its May 1834 resolutions concerning slavery, and in 1847 the managers issued a special report "on the Subject of Distributing Scriptures among Slaves" to address the concerns of northern abolitionists. This report defined the boundaries of the debate for the remainder of the antebellum period.[1]

The managers praised the "3,000 auxiliaries and branch societies, which now act with more or less efficiency," and argued that "motives of economy ... as well as the *rights* of the auxiliaries" dictated that decisions concerning Bibles for slaves belonged in the local domain. The American Bible Society, in the words of the board, "is not formed for purposes of education, or missions, or the corrections of civil laws." Rather, the managers invoked Article I of the ABS constitution, defining their mission as "circulating the Word of God without note or comment." They qualified this statement further, noting that distribution should occur "among all classes and conditions of men who are capable of using it." Slaves, owing to their widespread illiteracy and educational handicaps, remained excluded from this category. "Before Bible Societies, as such, can effect very much" among slaves, claimed the board, "there is a previous work to be done by the schoolmaster or other teacher."[2]

The managers reinterpreted their constitutional obligations in

1. Robert L. Cvornyek, "The Bible in Slavery and Freedom: The American Bible Society and the Afro-American Community, 1816–1960," Historical Essay, American Bible Society Working Papers, 1990-2, pp. 8–13. Several studies have treated the efforts to prod the Bible Society into taking a proabolitionist position. See especially Clifford S. Griffin, "The Abolitionists and the Benevolent Societies, 1831–1861," *Journal of Negro History* (July 1959), 195–216; and John R. McKivigan, "The Gospel Will Burst the Bonds of the Slave: The Abolitionists' Bibles for Slaves Campaign," *Negro History Bulletin* (July–September 1982), 62–64, 77. Minutes of Meeting of the Board of Managers, December 7, 1843, ABS Archives; American Bible Society, *Twenty-ninth Annual Report* (1845), p. 39; "Report of a Committee of the American Bible Society on the Subject of Distributing the Scriptures among Slaves," 1847, Corresponding Secretary's Papers, ABS Archives.

2. "Report on the Subject of Distributing the Scriptures among Slaves," 1847, ABS Archives.

narrow, constricted terms as limiting their mission and responsibilities. Perhaps more puzzling, they coupled this with high praise for the auxiliaries. In fact, complaints concerning the inefficiency, dormancy, and cumbersome nature of the auxiliary system dated to at least 1819. Further, the inability of auxiliaries to serve as effective distribution outlets stimulated the employment of paid Bible agents. By claiming that the local societies worked with thoroughness and efficiency and that they operated "independent of this Society, more so by far than are the several States in our Union, in relation to the Federal Government," the board hoped to counter the arguments of northern critics and reinforce its policy of avoidance and reaction. As abolitionists withdrew support from the ABS during the crisis of the 1830s, the Society found even less reason to placate more radical elements of the antislavery crusade. Beginning in 1850, therefore, the ABS placed a renewed emphasis on reviving its southern auxiliaries.[3]

Bible work in the South generally languished during the 1840s, despite the ABS's efforts to distance itself from abolitionists. Virginia maintained an active state auxiliary, and strong local affiliates existed in populated areas such as Charleston, but efforts throughout the region generally bore little fruit. Even the Society's annual reports, which served largely as public relations documents and always placed the ABS's work in the best light, reflected disappointment with the Bible cause in the South. The 1849 report, for example, noted that in Alabama "the returns of the distributers are so imperfect that it is difficult to give a satisfactory statement of them." In Mississippi, a new agent "has not been in the field sufficient time to furnish much for record." Florida was described as "this most difficult field, to advance the interest of the Bible Cause," while in Louisiana "comparatively little is effected," and in Arkansas "it is found exceedingly difficult to sustain an Agency." The reality of southern Bible work bore little relation to the rhetoric of the board's 1847 report.[4]

The managers sought to stimulate these auxiliaries by appointing a "Special Secretary of the South" in 1850. The Reverend Joseph C. Stiles (1795–1875), who accepted this responsibility, appeared well suited for the post. Despite his Yale degree (1814), studies at Andover Seminary (1821), and a two-year stint as pastor of Mercer

3. Ibid.
4. ABS, *Twenty-third Annual Report* (1849), pp. 58, 60, 62.

Street Presbyterian Church in New York City (1848–1850), Stiles remained a true son of the South. Born in Savannah, he labored largely in the low country of Georgia and Florida during the 1820s and 1830s and also served as an evangelist in rural Kentucky. After leaving the ABS in 1852, Stiles pioneered in establishing the Southern Aid Society, maintained a running verbal battle with the cautiously antislavery American Home Missionary Society, and published a popular study attacking abolitionists and similar "fanatics." The ABS's new special secretary could hardly be accused of "northern sympathies."[5]

The managers intended his appointment as a temporary expedient to reinforce their commitment to the southern field and to ascertain the actual state of the Bible cause throughout the region. Stiles's primary responsibilities involved touring the South, stimulating the auxiliaries to action, securing new and more effective agents to oversee the work, and providing a visible and local presence for the national effort. The ABS's corresponding secretary, John Brigham, subsequently described Stiles as "a son of thunder . . . a travelling Generalissimo of the Bible cause," who successfully exhorted southerners to support the great national effort.[6]

Stiles's mission started slowly. Beginning his southern tour in Washington, D.C., in an effort to induce some politicians to support the ABS's efforts, he found that Congress had already recessed for the Christmas holidays. Further, he preached in "an unpopular Church" on a rainy night, and his visit coincided with *"Jenny Lind's first* night" in Washington. As a result, "the house was not much more than half full and the congregation composed of those, in general, who were the least able to give." The situation worsened when he arrived in Mobile, Alabama, where the corresponding secretary of the local auxiliary "is in jail to respond to *twenty four* indictments for *forgery & embezzlement* & will doubtless be ere long transferred to the Penitentiary." At Blountsville, Knoxville, Nashville, and Chattanooga, Tennessee, "years, I think, had past since the Society . . . had met & in some of them it was difficult to ascer-

5. Franklin Bowditch Dexter, *Biographical Sketches of the Graduates of Yale College with Annals of the College History* (New Haven: Yale University Press, 1912), 6: 706–710; John W. Kuykendall, *Southern Enterprize: The Work of National Evangelical Societies in the Antebellum South* (Westport, Conn.: Greenwood Press, 1982), pp. 142–144.

6. John C. Brigham to James H. McNeill, January 25, 1855, Corresponding Secretary's Papers, ABS Archives.

tain who the officers of the Society were & when they held their last meeting." Bible work in the South differed considerably from the managers' lofty pronouncements and optimistic perceptions.[7]

Stiles persisted, and his efforts eventually produced some tangible results. By working with local Methodist conferences, the special secretary obtained the services of a new and energetic Bible agent in Georgia. He helped orchestrate "a genuine old-fashioned revival of religion in the Presbyterian Ch[urc]h[e]s of Mobile," and in the process he stimulated the complete reorganization of the local auxiliary. Stiles arrived in Montgomery, Alabama, to find "spiritual declension & anti-northern prejudice" but left with $21,000 in contributions toward a new Bible House. Eventually, the new secretary seconded the conclusions other Bible Society administrators reluctantly had embraced several years earlier: "First-rate State Agents must be employed to drill the people in systematic Christian habits." Only when southerners had been "brought up to systematic contribution & that from Christian principle" would Bible work flourish. When Stiles ended his whirlwind tour of the South early in 1852, he left local Bible Society staff to develop the appropriate administrative arrangements.[8]

Following Stiles's departure, the American Bible Society took several steps to solidify its southern strategy. Most notably, the managers appointed a native southerner, James H. McNeill (1825–1865), to a newly established position as corresponding secretary in 1853. Born in Fayetteville, North Carolina, McNeill was the son of a devout Presbyterian who served as ruling elder of the local church for forty years. The ABS's new secretary had attended local schools in Fayetteville, spent one year at the North Carolina University in Chapel Hill, and eventually graduated from Delaware College in Newark. Theological studies carried him to Union Seminary in New York, but he completed his course at Princeton, which long served as a training ground for southern Presbyterians. After ordination in 1848, he began his theological labors near Fayetteville, working throughout Chatham and Randolph counties in North Carolina. McNeill described himself in 1861 as "a *Southern Man* not only by birth and education but in present sympathies, and even in prejudices." He labored diligently with the Bible Society to see

7. Joseph C. Stiles to John Brigham, December 19, February 20, 1850, November 17, 1851, Corresponding Secretary's Papers, ABS Archives.

8. Stiles to Brigham, November 3, December 31, 1851, January 10, March 3, 1852, ibid.

that colleagues throughout his native region received ample attention and support.[9]

The managers allowed McNeill considerable freedom in supervising the southern work. Shortly after accepting his position at the ABS, McNeill informed an agent in Tennessee "of the new arrangement under which I conduct the correspondence of the Parent Society, over the Southern field." A clear division of labor developed among the Society's secretaries, with Joseph Holdich responding to letters from northern agents and abolitionist sympathizers, the aging John Brigham handling foreign correspondence and some miscellaneous domestic duties, and McNeill looking after the southern agents and auxiliaries. Three basic strategies governed McNeill's dealings with fellow southerners. First, he granted considerable autonomy to local societies, pioneering unique and innovative arrangements between the ABS and its local affiliates. Second, he encouraged agents to work carefully and closely with the auxiliaries, monitoring their finances but not interfering with their policies. Finally, he served as the Society's principal public relations spokesperson for the South, reminding correspondents of the ABS's neutrality and commitment to local control.[10]

McNeill clearly articulated his operating philosophy concerning southern auxiliaries in a November 1853 letter to an agent in Huntsville, Alabama: "Every local Soc[ie]ty, when *recognized* by the Parent Soc[ie]ty as auxiliary, has entire control over the work in its own field . . . and its Constitutional *'rights'* are denied when that work is taken out of its hands . . . we do not wish our agents to take this work into their own hands." Several strong southern societies developed under McNeill's tutelage during the 1850s. In New Orleans, for example, the South Western Bible Society was established in 1850. By 1855, this society had erected a substantial Bible House on Camp Street, annually issued nearly ten thousand Bibles and Testaments in thirteen languages, employed its own colporteurs and agents to circulate Scriptures, and claimed a network of auxil-

9. Joseph M. Wilson, ed., *The Presbyterian Historical Almanac . . . for 1866,* vol. 8 (Philadelphia: Presbyterian Board, 1866), pp. 356–361; James H. McNeill to P. M. Ozanne, January 29, 1861, Letter Book, Corresponding Secretary's Papers, ABS Archives. See also Kuykendall, *Southern Enterprize,* pp. 128–130.

10. James H. McNeill to J. Lyons, August 8, 1853, Letter Book, Corresponding Secretary's Papers, ABS Archives. The division of labor can be seen clearly by perusing the Letter Books of John Brigham, James McNeill, and Joseph Holdich in the ABS Archives.

iaries throughout Louisiana and western Mississippi. The ABS historically discouraged such autonomy among auxiliaries, but it welcomed this activity in New Orleans. McNeill even quietly arranged for the general agent of the South Western Bible Society to receive copies of a French Catholic edition of the Bible, not normally endorsed or circulated by the ABS, for distribution in Creole communities in New Orleans. Remittances for Bibles from the South Western Bible Society to the American Bible Society grew from less than $2,000 in 1851 to over $12,500 by 1859. Such success, in the managers' minds, validated their public contention that successful southern auxiliaries could function as active and efficient operations. Sacrificing some national control to achieve this local success seemed a shrewd and highly politic maneuver.[11]

Innovative relationships between the ABS and auxiliaries developed elsewhere throughout the South during the 1850s. The Alabama Bible Society secured a donation to build its own Bible House in Montgomery, "a *Three-Story Brick Building,* 25 feet wide, 100 feet deep with an alley on two sides . . . on as good a *business-lot* as there is in the City." By 1856, the ABS board agreed to place thirteen Alabama county auxiliaries that reported directly to the New York office under the jurisdiction of this state organization in Montgomery. Societies in Charleston, South Carolina, and Richmond, Virginia, negotiated agreements with the ABS to cosponsor joint agents, responsible to both the national society and the local affiliate. Remittances to the ABS from Virginia and Charleston were not as high as those from the South Western Bible Society but were among the highest south of the Mason-Dixon line. South Carolina even held its own state Bible conventions, where delegates from local auxiliaries met to coordinate and systematically plan work throughout the state. In Texas, the ABS authorized a special arrangement whereby "the societies located in the interior will be able to obtain their books directly from the depository in Galveston" to avoid the delays and inconvenience "when every individual order had to be shipped from New York." All these agreements il-

---

11. ABS, *Thirty-ninth Annual Report* (1855), p. 94; James H. McNeill to Agent Atkins, November 8, 1853, and McNeill to P. M. Ozanne, April 27, 1860, Letter Book, Corresponding Secretary's Papers, ABS Archives. For a good account of the growth and work of the South Western Bible Society, see the ABS, *Forty-third Annual Report* (1859), pp. 75–78.

lustrate an unmistakable trend toward greater sectional autonomy and diminished oversight by New York.[12]

McNeill did encourage distribution to slaves when local auxiliaries wished to do so. In 1854, he praised the annual meeting of the Abbeville, South Carolina, auxiliary, which included a keynote address "on the responsibility & duty of giving the Bible to slaves & teaching them to read it." The speaker, Reverend Robert A. Fair, combined a negative view of slaves' morals with a belief in the transforming power of the Gospel message. He argued that plantation owners should educate slaves in biblical principles to counteract their "gross ignorance and superstition" and "the degrading vices, immoralities, and pollutions prevailing amongst them." McNeill described Fair's condemnation of the slaves as "one of the most bold, manly, independent, truthful, & unanswerable arguments we ever listened to" and purported to "endorse every word that he uttered on that occasion." The Bible Society apparently found this view of slave life palatable because it reprinted and widely circulated the address.[13]

A few southern agents pursued an activist approach to distribution among the slaves. Andrew L. Hunter, a Methodist preacher who served the ABS in southern Arkansas between 1854 and 1860, spent June 1855 visiting the river town of Napoleon, "a place that abounds with every species of wickedness." There he addressed "a small congregation of Coloured people," informing them that all who could read would receive Bibles when the next shipment arrived from New York. He also offered the congregation "an opportunity to contribute to the funds of the County B[ible] S[ociety]," whereupon "one of them started round with a Hat and the sum of $4.70 was contributed." Hunter claimed that he never "found a man

12. Joseph C. Stiles to John Brigham, March 3, 1852; James H. McNeill to Agent Lyons, November 7, 1856, Corresponding Secretary's Papers, ABS Archives. The information concerning remittances was culled from ABS *Annual Reports*, 1856–1861. Charleston remittances peaked at $2,569 in 1857; the Virginia Bible Society remitted over $7,000 and contributed an additional $1,950 in 1857. ABS, *Thirty-ninth Annual Report* (1855), p. 97; McNeill to Edwin A. Bolles, January 17, 1861, Letter Book, Corresponding Secretary's Papers, ABS Archives; ABS, *Forty-first Annual Report* (1857), p. 76.

13. "Thirty-first Anniversary of the Bible Society of Abbeville District Auxiliary to the American Bible Society," August 4, 1854, Corresponding Secretary's Papers, ABS Archives; James H. McNeill to Agent Bolles, August 25, 1854, Letter Book, Corresponding Secretary's Papers, ABS Archives; Kuykendall, *Southern Enterprize*, pp. 135–136.

the owner of slaves that ever made an objection to their hearing the word of God." Traveling through Dallas County in November 1856, Hunter preached "to the Coloured people their owners letting them go to church for several days in succession." He recorded forty-three slave conversions in Dallas County, observing that "I have made it a point this year as far as practicable to preach to the blacks" and "I find that I have an influence with them and with their owners that I can turn to good account for the Bib. Society."[14]

Two years later, Hunter returned to Dallas County at the invitation of several plantation owners, and he informed McNeill that "with two or three exceptions," all of the slave converts remained faithful members of the Methodist and Presbyterian churches. He began a three-day revival meeting in the county, and his emotional account noted that "it was truly affecting to see masters and servants weeping and rejoicing together." Hunter reiterated that he "found the owners of these Blacks entirely willing that they should have the Bibles and Testaments," and he observed that "I find I get at the Whites through the Blacks in a way that I could not reach them without the Black people." Although expressing some concern whether his activities "may not be regarded as legitimately belonging to the Bible Agency," he asserted that "I felt I would not be doing right if I did not enter an open door pointed to directly by the finger of Providence." The Society's officers appeared thrilled with Hunter's work. His stories about distributing Bibles to slaves seemed to confirm the wisdom of their policy of local control, and his arrival in Dallas County at the instigation of Arkansas slaveholders did not jeopardize the ABS's reputation with southerners. The Society publicized Hunter's efforts through both its annual reports and the monthly *Bible Society Record* and privately encouraged his efforts.[15]

Hunter's ministry, however, proved virtually unique. Between 1840 and 1860, the American Bible Society granted a total of less than twelve hundred Bibles and slightly more than twenty-five hundred Testaments to free blacks and slaves. A high percentage of these Scriptures was supplied to "Colored Schools" in such places as New Jersey, Staten Island, and Canada. A few colporteurs in eastern Tennessee, the Carolinas, and Virginia requested

14. Andrew L. Hunter to James H. McNeill, June 1, 1855, November 1, 1856, Corresponding Secretary's Papers, ABS Archives.

15. Andrew L. Hunter to James McNeill, October 1, 1858, Corresponding Secretary's Papers, ABS Archives.

Scriptures for slaves during the 1850s, but references to such distribution in the correspondence appear very infrequently and irregularly. Christians ministering to slaves often enjoyed less cooperation from slaveholders than Hunter's well-publicized efforts suggest. Charles A. Proctor, a colporteur for the Knoxville Bible Society, noted that legal restrictions in Tennessee prevented anyone except slaveholders from providing Bibles to slaves and observed that most masters took "very little care to put the gospel in the hands of their servants." Similarly, a preacher working among slaves in the Ogeechee basin near Savannah requested a grant of Scriptures from the ABS's agent in Georgia in 1856 but cautioned that "these facts should not appear in print" for "reasons sufficiently apparent."[16]

McNeill spent more time reassuring southerners of the ABS's commitment to local control than he did encouraging agents to try to distribute Bibles among slaves. Despite his best efforts, correspondence from the agents and auxiliaries reveals an underlying suspicion toward the national headquarters. John Brigham, another corresponding secretary at Bible House, painted a generally depressing portrait while traveling through South Carolina in 1855. The Charleston Bible Society was one of the most successful ABS affiliates, but when Brigham moved inland he found a different attitude. "The Bible cause in this State is well-nigh dead," he lamented from Columbia. Brigham observed "an almost universal *coldness* . . . towards A.B.S. which they feel towards almost everything *northern.*" Rumors persisted throughout the South that the Bible Society planned a massive and indiscriminate distribution effort among slaves. McNeill denied stories that a "gen[era]l donation of 10,000 B[ible]s to the Coloured People South has been made." Evidence of mistrust and suspicion surfaced periodically. When the ABS was slow to acknowledge a $60 remittance for Bibles from the Tampa Bible Society in 1856, the local corresponding secretary demanded that McNeill research "what has become of our money or of our Bibles," adding sarcastically, "We hope you have not already con-

16. Cvornyek, "The Bible in Slavery and Freedom," pp. 13–16, includes the quotations from Tennessee and Georgia and provides an excellent overview of the question; Eric M. North and Dorothy U. Compagno, "Supply of Colored People and Slaves, 1841–1850," ABS Historical Essay 14, Part 4 (1964), pp. 136–142; and Eric M. North and Dorothy U. Compagno, "Distribution to Colored Persons and Slaves, 1851–1860," ABS Historical Essay 14, Part 5 (1964), pp. 62–66, provide detailed data on each grant of Scriptures to blacks during the 1840s and 1850s.

cluded to hold on to the money with a view to a dissolution of the Union."[17]

Impressionistic evidence offers one clue as to why the southern societies were distant and stagnant. Quantitative data confirm the limitations of the ABS's southern strategy. The number of local affiliates throughout the South grew dramatically during the 1850s. In 1849, the states of North Carolina, South Carolina, Georgia, Alabama, Florida, and Arkansas counted 257 auxiliaries within their boundaries. Ten years later, the number totaled 369. Financial contributions to the ABS's treasury, however, provide a very different perspective. Only in Arkansas, where forty-five of the sixty-two auxiliaries repaid the ABS for Bibles, and Florida, where fourteen of twenty-seven did likewise, did more than 50 percent of the local societies send any money to the national organization. Remittances amounted to 46 percent in South Carolina, 42 percent in Mississippi, 38 percent in North Carolina, 25 percent in Georgia, and 16 percent in Alabama. These figures stood in marked contrast to those for northeastern and midwestern states. Of Illinois's 114 auxiliaries, 92 percent remitted some money, for example, as did 77 percent of the 149 societies in Ohio, and 74 percent of Indiana's 110 affiliates. Figures for the Northeast included 75 percent for New Jersey, 79 percent for New York, 79 percent for Maine, and 50 percent for Massachusetts. On the eve of the Civil War the ABS was still financially dependent on the Northeast, the Middle Atlantic states, and the Old Northwest.[18]

Political tensions escalated during the 1850s, and the ABS's relationship with most southern societies deteriorated. McNeill tried to remain optimistic and continually stressed the national organization's neutrality. Writing to a skeptical South Carolinian in 1854, he described the ABS as "eminently Conservative and wholesome ... cherished by all who love their Country and their race ... an Institution [which] *never* in a *solitary* instance turned aside from that line, in obedience to the call of a blind and bigoted fanaticism."

17. John C. Brigham to James H. McNeill, March 26, 1855; Simon Furman to McNeill, October 12, 1856, Corresponding Secretary's Papers, ABS Archives; McNeill to E. C. Jones, October 19, 1855, Letter Book, Corresponding Secretary's Papers, ABS Archives.

18. These statistics were compiled from the ABS, *Forty-third Annual Report* (1859), pp. 113–136. The six leading states in payments in 1859 were New York, $140,420; Massachusetts, $30,153; Illinois, $28,530; Ohio, $26,642; Pennsylvania, $24,548; and Connecticut, $20,860.

During the height of the Kansas crisis in 1856, McNeill informed a southern agent that a recent board meeting had confirmed "the most sincere respect, and the cordial goodwill, towards the South! *Here*, at least, the agitating questions of the day find no entrance." Following the election of Abraham Lincoln, McNeill reassured the president of the Charleston Bible Society that the ABS "is as much & as truly the property & the Servant of Christians of the South as in the North ... nor will the Society, under any circumstances, be led into a course inconsistent with the principles wh[ich] have hitherto guided it."[19]

Incredibly, even during the early months of 1861 and following the formation of the Southern Confederacy, McNeill conducted regular business and exhorted the agents to continue their labors. He acknowledged to South Carolina Bible agent Edwin A. Bolles that a "strong prejudice" existed in January 1861 "against all institutions which happen to have their location in the North," but he expected that southerners might make "an exception" in the case of the Bible Society so that "we may continue to prosecute our benign work." McNeill instructed the ABS's agent in Goodman, Mississippi, to "go on with your work as formerly. Do all you can to reassure the minds of the people. Collect what funds you can, and order such Books as are needed," and expressed his hope that "the friends of God's Word in the South will not feel it necessary to withdraw from the Society." Similarly, the ABS's agent in California was informed in late January that "our friends in *all Sections* South as well as North, are manifesting the most cordial feelings toward the Parent Society. . . . Even if the two sections should become permanently separated, I do not think it at all likely, at least for the moment, that there will be any rupture of relations now existing." McNeill dutifully sent a certificate of recognition to a newly formed Bible Society in Coffeeville, Texas, observing on January 26, 1861, that "everything at present indicates a continued co-operation in every section of the country."[20]

McNeill even remained loyal to the Bible Society following the attack on Fort Sumter. He invited southerners to attend the annual

19. James H. McNeill to J. Coit, September 13, 1854; McNeill to Edwin A. Bolles, July 25, 1856; McNeill to N. R. Middleton, January 10, 1861, Letter Book, Corresponding Secretary's Papers, ABS Archives.

20. James H. McNeill to Edwin A. Bolles, January 17, 1861; McNeill to T. P. Johnston, January 25, 1861; McNeill to J. C. Blanton, January 26, 1861; McNeill to Frederick Buel, January 29, 1861, Corresponding Secretary's Papers, ABS Archives.

meeting in May, noting the importance of making the event "broad, catholic, & unsectional as well as unsectarian." The 1847 report regarding slaves and Scriptures was reprinted and circulated to southern agents in an effort to underscore the Society's historically neutral stance and to quell perceptions that it made any grants for this purpose "except to *Societies and respectable individuals* entitled to confidence *at the South.*" An agent in Tulip, Arkansas, was urged to "ignore the state of the country in your Public Addresses." One in Mississippi received notice that "we want to go on with our work as ever before, turning neither to the right nor to the left . . . and maintaining with [the auxiliaries] all the same cordial relations as heretofore."[21]

McNeill's efforts failed. Political and practical considerations proved insurmountable. Transportation and communication difficulties prevented the Society from filling the few orders it received from southern societies in the spring of 1861. When southern states seceded, relations with auxiliaries completely broke down. By July 1861, virtually all of the southern agents had resigned. For McNeill, personal tragedy became interwoven with the national crisis. Two of his children died on Christmas Eve and Christmas Day in 1860. After his native North Carolina joined the Confederacy, McNeill reluctantly resigned his ABS post on June 6, 1861, and decided to return south. His dual commitments to an essentially northern national benevolence and to southern society proved impossible to reconcile. He edited the *North Carolina Presbyterian* for one year, after which he entered the Confederate army, achieving the rank of colonel in the Fifth North Carolina Regiment. On March 31, 1865, shortly before the conclusion of hostilities, McNeill was killed at the battle of Petersburg, and he was interred in his native Fayetteville. His career with the ABS highlighted the difficulty of maintaining a national neutrality amid the moral and political crises of the 1860s.[22]

21. James H. McNeill to J. L. Girardeau, February 14, 1861; McNeill to H. A. Nelson, February 14, 1861; McNeill to Edwin A. Bolles, March 18, 1861; McNeill to J. S. McAlister, January 15, 1861; McNeill to T. P. Johnston, May 7, 1861, Letter Book, Corresponding Secretary's Papers, ABS Archives.

22. James H. McNeill to J. P. Moore, May 14, 1861, Letter Book, Corresponding Secretary's Papers, ABS Archives; *Bible Society Record,* June 1861, p. 84; *Southern Presbyterian,* June 21, 1862; Minutes of Meeting of the Committee on Agencies, July 3, 1861; *Bible Society Record,* July 1865, p. 107; Henry Otis Dwight, *The Centennial History of the American Bible Society* (New York: Macmillan, 1916), p. 256.

One recent historian of nineteenth-century America's "benevolent empire" has argued that the Bible Society was "the most successful" of the national philanthropies in "penetrating the wall of hostility" and maintaining cordial relations with the South during wartime. The board stressed neutrality in its public statements. Within one month of McNeill's resignation, the managers proclaimed that they "do not see cause to make any alteration in their practice or policy in regard to supplying auxiliary societies." The man charged with implementing this stated policy, as well as with coordinating the massive effort to supply northern troops and satisfying increased wartime demands, was a thirty-nine-year-old Dutch Reformed pastor named William J. R. Taylor.[23]

Taylor had been born in Rensselaer County, New York, and raised in Newark, New Jersey. A graduate of Rutgers College (1841) and the New Brunswick Theological Seminary (1844), he had been licensed by the Classis of Bergen and served Reformed churches throughout New Jersey and New York during the late 1840s and early 1850s. Immediately before accepting his appointment at the ABS in 1862, Taylor spent eight years as pastor of the prestigious Third Reformed Church of Philadelphia. The new corresponding secretary appeared an ideal candidate to negotiate the Society through its wartime tribulations. His membership in the Dutch Reformed church, which had taken an extremely conservative position on the slavery issue, seemed likely to placate southerners. Further, as a vocal advocate of "systematic beneficence," Taylor urged his denomination to develop an elaborate system of organized tithing, which "should be cultivated and systematized" in Sabbath school and include organized canvassing within each congregation.[24]

Taylor's denominational affiliation and his commitment to sys-

23. Kuykendall, *Southern Enterprize*, p. 149. John McKivigan notes that "the American Bible Society remained anathema to abolitionists during the war because the organization's managers not only refused to denounce slavery but also continued to supply southerners with the Scriptures" *(The War against Proslavery Religion: Abolition and the Northern Churches, 1830–1865* [Ithaca: Cornell University Press, 1984], p. 188). Minutes of Meeting of the Board of Managers, July 11, 1861, ABS Archives. Taylor was elected corresponding secretary on April 3, 1862.

24. William J. R. Taylor, *On Systematic Beneficence, with Facts and Forms Showing the Working of the System* (New York: Board of Publication of the Protestant Dutch Church, 1858), pp. 31, 37–48. Biographical material on Taylor is from his file in the Archives of the Reformed Church in America, New Brunswick Theological Seminary, New Brunswick, New Jersey.

tem, organization, and centralization were balanced by personal characteristics that made him particularly attractive to Bible Society administrators in the 1860s. When a memorialist writing Taylor's obituary in 1891 sought to emphasize "one trait of character that shone out more brightly than another, and threw its radiance over the others," he focused on his subject's *"amiability."* Taylor possessed a "gentleness and consideration for the feeling of others." He "never intentionally uttered a sentence that left a sting in its memory" and "was always careful in conversation and intercourse, by word or peer, to avoid whatever would conflict with the word of love." "Courteous and dignified in his intercourse with strangers," Taylor was "frank and warm-hearted with friends." In short, he combined the discipline and order of a good businessman with the supreme attention to manners and appearances necessary for a successful Bible Society administrator.[25]

Publicly, the American Bible Society maintained an amiable stance toward the Confederacy. Working through the Maryland Bible Society, Washington City Bible Society, and, to a lesser extent, local auxiliaries in Memphis and Louisville, the ABS delivered thousands of Bibles to the Confederate army. Annual reports told of large grants to the Southern Baptist Sunday School Board, Confederate generals, and southern chaplains, including the ABS's former special secretary Joseph C. Stiles. Circulars described the Society's efforts to supply southern troops and prisoners of war. Taylor urged agents in border states to publicize "this feature of our work," which "is making a strong impression on Southern people & troops & . . . doing much to soften feeling . . . of those who but a few months ago were full of venom against us."[26]

The ABS rigorously enforced its prohibition against agents and

25. William J. R. Taylor's biographical file, Archives of the Reformed Church in America. Taylor played a major role in attempting to stop the Sunday opening of the Chicago Columbian Exposition in 1893. He died on a railroad train en route from Colorado Springs to Utah to address the American Sabbath Union. See also *Bible Society Record,* November 1891, p. 171, and December 1891, p. 187.

26. ABS, *Forty-seventh Annual Report* (1863), pp. 37–39; *Forty-eighth Annual Report* (1864), pp. 39–40; *Forty-ninth Annual Report* (1865), pp. 40–41; Dorothy U. Compagno, "The Civil War, 1861–1865," ABS Historical Essay, 14, VI (1964), pp. 1–40; William J. R. Taylor to Frederick Buel, August 13, 1863, Letter Book, Corresponding Secretary's Papers, ABS Archives. Taylor's letterbook contains numerous examples of outgoing correspondence directed at publicizing the ABS's work with southerners. See also "The American Bible Society and the South," Circular, August 1865, Corresponding Secretary's Papers, ABS Archives.

other employees taking a public stance concerning either the conflict or domestic political affairs. Taylor noted that during the presidential campaign of 1864, the ABS "summarily dismissed" one agent for "making Republican speeches at political meetings" and observed that "the same result would have happened had he advocated the Democratic side." When a Methodist Bible agent from Kentucky criticized separatists and advocated union within his fractured denomination in 1865, Taylor warned him against "using his official position to propogate his partizan views." The most successful ABS employees during the conflict, noted Taylor, were those "who endeavor, in the spirit of that most decided of all men, the Apostle Paul, to become all things to all men that by all means they might save some."[27]

Privately, Taylor appeared to follow Paul's teachings when addressing southern auxiliaries, but he occasionally was more forthcoming with his personal anxieties and views concerning the Society's precarious position. Personally, the corresponding secretary clearly hoped for a quick restoration of the Union, and he supported Lincoln's initial limited aims during the early war years. Writing to a northern sympathizer in Kentucky in January 1862, Taylor expressed his "hope that the rebel will soon be so routed that all Kentucky may be opened to us." An agent for the South Western Bible Society who expressed distrust of northern philanthropies in 1863 received a terse reply from Taylor, agreeing that "you certainly do not misinterpret the loyal sentiment of the great mass of the people of the North."[28]

The bloody draft riots in New York City in July 1863, however, provoked Taylor's strongest wartime reactions. The draft riots crystallized the complex issues unraveling the fabric of American society during the 1860s. Despite the ABS's efforts to aid the South and remain neutral during the war, the Bible House was "openly threatened with destruction by the rioters in the streets." For many working-class draft resisters and Irish Catholic rioters, the Society undoubtedly represented the patrician, Protestant, Republican urban elite who controlled the city's economy and seemed determined to impose their own morality on the laboring classes. The Bible House, a symbol of consolidated evangelical power, was never

27. William J. R. Taylor to Drummond Welburn, November 4, 1865, Letter Book, Corresponding Secretary's Papers, ABS Archives.

28. William J. R. Taylor to S. M. Bayless, January 5, 1862; Taylor to P. M. Ozanne, April 23, 1863, Letter Book, Corresponding Secretary's Papers, ABS Archives.

attacked during the disorder, and Taylor triumphantly informed agents in New Hampshire, Kansas, and Ohio in late July that "it still stands." He excoriated the "vile politicians" and "Irish Romanists" seeking to "help the rebellion" through rioting and prayed that "this demonic spirit of plunder & murder be stopped effectively by the strong arm of the government!" Despite his amiability and good manners, Taylor clearly perceived the social stakes involved after the July rioting, and his private ruminations on this occasion were the strongest statements made by any Bible Society official during the Civil War.[29]

Rioting threatened the Society's operations on one immediate level. Three other developments had disturbing long-term implications for the national Bible movement. First, in 1862 a Confederate States Bible Society was organized at Augusta, Georgia, by disaffected southerners. James H. McNeill, the ABS's former corresponding secretary, initially spearheaded this movement, and his resignation from the ABS aided the organizing effort. Information concerning the organization was sketchy at the time. The Confederate society issued annual reports in 1862 and 1863 and published two editions of the Bible specifically for southern soldiers. An ABS informant in Louisville, however, claimed that the Confederate Congress received an application for funding from this new society with "cold indifference" in 1862 and that "though the child was brought to the birth, it fell dead from the womb of its conception.[30]

Despite this somewhat premature assessment, the Confederate society maintained an ongoing ministry for southern soldiers throughout the war years. In December 1865, the managers of this organization issued a circular "to the friends of the Bible Cause throughout the South" claiming that "our country is large enough to justify the maintenance of two great Bible centres" and pledging to examine the question of permanently establishing the Confederate society. This effort failed. Several state conferences of the

29. William J. R. Taylor to E. W. Smith, July 15, 1863; Taylor to Thomas H. Quinan, July 16, 1863; Taylor to J. B. Richardson, July 16, 1863; Taylor to L. B. Dennis, July 16, 1863; Taylor to Isaac Willey, July 22, 1863; Taylor to S. M. Bayless, July 24, 1863, Letter Book, Corresponding Secretary's Papers, ABS Archives. On the draft riots, consult Iver Bernstein, *The New York City Draft Riots: Their Significance for American Society and Politics in the Age of the Civil War* (New York: Oxford University Press, 1990).

30. C. B. Parsons to William J. R. Taylor, January 9, 1863, Corresponding Secretary's Papers, ABS Archives; Taylor to Thomas J. Quinan, January 10, 17, 1863, Letter Book, Corresponding Secretary's Papers, ABS Archives.

Methodist Episcopal church, South, decided not to support the organization's revival, and the Confederate society's leaders relented. Still, the specter of permanent sectional division hung heavily over the heads of the ABS's managers, and Taylor feared in 1866 that "there will be strong efforts to perpetuate [the Confederate society] by men of bitter prejudices—fire-eaters, disunionists, &c."[31]

Second, the British and Foreign Bible Society entered the American field during the Civil War. Shortly after McNeill's resignation, the Charleston Bible Society applied to the BFBS for a grant of Scriptures, citing its inability to acquire Bibles from New York. Just as the Confederate States of America looked to England for warships, rifles, and diplomatic recognition, southern Christians appeared eager to align their benevolent activities with those of the British as well. The ABS's managers publicly claimed to have "no objection whatever" to the Charleston society's purchase, but Bible Society administrators privately fumed. The British society, in Taylor's mind, "has no more right to interfere in this country than we have to operate in Wales or Yorkshire." The ABS and BFBS already had experienced considerable tension over their competitive missionary endeavors throughout the world, and this intrusion by a foreign Bible power appeared directly to threaten the ABS's domestic efforts. Relations worsened when Moses D. Hoge, the president of the Virginia Bible Society, visited England to procure Scriptures for distribution throughout the Confederacy. Further, the Virginia society refused to accept Scriptures from the ABS, and the BFBS entered a separate cooperative arrangement with the Confederate States Bible Society. Taylor bitterly resented these overtures, claiming that southerners "can get Bibles and Testaments far more readily from New York than from London & with actual permits and help of our own government instead of encountering the hazards of a blockading fleet." At the war's end, the ABS reluctantly recognized an unsettling "disposition on the part of some to seek aid from the Br[itish]. & For[eign]. B[ible]. S[ociety]."[32]

---

31. "To the Friends of the Bible Cause Throughout the South," Circular, December 10, 1865, Corresponding Secretary's Papers, ABS Archives; Compagno, "Civil War," pp. 4–7. William J. R. Taylor to W. J. Parks, December 8, 1865; Taylor to Moses N. Adams, June 26, 1866, Letter Book, Corresponding Secretary's Papers, ABS Archives.

32. William J. R. Taylor to William Ballantyne, February 18, 1862; Taylor to Thomas H. Quinan, January 10, 17, 1863; Taylor to Samuel J. Baird, March 6, 1866, Letter Book, Corresponding Secretary's Papers, ABS Archives; British and Foreign

The freedmen presented the most significant and challenging issue resulting from the Civil War. Material in the American Bible Society's archives confirms the judgments of northern missionaries, military observers, and subsequent historians. "The Freedmen," in the words of the ABS's army agent William H. Gilbert in 1865, "are rapidly learning to read," and "the considerate part of the community every where express the Conviction that there is an extensive demand for the Bible" among them. The former slaves' extraordinary educational appetites stimulated perhaps the most dramatic rise in literacy rates in American history. The Bible was both an important literacy tool for freedmen and a key stimulus in their desire to read. As Eric Foner has observed, "a craving 'to read the Word of God' provided the immediate spur to learning" for many adult blacks. The American Bible Society bore a special moral obligation to place the Bible in the hands of these new readers.[33]

Practical necessity intersected with sincere Christian commitment to shape ABS policy. The cause of educating the freedmen excited unprecedented support among philanthropic northerners. Religious and secular organizations established dozens of missionary agencies to aid the freedmen. Hubbard Beebe, an ABS agent writing from New Haven in September 1865, observed that "Connecticut is full of the activities of benevolent agencies, circulars, letters, addresses &c." Perhaps most unsettling to administrators at Bible House, Beebe admitted that "the new causes, especially those relating to the Freedmen, are quite popular" while "some of the older societies, like ours, are in some places set aside for a year." The Society recognized both the moral and practical reasons for highlighting and enhancing its ministry to the freed slaves.[34]

Bible Society, *Annual Report* (1863), pp. 248–250; (1864), pp. 247–249; and (1865), pp. 272–273.

33. William H. Gilbert to William J. R. Taylor, September 4, 1865, Corresponding Secretary's Papers, ABS Archives. Eric Foner, *Reconstruction: America's Unfinished Revolution, 1863–1877* (New York: Harper & Row, 1988), pp. 96–97. See Robert C. Morris, *Reading, 'Riting, and Reconstruction: The Education of Freedmen in the South, 1861–1870* (Chicago: University of Chicago Press, 1981), for an account of freedmen's education.

34. Hubbard Beebe to William J. R. Taylor, September 20, 1865, Corresponding Secretary's Papers, ABS Archives. On the proliferation of missionary organizations, see Joe M. Richardson, *Christian Reconstruction: The American Missionary Associa-*

Debates between advocates of special "missions to the freed-men" and proponents of sectional reconciliation seriously divided churches and northern benevolent agencies following the Civil War. The American Bible Society hoped to pursue a moderate course, balancing its missionary obligation to the freed slaves with its sectional commitment to the southern auxiliaries. Reconstruction imposed new realities on national agencies and forced difficult choices. The cause of the freedmen was the most emotional issue confronting the reunited nation in 1865. As the Society groped toward a policy during the immediate postwar years, it soon became obvious that the delicate balance would tilt toward sectional autonomy and local control.

Antebellum southern agents began reapplying to the ABS for work within four months of General Robert E. Lee's surrender at Appomattox. By the fall of 1865, the Society's direction appeared clear. Taylor observed in September that "we are gradually extending our Agencies into the Southern states—all but one of the appointees are our *old* Agents—& the exception [in North Carolina] ... is that of a native of that state & long a resident in it." Taylor informed one transplanted northern missionary interested in an ABS appointment in Georgia that "other things being equal, we prefer selecting Southern men for our Agencies there—and we wish to act with prudence, promptitude & energy." The one exception illustrates the general rule. Samuel J. Baird (1817–1883), an Ohio native and Presbyterian minister in southern New Jersey, expressed a desire to labor for the ABS in Tennessee. Taylor was reluctant, observing that "there is a strong prejudice throughout the South against Northern men." Baird's previous pastoral work in Kentucky and the Southwest, his successful efforts to establish a school in South Carolina and a female seminary in Louisiana, and his extensive connections "with Southern families &c." did earn him an ABS appointment for middle and western Tennessee in October 1865. Virtually every southern appointment, however, went to men born and bred in the region, and the Society decidedly preferred that its agents have prewar Bible Society experience.[35]

---

tion and Southern Blacks, 1861–1890 (Athens: University of Georgia Press, 1986), p. 71.

35. William J. R. Taylor to Drummond Welburn, September 11, 1865; Taylor to Alexander J. Baird, August 5, 1865; Taylor to Edward Oliver Dunning, August 5, 1865; Taylor to Henry Hardie, August 5, 1865; Taylor to W. T. Brantly, August 10, 1865,

Many southern agents had aligned openly with the Confederacy and occupied highly visible ministerial positions during the Civil War. This proved no hindrance to their rejoining the ABS. Edwin A. Bolles of South Carolina served as a district superintendent for the Confederate States Bible Society between 1861 and 1865 and boasted that "during my agency of four years . . . I found no difficulty in gathering funds by the thousands." William Crockett Johnson, laboring in northern Mississippi and western Tennessee, noted that "in this terrible Civil War, which is and was a great Sin, I sympathized with my own section," and Taylor described him privately as "on the rebel side during the war." Edward Oliver Dunning worked throughout the conflict with the secessionist Virginia Bible Society, an organization described by Taylor as "rather hostile" to the ABS in August 1865.[36]

Letter Book, Corresponding Secretary's Papers, ABS Archives. For a biography of Samuel J. Baird, see Alfred Nevin, ed., *Encyclopedia of the Presbyterian Church in the United States of America* (Philadelphia: Presbyterian Encyclopaedia Publishing Company, 1884), p. 50.

The list of postwar southern agents, in addition to Samuel J. Baird, includes Edwin Abiel Bolles (1812–1893), born in Charleston, South Carolina, and former agent for South Carolina, reappointed agent for South Carolina in June 1865; Gadwell Jefferson Pearce (1813–1876), born in Jackson County, Georgia, and former agent for Georgia, reappointed agent for Georgia in September 1865; William Crockett Johnson (1825–1902), born in Franklin, Tennessee, and former agent for Tennessee, appointed agent for northern Mississippi and western Tennessee in September 1865; Simon Peter Richardson (1818–1899), born in Dutch Fork, South Carolina, and former agent for Florida, appointed agent for Alabama and West Florida in October 1865; Edward Oliver Dunning (dates and place of birth unknown), former agent for West Virginia, appointed agent for the Valley of Virginia and East Tennessee in September 1865; Henry Hardie (1823–1868), born in Raleigh, North Carolina, and appointed agent for North Carolina in September 1865; Alexander J. Baird (1820–1874), born in southwestern Pennsylvania and former agent in Tennessee, appointed agent for middle and western Tennessee in October 1865; Reuben H. Luckey (1801–1875), born in Greene County, Georgia, and former agent for Florida and southern Georgia, appointed agent for Florida in January 1866; William P. Ratcliffe (1810–1868), born in Williamsburg, Virginia, appointed agent for Arkansas in August 1866; John Wesley DeVilbiss (1818–1885), born in Graceham, Maryland, appointed agent for Texas west of the Brazos River in December 1866; and Nelson P. Modrall (1811–1880), born in Tennessee, appointed agent for Texas east of the Brazos River in October 1866. Biographical information concerning all of these agents is available in Biographical Files, ABS Archives.

36. Edwin A. Bolles to William J. R. Taylor, January 31, 1866, and William C. Johnson to Joseph Holdich, August 3, 1865, Corresponding Secretary's Papers, ABS Archives; Taylor to Thomas H. Quinan, August 18, 1865, and Taylor to William F.

Reconstructing the southern agencies and reviving the southern auxiliaries was a high priority. Bible Society administrators complemented this policy with an effort to distribute Scriptures among the freedmen, and they expected southern agents to emphasize this ministry to former slaves. Taylor observed in a letter to the secretary of the Maryland Bible Society in September 1865 that "all the new Southern Agents are personally pledged to our great work among the Freedmen & poor whites. None other can be appointed." Correspondence from the agents in the field reinforces Taylor's claims. Edwin Bolles, who labored for the Confederate States Bible Society during the war, regularly requested grants throughout 1865 and 1866 for African Methodist Episcopal churches, freedmen's schools, and white auxiliaries wishing "to put the word of God into the hands of our people of color who can read." William C. Johnson, despite his well-known rebel sympathies, acknowledged after the war that "the Bible must be furnished to all men, irrespective of color, and the blacks must be cared for as the most needy at this time." Within two months of his appointment, Johnson reported preaching "to the colored people" in Holly Spring, Mississippi, and informing "them fully as to the Society's purposes in their behalf." The Society published a special Gospel of John in large type as an educational tool for freedmen's schools in 1865, and correspondence files indicate various cooperative efforts with northern missionary programs and educational efforts.[37]

Baird, September 14, 1865, Letter Book, Corresponding Secretary's Papers, ABS Archives.

37. William J. R. Taylor to Thomas Quinan, September 13, 1865, Letter Book, Corresponding Secretary's Papers, ABS Archives; Edwin A. Bolles to Taylor, September 20, November 30, December 30, 1865, January 30, March 30, April 27, August 27, 1866, April 1867; William C. Johnson to Taylor, August 3, November 20, 1865, Corresponding Secretary's Papers, ABS Archives. A thorough reading of all the southern agents' correspondence during the immediate postwar years leads to the conclusion that considerable efforts were made to distribute Bibles among the freedmen. Such work appeared to receive a greater emphasis from agents in North Carolina, South Carolina, Texas, and Tennessee than in Florida, Louisiana, and Virginia. See Minutes of Meeting of the Board of Managers, September 7, 1865, ABS Archives; and Bible Society Record, September 1865, pp. 39–40, for information concerning the special Gospel of John. A file folder marked "Freedmen's Correspondence, 1863–1869," Corresponding Secretary's Papers, contains examples of cooperation with various missionary and educational agencies.

The ABS's most extensive and well-publicized effort to supply southern blacks involved the employment of an "Agent to Superintend Bible Work among the Freedmen." General Clinton B. Fisk, who headed the Freedmen's Bureau in Tennessee, and the Reverend William F. Baird (1818–1892), a Cumberland Presbyterian preacher from Iowa who served as an ABS agent for the northern army during the war, first suggested this initiative to the managers in 1865. The board moved slowly and cautiously before approving this agency. The managers recognized the advantages of a special agent but were reluctant to supersede or abandon their commitment to local control in the South. William Baird finally received approval to tour the South and begin working among the freedmen in October 1865, but Taylor clearly outlined and carefully circumscribed the position's responsibilities and boundaries.

Three themes emerge from Baird's commission and detailed instructions: the need to work within the ABS's agent and auxiliary structure; an overriding emphasis on discretion and prudence; and the temporary, limited nature of the task. The board defined this special agency, in William J. R. Taylor's words, to "secure thoroughness, wisdom & efficiency" in supplying the freedmen. He especially emphasized that work among the freedmen should progress "without any clashing with the newly appointed State Agents." Taylor underscored the fact that Baird's responsibility "expressly associates you with the State Agents. . . . You are to cooperate with them & they are requested to aid you. . . . They are not to be regarded as subordinate to you—but as brethren in the same work." Taylor urged Baird to proceed with "Christian candor & courtesy" among the southerners, taking special care to use "discretion for dealing with them on a subject so delicate." Most important, the board mandated that Baird's agency "is to have no direct connection with the Freedmen's Bureau." Association with controversial government and missionary endeavors "does not strike us at all favorably." The ABS wished to maintain its independence, coming "into contact with the government only incidentally" and not jeopardizing its relations with southern auxiliaries. Baird's primary responsibilities involved working with agents, auxiliaries, and local Bible committees to institutionalize the mission to the freedmen within the ABS's existing structural framework. The Agency for the Freedmen, in Taylor's mind, "is designed not to give undue prominence to the work among the Freedmen . . . is not so much a specialty as a new development of our work for which you and the Agents are to lay broad & deep & strong foundations."[38]

Several factors undermined both Baird's agency and the Society's general efforts among freedmen. Strict reliance on local agents and auxiliaries kept the Bible cause subject to local prejudices. Conditions varied throughout the South, but preachers and laypersons sympathetic to the freedmen offered a generally dismal assessment. When the ABS donated several hundred Bibles and Testaments to the Atlanta Bible Society in 1865, a local Methodist missionary "could find no White Citizen willing to risk his reputation . . . to circulate the word of life as printed and sent out by the Yankees." This minister noted that "the leading members of the churches are and have been decidedly *Secesh* . . . they are not prepared to acknowledge the defeat of the South and the emancipation of the slaves. . . . They are soured in their feelings and will be sure to stand aloof for the present."[39]

The New Orleans Ministerial Association lodged a formal complaint against the South Western Bible Society, observing that this auxiliary refused to grant or sell Bibles to northern soldiers and that "Christian men from the North, loyal to the Federal Government & favorable to the present administration," were excluded from participation. South Carolina Bible agent Edwin A. Bolles reported in 1867 that "the Charleston Bible Society will not cooperate with the A.B.S. in giving the Word of God to the freedmen," and he avoided visiting the city, preferring to concentrate his efforts inland. Bitter disunion split the Bible Society in Memphis, where secessionists controlled the auxiliary, stored their stock of Bibles in the basement of a church noted for its disloyalty, and excluded Union supporters from the work. The Memphis and Shelby County Bible Society's only positive reaction to the freedmen's agency, noted William Baird, came from a local pastor who "stated at the last anniversary meeting of the Society that he was in favour of giving the Bible to the colored people in order that they might learn from it their inferiority to the White race."[40]

38. William J. R. Taylor to William F. Baird, September 29, October 6, 21, 1865; and Taylor to Edward Oliver Dunning, October 28, 1865, Letter Book, Corresponding Secretary's Papers, ABS Archives.

39. D. Young to William J. R. Taylor, July 10, 1865, Atlanta Bible Society Correspondence, Corresponding Secretary's Papers, ABS Archives.

40. New Orleans Ministerial Association to Joseph Holdich, December 8, 1864, Southwestern Bible Society Correspondence; Edwin A. Bolles to William J. R. Taylor,

Baird, the regular Bible agents, and the ABS's board of managers carefully avoided any confrontation with reluctant and hostile local auxiliaries. Taylor regretted the Charleston Bible Society's refusal to supply freedmen, but he instructed agent Bolles that "the only course is to let them severely alone." Baird received a letter from the corresponding secretary lamenting that the South Western Bible Society "will do little or nothing for the Freed people" and noting some pressure from northern ministers in New Orleans to establish a completely new auxiliary. Taylor acknowledged these problems but affirmed the ABS's stance that "we do not feel disposed unduly to take the work out of their hands." Baird's correspondence to the Society reflects a sincere desire to supply the freedmen, a general distress at prevailing racist feelings among many leaders of the local auxiliaries, and some gentle attempts to reshape southern attitudes. Gratifying success alternated with depressing failure. Arriving at Houston in late August 1866, Baird concluded that "the brethren here are fortunate in the Salvation of officers of this Society. They have chosen some of the most religious and active businessmen. . . . I am much pleased with the organization." One week earlier, Baird penned a more sober letter from a Galveston hotel, sitting "in a hot room with a dim light, and surrounded by a large company of bugs and mosquitoes," that documented the "bitter feeling toward the Northern people." A leading Christian in this river town warned that if the Galveston Bible Society "was to be *radical,* they didn't want it," and Baird reluctantly decided "not to resuscitate" the local auxiliary. Baird's mission, like the Bible Society's southern strategy generally, relied purely on local circumstances and the goodwill of leading white Christian southerners.[41]

Reconstructed southern auxiliaries were often ambiguous or overtly hostile toward work among the freedmen, and black citizens received minimal opportunities to participate in the Bible cause. The Bible Society's agents preached to the freedmen, solicited their financial contributions, and encouraged their educa-

---

April 4, 1867; William F. Baird to Taylor, July 5, 1866, Corresponding Secretary's Papers, ABS Archives.

41. William J. R. Taylor to Edwin A. Bolles, March 14, 1866, and Taylor to William F. Baird, December 18, 1865, Letter Book, Corresponding Secretary's Papers, ABS Archives; Baird to Taylor, August 20, 13, 1866, Corresponding Secretary's Papers, ABS Archives.

tion. ABS representatives generally discouraged black initiatives to affiliate directly with the Society, preferring to work through southern societies and established missionary agencies. Taylor articulated this policy in an October 1865 letter to East Tennessee agent Edward Oliver Dunning: "We will gladly supply the Colored people either through our Auxiliaries or through other responsible channels of distribution—as the Freedmen's Bureau Association or Bds. of Missions &c. when it may be desirable." Some agents discouraged the Society from granting books to blacks, claiming that the freed people could not responsibly coordinate distribution. Reuben H. Luckey, representing ABS interests in Florida, warned that "the Freedmen of the South if they had unrestricted access to the Bible House in New York would soon relieve its stores of all the books, and would almost as soon loose or destroy them." The Society heeded such cautionary advice.[42]

The American Bible Society appeared especially reluctant to encourage and recognize "Colored Bible Societies." Despite their poverty, southern blacks engaged in what one historian has described as "an explosion of institution building" in the years following emancipation. Churches, schools, fraternal organizations, mutual benefit societies, and equal rights leagues sprang up throughout the South during the 1860s, testifying to black enterprise, organizational ability, and institutional sophistication. With few exceptions, Bible societies remained outside this impressive framework. Henry Hardie, the ABS's agent in North Carolina, expressed interest in advancing this work after learning of the establishment of the Knoxville Colored Bible Society in Tennessee in December 1865. Taylor urged caution: "There are few places where the blacks have enough men of intelligence & other requisites for maintaining such an organization, & only in such places should the attempt be made." Hardie persisted, however, and six months later he again petitioned the corresponding secretary to organize such a society in New Bern, North Carolina. Taylor relented, but his response hardly constituted a ringing endorsement: "You will do well to organize the B[ible]. S[ociety]. of colored people

42. William J. R. Taylor to Edward O. Dunning, October 28, 1865, Letter Book, Corresponding Secretary's Papers, ABS Archives; Reuben H. Luckey to Taylor, August 29, 1866, Corresponding Secretary's Papers, ABS Archives.

... if you can get trustworthy & competent men at the helm of it. So also elsewhere—but always with caution."[43]

The Society's conservative policy prevented it from establishing a strong connection with the newly freed black community. Bible societies remained outside the complex institutional network created by freed people. The few "Colored Bible Societies," like those at Knoxville and New Bern, soon sank into inactivity and expired. William Baird concluded his agency early in 1867, and the Society thereafter reinstituted its commitment to local control. The ABS's policy of working through its white auxiliaries took precedence, and a generally negative attitude toward blacks' administrative abilities and intellectual competence caused the ABS to retreat from this work. Bible Society administrators wanted the freedmen to receive the Scriptures, but they preferred to funnel Bibles through the hands of white southerners. Perhaps William J. R. Taylor best summed up the Society's official view in a letter to an agent laboring in middle Tennessee. If white southerners failed to provide freedmen with the Bible, he warned, "the colored people will be educated by others." This could prove especially unfortunate, in Taylor's view, for "surely it seems that Providence indicates their old Employers & the people among whom they have always lived as the proper persons to elevate them for the enjoyment of their freedom & to train them for the skies."[44]

The Bible Society weathered the storms of the 1850s and 1860s with its institutional structure largely intact. Residual southern hostility prevented it from establishing strong southern auxiliaries after the war, but northerners traditionally provided the bulk of ABS support in any case. Southern work remained largely in the hands of prudent and loyal local agents, who discreetly carried out their responsibilities and worked to minimize sectional tension. The Society's experiences proved that a national nonprofit corporate bureaucracy could eventually accommodate and absorb local diversity. Maintaining a national focus, however, exacted a significant moral cost. If the Society aspired to a higher purpose, it could not merely gauge its success by perpetuating its own institution. The cause of the freedmen and the issue of race proved too contro-

43. Foner, *Reconstruction*, p. 102; William J. R. Taylor to Henry Hardie, December 16, 1865, June 21, 1866, Letter Book, Corresponding Secretary's Papers, ABS Archives.

44. William J. R. Taylor to Alexander J. Baird, November 15, 1865, Letter Book, Corresponding Secretary's Papers, ABS Archives.

versial for serious and sustained missionary effort. Irreconcilable domestic divisions threatened any philanthropy claiming both a national constituency and a moral focus. Christian unity appeared more elusive than ever at midcentury. The Society needed a bold, new, noncontroversial initiative to reclaim its broader sense of purpose. The managers wisely directed their gaze overseas.

9

Bringing System and Order to the Agency: Bible Work in the Levant, 1854–1889

One final transformation in the history of the American Bible Society requires analysis. Beginning in the 1850s, as sectional tensions and domestic disturbances heightened at home, the managers reopened their Levant agency. By the late nineteenth century, the ABS had shifted its priorities. The "Christian Public" increasingly identified the ABS as fundamentally a foreign mission organization. New Bible translations, supported and developed by the ABS, appeared in scores of languages. Overseas agents acquired significant influence within the Society and built substantial organizations abroad. Missionary work provided an important outlet for the Society's energies, allowing it to alter its role and assume a critical position within the global Protestant crusade. As work in the Levant matured, the contrast between Simeon Calhoun's "mission to the heathen" in the 1830s and the organized, systematic, businesslike nature of late nineteenth-century religious life grew ever greater. The ABS resolved its earlier tensions, and the new style of missionary labor spoke volumes about its transformation.

Chester Newell Righter, the Society's second representative in the Levant, served the ABS for only two years. In December 1856, while touring ABCFM stations in Asiatic Turkey, the thirty-two-year-old agent fell ill with a mysterious disease and died suddenly at the home of an American missionary. His short career contained few noteworthy accomplishments or innovative approaches to Bible work and would appear marginally significant, even for a chronicler of mission history. Yet Righter's brief life inspired the prominent evangelical editor and Bible Society life director Samuel I. Prime (1813–1885) to compile and publish *The Bible in the Levant; or the Life and Letters of the Rev. C. N. Righter, Agent of the American Bible Society in the Levant* in 1859. A careful consideration of Prime's biographical tribute, combined with an examination of Righter's cultural and familial milieu, offers the historian unanticipated insights into the social and economic forces transforming midcentury American Protestantism.[1]

Righter was born in the village of Parsippany, in Hanover Township, Morris County, New Jersey, on September 25, 1824. A local historian, writing in 1882, observed that the township was inhabited "chiefly [by] the offspring of the primitive settlers . . . mainly from the New Englandish settlements of Newark and Elizabeth." Since its founding in 1710, the community's fertile soil and pleasant climate attracted a stable farming population, and its rural solitude "prompts the Hanoverians to cling to the homesteads of their fathers." Census statistics appear to reinforce the image of a sleepy, stable country village. Between 1810 and 1870, the population fluctuated between thirty-four hundred and thirty-nine hundred, with a net decline of two hundred residents over the sixty-year period. Every indicator suggests that the township and the "rambling settlement" of Parsippany were traditional communities where town, church, and family constituted the focal points of social existence.[2]

But the local historian's bucolic portrait obscures some farreaching socioeconomic changes that were transforming the nature of Morris County life as Chester Righter approached maturity.

1. Samuel Irenaeus Prime, *The Bible in the Levant; or the Life and Letters of Rev. C. N. Righter, Agent of the American Bible Society in the Levant* (New York: Sheldon & Company, 1859).

2. Monroe Howell, "Hanover Township," in E. D. Halsey, *History of Morris County, New Jersey, with Illustrations and Biographical Sketches of Prominent Citizens and Pioneers* (New York: W. W. Munsell, 1882), p. 221. Hal S. Barron, *Those Who Stayed Behind: Rural Society in Nineteenth-Century New England* (New York: Cambridge University Press, 1984), argues that stable, traditional, "preindustrial villages" constituted an important form of social organization on the nineteenth-century American rural landscape. But see Darrett B. Rutman's comments in "Behind the Wide Missouri," *Reviews in American History* (June 1985), 232–235.

In 1831, the Morris Canal was completed, linking Easton, Pennsylvania, and Newark, New Jersey. Anthracite mined in the Pennsylvania coal fields arrived in Morris County and stimulated a booming local iron industry. By 1838, the Morris and Essex Railroad linked Morristown to Newark, and within ten years the terminus moved north to Dover. These improved transportation facilities encouraged extensive mining operations throughout the area, created new opportunities for an export trade, and moved the small towns and agricultural villages of north central New Jersey into an increasingly integrated national commercial capitalist economy.[3]

Chester Righter's father occupied an important place in the expansive regional economy. John A. Righter (1782–1857) parlayed a complicated series of mercantile dealings and real estate speculations into a substantial family fortune. By 1850, he owned $60,000 worth of real estate throughout the area. His varied investments included a flour mill at Boonton, an iron forge on the Meriden River, an iron mine in Hibernia, and unimproved land in Rockaway Township. His Parsippany hotel accommodated both travelers and workmen attracted to the booming region, and his general store marketed the fruits of his Hanover Township farm. John Righter's diversified economic activities, his participation in regional trading networks, and his speculation in manufacturing and mining enterprises linked him socially and temperamentally to a new generation of American merchant-capitalists whose activities and interests transcended the traditional boundaries of the corporate family economy and the covenanted religious community.[4]

3. On canals, see George Rogers Taylor, *The Transportation Revolution, 1815–1860* (New York: Rinehart, 1951); Stuart Bruchey, *The Roots of American Economic Growth, 1607–1861* (New York: Harper & Row, 1968), pp. 158–160; and Allan R. Pred, *Urban Growth and the Circulation of Information: The United States System of Cities, 1790–1840* (Cambridge: Harvard University Press, 1973).

4. Information on John Righter and his family has been compiled from a variety of sources, including Halsey, *History of Morris County*, pp. 46, 223, 281; Vincent Bello, Patricia Flavelle, and Lora Geftic, eds., *None Outsings Parsippany* (Parsippany: Parsippany–Troy Hills Board of Education, 1976), pp. 124, 137; and the U.S. Census, Morris County, New Jersey, 1850. On the implications of the new economy, the commercialization of agriculture, and trading networks, see especially Mary P. Ryan, *Cradle of the Middle Class: The Family in Oneida County, New York, 1790–1865* (New York: Cambridge University Press, 1985), p. 59; Paul E. Johnson, *A Shopkeeper's Millennium: Society and Revivals in Rochester, New York, 1815–1837* (New York: Hill and Wang, 1978), pp. 16–28; Diane Lindstrom, *Economic Change in the Philadelphia Region, 1810–1850* (New York: Columbia University Press, 1977); and Pred, *Urban Growth*.

John Righter worked in part so that his children might benefit from, and extend, his economic achievements. He could not, of course, settle all six in Parsippany, or even in the broader confines of Morris County. For his two daughters, the family patriarch probably hoped to arrange favorable marriages through sizable dowries. They would follow their husbands and establish new households elsewhere. Even some of his male children might seek economic success away from the town of their birth. The antebellum economy that allowed men like Righter to accumulate substantial amounts of capital created opportunities that would entice their male heirs far from the family homestead. John provided an education for his second son, William (1826–ca. 1895), who graduated from Union College in 1842. Shortly thereafter, William departed for Newark, where commercial and industrial expansion created an unprecedented demand for middle-class, white-collar clerks and professionals. William entered the law office of a prominent local philanthropist and attorney, was admitted to the Essex County bar in 1848, and soon began his own legal practice on Broad Street. Like many members of the mid-nineteenth-century urban elite, he coupled his economic achievements with a sense of public responsibility. William Righter served on the Newark Board of Education (1851, 1853, 1854), helped establish the city's Board of Health, was named a director of the Security Savings Institution, and ran unsuccessfully for Congress in 1876. He effectively used the head start his father had provided to establish a lucrative and rewarding career in the competitive mid-nineteenth-century world.[5]

John Righter also provided early educational training for his eldest son, Chester, allowing him to board with his uncle E. A. Stiles, who conducted a classical school at Wantage, Sussex County, New Jersey, in 1836. The school was suspended a few months later, and

5. William A. Righter's career is summarized in William H. Shaw, *History of Essex and Hudson Counties, New Jersey* (Philadelphia: Everts & Peck, 1884), pp. 283–284. For antebellum Newark, see Susan E. Hirsch, *Roots of the American Working Class: The Industrialization of Crafts in Newark, 1800-1860* (Philadelphia: University of Pennsylvania Press, 1978); and Raymond Ralph, "From Village to Industrial City: The Urbanization of Newark, New Jersey, 1830–1860" (Ph.D. dissertation, New York University, 1978). Allan Stanley Horlick, *Country Boys and Merchant Princes: The Social Control of Young Men in New York* (Lewisburg: Bucknell University Press, 1975); Joseph F. Kett, *Rites of Passage: Adolescence in America, 1790 to the Present* (New York: Basic Books, 1977), pp. 86–108; and Ryan, *Cradle of the Middle Class*, pp. 132–141, discuss the new opportunities opened to young men by the antebellum economy.

Chester returned home, but he left for Wantage again in 1839, when Stiles reopened the academy. In 1840, at age sixteen, Chester experienced conversion during a revival at the Clove Church in nearby Newton. His cousin recalled that this reborn Christian became "a new creature." His natural nervousness, haste, and selfishness gave way to new personality traits such as "patient perseverance" and "moral courage."[6]

Although he recognized that the evangelical virtues of patience, prudence, and perseverance might serve his eldest son well in the world of business, John Righter felt uneasy about the boy's commitment to constant prayer. Samuel Prime observed that the elder Righter, "if a Christian, was reserved in regard to his feelings, and made no profession, even to his nearest friends, of being interested, personally, in religion." Rather, "he was a man of the world." Business engagements and the regulation of his agricultural, manufacturing, and mercantile concerns occupied his time. Many mid-nineteenth-century businessmen viewed the sacred and the secular as separate and distinct spheres. An increasingly well-defined barrier separated the two, and religion, to remain pure, must avoid contamination from worldly affairs and temporal concerns. The church served principally as a refuge, a moral training ground, and a place to learn such sound, reliable, middle-class virtues as orderly behavior, personal discipline, and self-control.[7]

For Chester Righter, like many young men maturing in the 1840s, the critical moment in his life revolved around his choice of a career or profession. By 1841, he increasingly turned his attentions to the ministry. A generation or two earlier, his family might have rejoiced at this proclivity. Religious work then implied a position of social leadership, status within the local community, and visible evidence of salvation. John Righter reacted in a more modern fashion. As a man of the world, he wished his eldest son to share in his secular success and enter a business partnership with him. He "set before his son inducements of a worldly nature," and Chester recalled this period as "a temptation and trial." Entering religious life now meant a withdrawal from, rather than participation in, the

6. Prime, *Bible in the Levant*, pp. 12–16.

7. Ibid., p. 19. Donald M. Scott, *From Office to Profession: The New England Ministry, 1750–1850* (Philadelphia: University of Pennsylvania Press, 1978), pp. 148–155, develops this argument about changing perceptions of the ministry at midcentury and the creation of separate sacred and secular spheres. See also Ann Douglas, *The Feminization of American Culture* (New York: Knopf, 1977), pp. 33–43.

affairs of the world. A young man entering the ministry in the 1840s, for example, could hardly hope to obtain the public influence and political opportunities open to William Righter as a successful Newark attorney. Preaching the Gospel meant sacrificing "the prospect of wealth and future ease." Turning his back on the world of commercial, competitive capitalism, Chester must "leave houses and lands, father and mother, for Christ's sake." He must rebel against the wishes of the family patriarch. Ultimately, he decided that "no wealth was more precious . . . than the unsearchable riches of Christ," and he elected to devote his life to saving souls.[8]

Chester's choice involved an explicit rejection of the secular, worldly temptations of the Jacksonian economy. Closely tied to this question of money was a related issue of gender. When he penned his tribute to the fallen missionary, Samuel Prime dedicated the volume to Righter's "Mother who freely gave her beloved son TO THE SERVICE OF GOD IN A FOREIGN LAND and did not regret the gift when he died far away." The author described Lockey Righter as "a devout woman, full of faith and prayer, and consecrating her children with all the ardor of a mother's love and the confidence of a firm belief in the promises, to the service of God." A historian of the First Presbyterian Church in Parsippany remembered her as "a woman zealous for the spread of missions." Born in New Jersey in 1786, she was a founding member of the Female Evangelical Society of Parsippany in 1816, occupied a prominent pew in the Presbyterian parish, and apparently lived a devout Christian existence. Local community institutions reinforced her religiosity. One nineteenth-century observer noted the "sturdy moral and religious character" of Hanover dwellers and characterized the township as "one of the best church-going communities of the state." The founders of Parsippany's Presbyterian and Methodist congregations took special care to locate their churches "on commanding eminences," where they monitored the bustle of local life below.[9]

Lockey Righter occupied a new social space in nineteenth-century society. Unlike the women of earlier generations, she played no role in the family economy. Her husband's varied business interests frequently removed him from the household. Further,

8. Prime, *Bible in the Levant,* pp. 19–20.

9. Ibid., pp. i, 12; Annette C. Ball, *History of the Parsippany, New Jersey, Presbyterian Church from the First Log Structure to the Present Time* (N.p.: Privately published, 1928), pp. 49, 51; U.S. Census, Morris County, New Jersey, 1850; Howell, "Hanover Township," p. 221.

John's world of cash, credit, commerce, and managerial capitalism involved performing activities which the culture defined as masculine. As he expanded his economic role, however, John forfeited a degree of patriarchal control in the family circle. Middle-class women found no place in the acquisitive commercial world of their husbands, but they assumed greater responsibility for regulating the privatized, domestic sphere of the household. As the historian Mary P. Ryan has observed, the dual ideals of responsible breadwinner father and loving mother lay at the heart of mid-nineteenth-century social mythology. Manly independence, individualism, and aggression contrasted with feminine affection, self-sacrifice, and passivity.[10]

Nurturing six children and caring for her substantial home occupied much of Lockey's time, although her husband's wealth did allow her to hire an Irish-born maid. Like many wives of merchants and professionals in antebellum America, she fused her maternal chores with an intense evangelical commitment. She found common cause with other women of her class in the associational networks of women's evangelical and benevolent societies which proliferated between 1816 and 1840. These evangelical women donated money to save the heathen and reform unregenerate Americans, but they also expended considerable time, effort, and thought toward the task of converting their husbands and children. If it angered his businessman father, Chester's choice constituted a significant domestic triumph for his loving mother.[11]

Women may have dominated local congregations and church life long before canals and railroads altered the American landscape. What is significant and new is the way the public rhetoric of mid-nineteenth-century evangelical culture extolled virtues commonly defined as feminine. When they forfeited their economic roles and public relevance, middle-class mothers and ministers described their own importance in a new language of sacrifice and denial.

10. On the changing economic role of women in antebellum America, see especially Nancy Cott, *The Bonds of Womanhood: "Woman's Sphere" in New England, 1780–1835* (New Haven: Yale University Press, 1977), pp. 19–62; Ryan, *Cradle of the Middle Class*, pp. 153–154; Kathryn Kish Sklar, *Catharine Beecher: A Study in American Domesticity* (New Haven: Yale University Press, 1973); and Douglas, *Feminization of American Culture*, pp. 60–74.

11. Women's evangelical societies are discussed in Ryan, *Cradle of the Middle Class*, pp. 105–112; Anne M. Boylan, "Women in Groups: An Analysis of Women's Benevolent Organizations in New York and Boston, 1797–1840," *Journal of American History* (December 1984), 497–523; and Cott, *Bonds of Womanhood*, pp. 155–159.

Samuel Prime characterized Chester Righter as "self-sacrificing and obliging, when the feelings of others were involved, he was the first in every movement to promote the general comfort of the company, the last to yield when difficulties were to be overcome." Righter's extreme sense of selflessness led his biographer to reflect that "I do not know that the fires of an earth-born, selfish ambition, a paltry spirit of self-glory, ever burned for a moment in his manly breast." Though Prime carefully described Righter as "manly," his account continually returned to the "feminine" virtues of self-denial, sacrifice, and humility. He even recounted an ocean voyage on which Righter spent mornings in exercise but followed up this physical regimen with an afternoon of "reading or talking French with the ladies."[12]

Once Chester decided to enter the ministry, his family's socio-economic status ensured that he would receive the best available training. He entered Yale College in the fall of 1842. Yale's student body had changed significantly over the past several decades. Its students were older and poorer, came from a greater diversity of geographical backgrounds, and appeared more interested in law and education than in religious training. But the college still offered aspiring Presbyterian ministers a sufficiently orthodox education to prepare them for New England pulpits and ample social opportunities for commingling with the children of America's evangelical elite. At Yale, the young ministerial hopeful soon struck up a friendship with George Hill, son of ABCFM treasurer Henry Hill.[13]

After graduating with honors, Righter studied theology at the

12. Prime, *Bible in the Levant*, pp. 9, 10, 25. On religion and perceptions of feminine virtues, see Douglas, *Feminization of American Culture*, pp. 44, 60, 98–99; Sklar, *Catharine Beecher*, pp. xii–xiv; Jane Hunter, *The Gospel of Gentility: American Women Missionaries in Turn-of-the-Century China* (New Haven: Yale University Press, 1984), p. 38; Scott, *From Office to Profession*, pp. 133–140; Barbara Welter, "The Feminization of American Religion, 1800–1860," in *Dimity Convictions* (Athens: Ohio University Press, 1976); and Joan Jacobs Brumberg, *Mission for Life: The Judson Family and American Evangelical Culture* (New York: New York University Press, 1984), pp. 79–106. A suggestive article on women's religious roles during an earlier period is Gerald F. Moran, "Sisters in Christ: Women and the Church in Seventeenth Century New England," in Janet Wilson James, ed., *Women in American Religion* (Philadelphia: University of Pennsylvania Press, 1978).

13. Peter Dobkin Hall, *The Organization of American Culture, 1700–1900: Private Institutions, Elites, and the Origins of American Nationality* (New York: New York University Press, 1982), pp. 161–163, discusses the transformation of Yale.

Yale (1848–1851) and Andover (1853) seminaries. Failing eyesight, perhaps a self-induced psychosomatic illness indicating vocational anxieties, forestalled his plans to obtain a settled ministerial post. In 1853 he spent a year traveling abroad for health reasons. He toured England, France, Switzerland, Italy, Greece, and Turkey, and his experiences piqued his interest in the Near East. During his overseas travels, Righter met Samuel Prime, whose connection with the American Bible Society undoubtedly helped the young man obtain the position of Bible agent for the Levant in 1854.[14]

Righter's socioeconomic background enabled him to pursue a more straightforward path to the Levant than Simeon H. Calhoun, but his missionary approach approximated that of his predecessor in the Near East. Righter traveled widely throughout the Holy Land, spent considerable time tending to British and Russian soldiers after the outbreak of the Crimean War in 1854, and enjoyed amicable relationships with British and American missionaries. His curiosity concerning the region, stimulated by his year abroad, and the declining opportunities for settled pastorates in America, appeared to be the principal reasons he desired a post overseas. He exhibited no talent or evidence of extraordinary linguistic abilities, and his letters to Corresponding Secretary John Brigham principally described the culture and peoples of the Levant. His major qualifications for the agency appeared to be endorsements from Samuel Prime and Yale's president, Chauncey Goodrich. The ABS's board of managers had not yet defined precisely what they expected from a Bible agent, but the abrupt conclusion of Righter's work probably spared him and the board from the conflicts that characterized Calhoun's tenure.[15]

Righter's premature death provided the ABS with its first fallen missionary, and it also marked a watershed in the Society's approach to overseas labor. The managers chose an agent with a very different philosophy to carry on the work in 1857. Isaac Grout Bliss would remain in the Near East for thirty-two years and would help revolutionize the way the Society conducted its business. His philosophy would prove compatible with the board's increasingly modern, bureaucratic approach to Bible work. His success also

14. Prime, *Bible in the Levant,* pp. 21–45.

15. Chauncey Goodrich to John C. Brigham, March 15, 1854, Levant Correspondence, Corresponding Secretary's Papers, ABS Archives. See also the following letters from Righter to Brigham in the same collection: February 1855, October 20, December 18, 24, 1855, August 25, 1856, for typical accounts of his work.

epitomized a transformation that would accommodate the values of Protestantism with the society of the Gilded Age and restore religion to a central place in American culture. Effecting the new rapprochement between sacred and secular involved a series of compromises, however, and the long-term implications should have caused committed evangelicals to pause a bit longer than they did.

From 1889 through 1891, Isaac Bliss's son Edwin M. Bliss (1848–1919), along with Henry Otis Dwight, also the son of a Levant missionary, compiled *The Encyclopedia of Missions*. One of their biographical subjects was Edwin's father, who served as the Bible agent at Constantinople between 1857 and 1889. Reviewing the situation at the time of his appointment, the authors observed that the agency operated "without any organization at all." Isaac found "no rules as to the distribution of Bibles" and soon discovered that "the greater part of the funds received from their sale was applied to general missionary work." As a responsible ABS employee, Bliss could not allow this state of affairs to continue. Using "great tact and patience," but with an "indomitable will" to set things right, he soon brought a new system to Bible affairs. As the editors described it, his principal accomplishment involved bringing "order out of this confusion."[16]

Righter had exemplified the self-effacing nineteenth-century Protestant missionary who denied himself worldly pleasures and isolated himself in a foreign land, ultimately sacrificing even his life for the cause of Christ; by contrast, Bliss symbolized the future course of American religion. He was born in the village of Springfield, Massachusetts, on July 5, 1822. The Bliss family could trace its New England ancestry into the seventeenth century, but declining economic opportunities and the burden of supporting a large family on Vermont's rocky soil had prompted Isaac's father to move from Putney to Springfield shortly before the future missionary's

16. "Isaac Grout Bliss," *The Encyclopedia of Missions: Descriptive, Historical, Biographical, Statistical*, ed. Henry Otis Dwight, H. Allen Tupper, and Edwin Munsell Bliss, 2d ed. (New York: Funk & Wagnall's, 1904), pp. 94–95. Edwin Bliss had served as assistant agent for the Levant under his father from 1872 to 1875 and 1877 to 1888. Dwight functioned as the Society's recording secretary between 1907 and 1917. The biographical sketch in the following paragraphs derives from information in this article, as well as the entry "Edwin Elisha Bliss" on page 94 in the same volume. See also "Isaac Grout Bliss," in *Amherst College Biographical Record of the Graduates and Non-Graduates*, ed. Robert S. Fletcher and Malcolm O. Young (Amherst, Mass.: Trustees of Amherst College, 1939).

birth. Even a western Massachusetts farm could not permanently support Isaac and his eight siblings, and many of the children necessarily looked beyond agriculture to other careers. Exceptional piety must have pervaded the Bliss household because three of the progeny turned to overseas missionary labor. Isaac's educational career included study at Amherst College, followed by the Andover and Yale theological seminaries. He was ordained by the West Springfield Presbytery in 1847 and departed for Turkey under the auspices of the ABCFM shortly thereafter.

Thus far, his ministerial career appears relatively traditional: a rural New England birth; maturation in an economically marginal, declining agricultural region; educational training in a recently established antebellum college designed to serve farm youths seeking middle-class status; orthodox theological training; ordination. He apparently avoided the many starts and stops that impeded Simeon Calhoun's path. But Bliss's career seemed indistinguishable from those of many ministerial colleagues beginning their "mission for life" in the 1840s.

A personal crisis awakened Bliss to the precarious nature of clerical existence in midcentury America. In 1852 he took ill and reluctantly resigned his position with the ABCFM to return to the United States. He probably planned to settle in a permanent pastorate, but his experiences confirm historian Donald Scott's characterization of the 1840s and 1850s as "a nadir for the pastoral clergy." For three years he remained "without charge," clinging to his profession but unable to find a parish in which to practice. Congregations, suspicious of clerical careerism, frequently proved unwilling to engage pastors permanently—especially young men like Isaac Bliss, who appeared more interested in the glamour of missionary labor and employment by the large benevolent boards than in the routine duties of a country church. A mobile mass of unemployed ministers apparently roamed throughout New England during this period, occasionally performing clerical services for fees but living an uncertain existence.

Bliss, a married man with children, required greater stability. His troubles did not end when he found a pastoral charge in 1855. For two years, he served as a "stated supply" minister at Presbyterian parishes in Southbridge and Boylston, Massachusetts. Congregations increasingly used this device to retain clergymen without installing them as permanent pastors. An individual could remain on the "stated supply" for any length of time, and the parish had no permanent obligation to support him. In 1856, as Chester Righter embarked on his fateful and final journey to Asiatic Turkey, Isaac Bliss's personal and professional prospects in western Massachusetts appeared bleak.[17]

Shortly after the news of Righter's death reached America, Isaac maneuvered for the vacant position. He asked former ABCFM colleagues in Constantinople to place his name before the board of managers. Bible translator William G. Schauffler contacted John Brigham on February 11, 1857, and, in proposing Bliss's appointment, urged the ABS to use new criteria in selecting a Bible agent. Bliss, he observed, would prove exceedingly useful "in a country whose languages he has acquired much more fully than Mr. R[ighter]. ever did." Further, Schauffler praised the applicant's familiarity "with the people & the customs." General virtues and evidence of proper "character" no longer seemed adequate to carry on the "regular & systematic duties of a Bible Agency." Experience, linguistic skills, and a proven record ought to carry greater weight. Bliss's application was even more explicit. He scorned the "students or young men just through with their studies" who also applied for the agency. Lacking real-world experience, they offered little more than "urgent recommendations from D[octors of] D[ivinity]" to support their candidacies and were merely "desirous of perfecting themselves by foreign travel." Isaac presented himself as a seasoned, professional missionary, with the proper blend of administrative acumen and scholarly credentials to ensure a successful appointment. Further, he implied that he would make a permanent commitment to the work. Journeying to Turkey was not a youthful whim or a way to satisfy an unfulfilled sense of adventure. Rather, it was a professional commitment, as well as an antidote to the instability and frustration of ministerial life in mid-century America.[18]

The ABS expanded its work overseas following the Civil War, and its managers increasingly turned to men like Bliss to administer their foreign agencies. By 1889, the year Bliss died, the Society staffed agencies in the Levant, Argentina, Mexico, Persia, China, Japan, Cuba, Brazil, Peru, and Venezuela. The ten Bible men active

17. Scott, *From Office to Profession*, p. 113. This discussion owes much to Scott's remarks on pp. 113–121.

18. William Schauffler to John C. Brigham, February 11, 1857, and Isaac Bliss to Schauffler, September 21, 1857, Levant Correspondence, Corresponding Secretary's Papers, ABS Archives.

in 1889 served the ABS for an average of nearly twenty-four years each. If we exclude William Patterson, who died during his first year of work in Venezuela, the average increases to twenty-six and a half. Eight of the ten died or retired in the service of the Society; the ABS subsequently discontinued a ninth agency and removed the tenth agent for "gross neglect of duty, and also of dishonesty in the keeping of the accounts with the Society." Nine of the ten amassed considerable missionary experience before accepting a Bible agency, and only one began his ABS career immediately after graduating from seminary. Several occupied important administrative posts with other evangelical organizations before committing themselves to the ABS. Henry Loomis was an assistant secretary of the Presbyterian Board of Foreign Missions in New York, and Luther Gulick functioned as secretary of the Board for Home and Foreign Missions of the Hawaiian Evangelical Association for seven years. Except for Bliss, only one apparently possessed significant pastoral experience in the United States.[19]

19. The nine agents, in addition to Bliss, were as follows:

Henry Loomis, b. 1839, Burlington, New York; Presbyterian; graduate of Hamilton College and Auburn Theological Seminary; assistant secretary, Presbyterian Board of Foreign Missions in New York; Presbyterian Missionary in Yokohama, Japan, 1872–1876; resigned owing to ill health and pursued entomological studies in California, 1876–1881; ABS agent in Japan, 1881–1911; resigned owing to ill health, 1911; d. 1920, Yokohama, Japan.

Hiram Philetus Hamilton, b. date unknown, Shekoneko, New York; Presbyterian; graduate of Princeton College and Union Theological Seminary, 1879; ABS agent for Mexico, 1879–1905; d. 1905, Mexico.

Luther Halsey Gulick, b. 1828, Sandwich Islands, to missionary parents; came to United States as a youth, pursued private course of study with Luther Halsey (his foster father); graduated from University of the City of New York with a medical degree, 1850; ordained by Congregational Council in New York at Broadway Tabernacle Church, 1851; began missionary work in Micronesia, 1851; secretary of Board for Home and Foreign Missions of Hawaiian Evangelical Association, 1864–1871; affiliated with ABCFM mission in Spain, 1871–1875; ABS agent in China and Japan, 1875–1881; ABS agent in China, 1881–1889; retired because of ill health, 1889; d. 1891.

William L. Whipple, b. 1844, Mount Vernon, Ohio; graduated from Marietta College and Lane Theological Seminary, 1872; Presbyterian missionary in Persia, 1872–1879; ABS agent in Persia, 1880–1897; agency discontinued, 1897; appointed to East Persia Mission by Presbyterian Board of Foreign Missions, 1899–1901; d. 1901.

Andrew J. McKim, date and place of birth unknown; agent for American and Foreign Christian Union in Peru, date unknown–1884; ABS agent in Cuba, 1884–1896; work suspended, 1896–1898; ABS agent in Cuba, 1898–1899; ABS agent in Puerto Rico, 1899–1901; resigned, 1901, under pressure from board of managers; subsequent career unknown.

The trends appeared clear, and they paralleled the developments that simultaneously shaped the nature of domestic agencies. The ABS sought out men who would commit themselves to Bible work for life, and the board offered adequate inducements to attract them away from other missionary organizations. The managers settled on experienced men, career missionaries who had spent time abroad and possessed some familiarity with the cultural groups they would encounter. Administrative experience appeared especially desirable, whereas pastoral work seemed only marginally important. Ordination and theological training were the formal entry requirements, but specific denominational or collegiate ties counted for less than a proven work record of missionary commitment and administrative skill.

More had changed than simply the types of men who administered the Society's overseas affairs. The very nature of their labor, their own expectations, and the demands the home office placed on them seemed very different in the post–Civil War period. Perhaps the most effective way to elucidate these changes is to examine Bliss's greatest accomplishment and most lasting monument. In 1872, Isaac Bliss proudly presided at the dedication of a new Bible House in Constantinople. Like the Bible House on Astor Place, the Turkish structure was designed to headquarter several evangelical agencies. It would serve as the center for Protestant missionary efforts throughout the Near East. Bliss carried the project from conception to completion, overseeing every detail of the construction and managing the facility after it opened. By analyzing the

---

Andrew M. Milne, b. 1838, Aberdeenshire, Scotland; businessman who dedicated his life to Christ at a meeting of the YMCA in London, 1858; came to Buenos Aires as representative of the business firm of Robert Begg to supervise fruit shipments, 1863; began work as colporteur, 1863–1864; ABS agent for La Plata, 1864–1907; d. 1907.

Francisco Penzotti, b. 1851, northern Italy; came to South America with his brother in 1864; Waldensian missionary in Uruguay, 1879–1886; ABS agent for "Pacific Coast" of Peru, 1888–1892; ABS agent for Central America and Panama, 1892–1907; ABS agent for La Plata, 1907–1921; d. 1925.

Hugh C. Tucker, b. 1856, Tennessee; Methodist circuit rider in Tennessee and pastor in Nashville; went to Brazil as missionary of Methodist Episcopal church, South, 1885–1887; ABS agent for Brazil, 1887–1934; secretary emeritus of ABS agency in Brazil, 1934–1956; d. 1956, Media, Pennsylvania.

William M. Patterson, b. 1838, St. Louis County, Missouri; Methodist; Civil War service; pastoral work in and around St. Louis, 1865–1878; missionary of Methodist Episcopal church, South, in Mexico, 1878–1888; ABS agent for Venezuela, 1888–1889; d. 1889, Venezuela.

THE BIBLE HOUSE AT CONSTANTINOPLE.

Constantinople Bible House, 1872. *Courtesy of the American Bible Society Archives.*

motivations that prompted him to plan the Bible House and considering the practical and symbolic purposes that he intended the structure to serve, we can understand why the transformed American Bible Society remained a thriving philanthropy in the Gilded Age.

Several practical considerations stimulated Bliss to press the board for improved physical facilities. Crowded storage conditions, problems securing reasonable rental arrangements in Constantinople, and an innocuous, unattractive Bible depository bothered the new agent. In 1863, he complained that "our books get injured & our sheets are eaten by rats & mice" in the damp depository basement, and he urged the board to consider purchasing, or at least securing a long lease on, another building. Bliss agitated for a new structure over the next several years but did not begin his campaign in earnest until 1866. That spring he secured permission to return to New York under the guise of attending the Society's Golden Jubilee celebration, but his real purpose was to promote the cause of his proposed Bible House.[20]

The board of managers reviewed his proposal but reacted with caution. Endorsing the concept and encouraging him to explore the possibility of securing outside funding, the board questioned "the propriety of raising funds for this special object" under ABS auspices and voted to "disclaim all pecuniary responsibility . . . as not within the constitution or policy of the Society." Owning real estate in a foreign land would be a real departure from past practice. A special appeal for this purpose might detract from other worthy projects such as supplying the freedmen, and the managers emerged from the Civil War in a precarious financial state. The schism that prompted the closing of all the southern agencies and stimulated rebel evangelicals to form the Confederate States Bible Society had slashed the Society's income. The bold new departure which Bliss proposed, including his request for funds in excess of $50,000, could not be entertained.[21]

If they did not enthusiastically embrace his appeal, the managers did not completely close the door. They granted Bliss an extended, paid leave of absence to raise funds for the project privately and approved the concept as "of great advantage and benefit to the Bible work in the East" and a "worthy and important undertaking."

20. Isaac Bliss to John Brigham, February 5, 1858; Bliss to Henry Fisher, February 11, 1858; Bliss to Joseph Holdich, December 21, 1863, January 21, February 20, 1864, Levant Correspondence, Corresponding Secretary's Papers, ABS Archives.

21. Minutes of Meetings of the Board of Managers, June 7, September 6, 1866. See also Joseph Holdich to Isaac Bliss, July 7, 27, August 30, 1866, December 14, 1867, Letter Book, Corresponding Secretary's Papers, ABS Archives. The Minutes of Meeting of the Board of Managers, January 2, 1890, provides a historical overview of the proposal, as does the ABS's *Fifty-second Annual Report* (1868).

During the next year, Bliss demonstrated his extraordinary capacity as a fund-raiser. He addressed wealthy congregations, organized a nationwide speaking tour, and promoted his cause in print. He also engaged seven wealthy New York financiers and evangelical philanthropists to act as trustees: William E. Dodge (1805–1883), a founder of the Phelps, Dodge and Company metal importing firm; William A. Booth (1805–1895), sugar merchant and past president of the American Exchange Bank; David Hoadley (1806–1874), president of the Panama Railroad Company; William H. Aspinwall (1807–1875), partner in the Howland and Aspinwall business house; Robert Carter (1807–1889), owner of Robert Carter and Brothers, book publishers; Samuel B. Schieffelin (1811–1900), religious author and businessman; and William G. Lambert (1797–1882), head of the New York branch of A. and A. Lawrence Company. By July 1867, Bliss had met his goal of $50,000 and the trustees incorporated in New York State as the Bible House of Constantinople. Shrewd investments soon increased the Bible House Fund to well over $60,000, and Bliss returned to Constantinople secure in the knowledge that his dream would become a reality.[22]

His accomplishment redefined the job of a foreign Bible agent. Bliss used shrewd business sense, personally cultivated a wealthy philanthropic clientele, established and managed a private corporation to effect his designs, and adeptly loosened purse strings throughout the country. The board remained in the background, cautiously and carefully watching his progress. His successes suggested the new possibilities and roles which even a man of religion might assume in the capital-intensive, corporate economy of the Gilded Age.

Bible House opened its doors in 1872, and all evangelicals welcomed it as an impressive achievement. Missionary and Bible societies in England and America shared office space in the four-story structure. A ground-floor salesroom attracted a walk-in clientele, and translators prepared new versions of the Bible on the upper floors. Bliss successfully prodded the board into transferring

22. Minutes of Meeting of the Board of Managers, September 6, 1866; Joseph Holdich to Isaac Bliss, November 28, 1866, and Holdich to Richard Storrs, November 13, 1866, Letter Book, Corresponding Secretary's Papers; "Bible House for Constantinople," Circular, January 11, 1867, Constantinople Bible House file, Treasurer's Papers, ABS Archives; Constitution and By-Laws, Constantinople Bible House (microfilm available at ABS Archives, original at Houghton Library, Harvard University).

electrotyping equipment to the Levant in 1870, and typesetting, printing, and binding were done within the Bible House's walls. Built of stone and supported by iron girders, the building contained a notable central doorway supported by columns of black marble. *Harper's Weekly* observed in August 1873 that "its site commands a full view of the magnificent harbor, the Golden Horn, and a portion of the Bosphorus." Bliss must have been especially pleased to read that the editors considered this location "well chosen with reference to business purposes."[23]

What motivated the Bible agent to undertake this massive and time-consuming project? Mundane considerations of space, security, and high rentals might have been resolved in other ways. Bible House in Constantinople functioned as a monument and cultural symbol. The promotional literature Bliss prepared to sell his idea to the philanthropic public offers insight into his thinking, and, more important, into the values a Victorian Protestant generation found appealing.

"The object of the building is to furnish a permanent location for the depository," Bliss explained in 1866. Every description and endorsement of the project stressed its permanence. The translator Elias Riggs noted "the desirableness of securing something more commodious and permanent" than the older makeshift depository, and ABCFM missionaries at the western Turkey station praised Bible House as "a material symbol of the increasing strength and prospective permanence of Evangelical Christian work." Perhaps permanence was an especially desirable virtue for the ministers of Bliss's generation. A search for permanence is a recurring theme in Isaac's own life: recall his parents' removal from Vermont, the difficulties of supporting a large family on New England soil, the failure to obtain a settled pastorate, the precarious existence of a Protestant preacher at midcentury.[24]

Permanence in missions was a fundamentally new goal. Antebellum missionaries viewed their personal commitment as lifelong

23. The best descriptions are in Isaac Bliss to Edward Gilman, March 12, 1887, Levant Correspondence, Corresponding Secretary's Papers, ABS Archives; *Harper's Weekly*, August 9, 1873; and "The Bible House at Constantinople," *Bible Society Record*, March 1873, pp. 37–38.

24. The quotes by Isaac Bliss and Elias Riggs are from "Bible House for Constantinople," circular, January 11, 1867. The ABCFM missionaries expressed their views in "Annual Report of the West Turkey Mission," June 10, 1872, Levant Correspondence, Corresponding Secretary's Papers, ABS Archives.

but expected their efforts to bear quick fruit abroad. They sought to instill a Christian spirit among their clients, then retreat from the field while natives organized their own churches and congregations. Preaching and itineracy were the hallmarks of the older system. By midcentury, it became obvious that the heathen would respond slowly, if at all. Mission stations assumed a more permanent form and functioned as stable foreign subcommunities within their broader national cultures. As evangelicals dug their trenches for a long struggle with the forces of infidelity, they erected substantial institutions to assist them. Bebek Seminary in Turkey (1840), Abeih Academy in Syria (1843), Robert College in Constantinople (1863), Syrian Protestant College, subsequently renamed the American University in Beirut (1866), and Constantinople Woman's College (1871) served as monuments to this age of Western philanthropy and implied a permanent Protestant presence in the Near East. Educational institutions, designed to serve both the growing Western populations of these lands and the relatively small number of native converts, proliferated. The Bible House was conceived and developed within this context.[25]

If it owed much to a new sense of missionary permanence, the Bible House also constituted an experiment in ecclesiastical marketing. As early as February 1858, Bliss informed the ABS's treasurer of plans "for a better salesroom." He intended to prepare "placards in all the languages in which we have Bibles for sale ... have them put neatly upon paste board & hung by the window & door outside" in hopes that this advertisement would "attract the attention of the multitude that pass by." The new Bible House offered even greater potential. One Protestant Armenian merchant, after subscribing $1,000 to the cause, could "not think of any one thing which would have so good an influence on the Oriental mind in favour of the Bible as this projected Bible House." A Methodist

25. See the treatment of Rufus Anderson in James A. Field, "Near East Notes and Far East Queries," in John K. Fairbank, *The Missionary Enterprise in China and America* (Cambridge: Harvard University Press, 1974), p. 42. Robert L. Daniel, *American Philanthropy in the Near East, 1820–1960* (Athens: Ohio University Press, 1960), pp. 41–70; and Joseph L. Grabill, *Protestant Diplomacy in the Near East: Missionary Influence on American Policy, 1810–1927* (Minneapolis: University of Minnesota Press, 1971), pp. 8–11, discuss Protestant institutions in the Near East. Rufus Anderson, *Memorial Volume of the First Fifty Years of the American Board of Commissioners for Foreign Missions* (Boston: ABCFM, 1862), pp. 247–252, discusses the question of permanence under the title "How the Work May Be Completed" and suggests the ambiguities surrounding the issue at midcentury.

missionary praised it for providing "a conspicuous centre of operations," and Edwin Bliss called it "one of the most noticeable objects in the city, forming with its neat walls a marked contrast to the irregular piles one sees on every side." The building and the first floor salesroom functioned as an advertisement for the powerful, orderly, evangelical impulse. By the 1860s, American businessmen had begun developing novel techniques for attracting consumers. Urban department stores, modeled after Alexander T. Stewart's Marble Dry Goods Palace in New York, attracted city shoppers in ever-increasing numbers. By the 1870s, R. H. Macy's, Lord & Taylor, B. Altman's, Stern Brothers, Bloomingdale's, Abraham & Straus, and Best & Company all lured Manhattanites into their showrooms. Large-scale newspaper advertising, promotional gimmickry, monumental architecture, and lavish display heralded the birth of an age of unprecedented consumerism. The place of business became a place of show—an enormous self-advertisement—and even pious Presbyterians such as John Wanamaker conducted their affairs after the new fashion.[26]

Evangelicals traditionally valued simplicity and a "plain style" of worship, but perhaps a new age required new ideas. Bliss claimed that the idea for a grand Bible House materialized in his mind while walking home from work one day, when he overheard two Turks evaluating Protestant missionaries. One criticized them for not knowing "how to do business. They have no permanent place. One year they are here, and another there." The Turkish observer then proceeded to contrast this disorganization with the superior purposefulness of another religious denomination. "The Catholics," he concluded, "evidently intend to stay. They are putting up substantial buildings for schools and churches." Cyrus Hamlin, the president of Robert College, also observed that the Roman Catholics erected dozens of "solid structures ... schools, colleges, churches, convents, &c." Protestants, he lamented, had "nothing of the kind." A Bible House "would offer a stable and reliable centre which everybody would find out, and the hundreds of thousands

26. Isaac Bliss to Henry Fisher, February 11, 1858, Levant Correspondence, Corresponding Secretary's Papers, ABS Archives; S. M. Minasian (the Armenian merchant) and Albert L. Long (the Methodist missionary) quoted in "Bible House for Constantinople," circular, January 11, 1867; Edwin Bliss quoted in "The Bible House at Constantinople," *Bible Society Record,* March 1873, p. 38. Alfred Chandler, *The Visible Hand: The Managerial Revolution in American Business* (Cambridge: Harvard University Press, 1977), discusses department stores on pp. 224–229.

The Bill Poster's Dream, 1862, B. Derby lithograph. By the mid-nineteenth century, the American Bible Society competed with other cultural institutions for space in New York City's highly commercialized and publicity-conscious urban milieu, as this cartoon aptly demonstrates. *Courtesy of the Eno Collection, Miriam and Ira D. Wallach Division of Art, Prints and Photographs. The New York Public Library. Astor, Lenox and Tilden Foundations.*

who go and come over all the land would know it, and more or less gather to it."[27]

Victorian Protestants studied Roman Catholicism with good reason. Catholics not only constituted formidable foes in mission lands but also had constructed a vast institutional network ministering to over 6 million Americans by 1880. Catholic steeples dominated the skylines of industrial American cities. As the church developed a growing Irish middle-class lay leadership, Roman Catholic architects secured lucrative diocesan patronage. Neo-Gothic structures, with their stark but monumental exteriors physically proclaimed the permanence of Irish Catholicism on the American landscape. In New York, where the bell tower of Most Holy Redeemer German Church presided over the Lower East Side after 1851, Irish Catholics constructed their most important symbol. Archbishop John Hughes laid the cornerstone of St. Patrick's Cathedral on Fifth Avenue in 1858. When it opened twenty-one years later, it rivaled the great cathedrals of Europe. Costing nearly $3 million and seating over twenty-five hundred people, the white marble structure contained elaborate statuary and carvings, a magnificent rose window, and twin spires that rose 328 feet in the air.[28]

An earlier evangelical generation might have labeled such monumentalism idolatry and scorned the wasteful decoration and ornamentation as bordering on paganism. Protestant leaders by 1880 appeared less interested in reforming the Romanists than in studying their success and adapting Catholic institutional forms to their own purposes. In New York, Protestants established new "Institutional Churches" like St. Bartholomew's Episcopal, Madison Square Presbyterian, and St. George's Episcopal. With their social and educational outreach programs, stress on the physical plant as the center of neighborhood life, and inspiring edifices, these churches closely resembled the nineteenth-century Roman Catholic parish. Judson Memorial Church in New York, the movement's

27. Bliss's story appears in "The Bible House at Constantinople," *Bible Society Record*, March 1873, p. 38. Hamlin is quoted in "Bible House for Constantinople," circular, January 11, 1867.

28. Jay P. Dolan, *The Immigrant Church: New York's Irish and German Catholics, 1815–1865* (Baltimore: Johns Hopkins University Press, 1975), pp. 166–168; James Hennesey, *American Catholics: A History of the Roman Catholic Community in the United States* (New York: Oxford University Press, 1981), pp. 172–176; Donna Merwick, *Boston Priests, 1848–1910: A Study of Social and Intellectual Change* (Cambridge: Harvard University Press, 1973), p. 108.

Mandarin Revision Committee, Shanghai, 1901. Overseas work occupied an increasing percentage of the Society's time and monetary resources by the late nineteenth century. Missionary translators, often funded by the ABS, had translated books of the Bible into over five hundred languages by 1900. *Courtesy of the American Bible Society Archives.*

ultimate expression, even used Italianate architecture in its effort to attract Lower East Side Italian immigrants. In a way only partly realized at the time, the construction of Bible House on Astor Place in 1853 was a premonition of these patterns of development, in which physical structures and bureaucratic institutions became central. Religion had become a problem of effective marketing.[29]

If it contained important symbolic significance, the Constantinople Bible House also fulfilled a critical administrative function. The translator William Schauffler complained in 1864 that missionaries in Turkey had "wearied ourselves in experiments on a *circumference without a center*," and Bliss intended Bible House to become that center. Shortly after the building's completion, he pressured the managers to employ an assistant agent to "help me in my office work . . . [and] to take my place in visiting the different parts of the field when it is a necessity & I am not able to go." Bliss traveled less

29. This discussion owes much to Brumberg, *Mission for Life*, pp. 184–191.

than his predecessors, spending more time in the office coordinating distribution and production. The ABS appointed Edwin Bliss as assistant agent to his father in 1872 and established subagencies in Greece (1867), Egypt (1875), and Syria (1875). Isaac Bliss increasingly functioned as a middle-level administrator, managing the flow of funds between the board and his own field representatives.[30]

On assuming responsibility for the Levant in 1858, Bliss complained that the ABS often granted Bibles to missionaries and colporteurs without the agent's knowledge. He explained his role to John Brigham as one of overseeing "the superintendence of the distribution, the receiving & answering all orders for Bibles &c, keeping the accounts &c &c" and defined his major goal as bringing Bible affairs "into a better business shape." By introducing "regularity" to financial affairs and coordinating the flow of Scriptures between the board and missionaries, he sought "to know more accurately than before the amount & cost of distribution & the avails over & above such cost." As his agency progressed, Bliss increasingly relied on a complex network of missionaries, local societies, colporteurs, and Bible readers to spread the Word. Only twelve native-born colporteurs received Scripture grants in the Levant in 1861, but this number grew dramatically during the next two decades, reaching a peak of 129 in 1881. Developments in the Near East reflected the ABS's new worldwide reliance on local missionaries. By 1889, the Society's foreign agents employed 386 individuals as Bible distributors, each of whom spent approximately seven and one-half months of the year in the ABS's employ.[31]

Bliss consciously distanced himself from direct missionary labors. He developed standardized report forms for the colporteurs, monitored their progress from Constantinople, and prepared elaborate statistical compilations for the New York office. Calhoun and Righter had prepared articles based on their travels and experiences for the Society's *Monthly Extracts;* Bliss accumulated and edited reports from his laborers in the field, submitting these for

30. William Schauffler to Isaac Bliss, February 3, 1864, and Bliss to Joseph Holdich, April 5, 1872, Levant Correspondence, Corresponding Secretary's Papers, ABS Archives.

31. Isaac Bliss to John Brigham, August 27, 1858, Levant Correspondence, Corresponding Secretary's Papers, ABS Archives; Rebecca Bromley, "Distribution Abroad: The Levant, 1861–1900," ABS Historical Essay 15, Part V-D (1965), pp. 23–24; ABS, *Seventy-third Annual Report* (1889), p. 89.

publication. His own work involved minimal contact with Moslems, Jews, or Orthodox Christians. He controlled the buying, selling, shipping, and storage of Scriptures from a central location, based on market information received from his subordinates. By May 1873, missionaries at the West Turkey station could inform Joseph Holdich "with pleasure" that Bliss succeeded in "uniting Bible work with everyday business, introducing Bibles as a commodity for exchange into the markets and district fairs." As time wore on, Bliss behaved less and less like a traditional missionary and more and more like a modern businessman.[32]

Late nineteenth-century foreign agencies functioned in a bureaucratic, business-oriented fashion, and this transformation held important implications for the way the ABS conducted its affairs. First, it explains one apparent anomaly. The Society's foreign agents were exclusively male throughout the remainder of the century, although the general missionary force grew increasingly feminized. As secular careers offered men greater rewards, monetary compensation, and status after midcentury, they increasingly turned away from missionary labor. Single women and widows found new vocational opportunities in the foreign field, and they dominated denominational agencies by 1890. The traditional missionary virtues of self-abnegation, sacrifice, service, and denial were viewed as essentially "feminine" qualities, well suited to Gilded Age perceptions of women's "proper" sphere. Women evangelicals abroad taught school, nursed the sick, and effected conversions in heathen households; in one sense they transferred their traditional domestic responsibilities to a new context. Despite the new status and opportunities mission work provided, women usually remained distant from the governing boards of denominational agencies and societies.[33]

Isaac Bliss did none of this. He employed some Bible women to spread the Scriptures, but his world revolved around competition, ambition, and managerial capitalism. He aggressively raised

32. West Turkey Mission to Joseph Holdich, May 20, 1873, Corresponding Secretary's Papers, ABS Archives.

33. On the feminization of missionary work, see Hunter, *Gospel of Gentility*, pp. 11–26, 32–38, 83–88, and 174–186; Barbara Welter, "She Hath Done What She Could: Protestant Women's Missionary Careers in Nineteenth-Century America," in James, ed., *Women in American Religion*, pp. 111–125; and R. Pierce Beaver, *American Protestant Women in World Mission: A History of the First Feminist Movement in North America* (Grand Rapids: William B. Eerdman's, 1980).

funds, manipulated subordinates, administered budgets, developed novel marketing techniques, calculated receipts and expenditures, allocated resources, supervised production, and sought new distribution outlets. His pragmatic perception of a Bible agency offered little evidence of self-sacrifice, quiet Christian duty, and contemplative withdrawal. Bible work, in contrast to other missionary labor, had indeed become a man's work.

It also became an American enterprise. As the ABS assumed a central place in the American missionary community, the world Bible movement fragmented. By the late 1870s, ABS officers and agents viewed the British and Foreign Bible Society in increasingly adversarial terms, as a market competitor. Bliss warned the managers as early as August 1859 that the BFBS "will crowd us out altogether unless we are awake in all respects" and expressed his "wish [for] the American Society to have an equal share in the work of supplying [the Turks] with the word of life with the British & Foreign Society." Comity broke down completely at several points, and the British even charged that the Constantinople Bible House constituted an effort at establishing American national supremacy. Members of the West Turkey mission did attribute symbolic significance to the fact that "the Great Powers of Europe are represented here by gorgeous palaces, the Great Republic of America, more fittingly, by noble structures dedicated to the Bible and Learning."[34]

Problems arose in every region where the two societies stationed agents, and the basic sources of conflict remained constant. Questions concerning ownership of specific versions which both societies funded, efforts to achieve an equitable division of territory, and complaints about pricing policies generated the most tension. Representatives of the ABS and the BFBS agreed on the desirability of reaching an accommodation, but each group sought to protect its own interests and markets, and neither took the lead in fostering a cooperative, coordinated approach to world Scripture distribution. As Corresponding Secretary Edward Gilman argued in 1877, the ABS "feels called upon to supplement the work of American missionaries wherever they may be laboring for the dissemination of the truth." The Society now existed to serve an American mission-

34. Isaac Bliss to John Brigham, August 16, 1859, and "Annual Report of the Western Turkey Mission," June 10, 1872, Levant Correspondence, Corresponding Secretary's Papers, ABS Archives.

ary constituency and was responsible to an American Christian public for its actions. It shunned any activity or policy that might jeopardize its standing with these groups and viewed itself as an integral component of a vast effort to export American Protestantism to foreign lands. Membership in an international Christian community seemed less critical to the ABS's new definition of success than maintaining its credibility within the United States and demonstrating its effectiveness on foreign terrain.[35]

The Society's increasing overseas operations stimulated it to make common cause with American nationalism for another reason. Changing political conditions in the Ottoman Empire occasionally plagued ABS efforts. The Turkish government periodically seized books, arrested colporteurs, placed new restrictions on distribution, and raided the depository. As it committed more of its resources to the Levant and increased its investments in personnel and equipment throughout the region, the Society sought to secure government protection. By the 1880s, when Turkish authorities increased actions against colporteurs, the Society actively lobbied American ambassador Lew Wallace and secretary of state and future ABS president Frederic T. Frelinghuysen.[36]

By 1884, the ABS secretaries agreed to join representatives of the ABCFM and Presbyterian Board of Missions in drafting a joint protest to President Chester A. Arthur. Significantly, they based their argument on the importance of "the business enterprises of American missionaries in Turkey." The *business* aspect of their operations, not their *religious* functions, made them "legitimate objects for [the] watchful care" of consular officials. Scripture and tract exports, claimed these Protestant leaders, were "quite on a par in importance with any branch of trade," and they sought retribution and redress for past grievances against the Turks. Further, the secretaries suggested that "in the disposition of the Mediterranean fleet," several vessels should patrol the Turkish coast, "mak-

35. Edward Gilman's report in Minutes of Meeting of the Committee on Distribution, June 6, 1877, ABS Archives, summarizes the problems. Conflicts between the ABS and BFBS are treated in Bromley, "Distribution Abroad," pp. 33–48; Dorothy U. Compagno, "Distribution in Latin America, 1861–1900," ABS Historical Essay 15, Part V-C (1965), pp. 18–27; and Eric M. North, "Distribution Abroad, 1861–1900: Japan," ABS Historical Essay 15, Part V-F-1 (1965), pp. 65–67, 79–100.

36. Problems between the ABS and Turkish authorities are summarized in Bromley, "Distribution Abroad," pp. 49–59. See also "Government Agencies Correspondence," 1873–1888, Isaac Bliss Papers, Levant Agency Files, ABS Archives.

ing frequent visits to Constantinople." Gunboats were considered legitimate vehicles to safeguard the Scriptures, and perhaps national demonstrations of force would reform the heathen where proselytization and other educational efforts had failed.[37]

By any Gilded Age definition, the American Bible Society functioned successfully. It distributed over one million volumes annually, received hundreds of thousands of dollars in donations, maintained substantial legacies, and conducted its affairs in a proper, businesslike spirit. It remained an innovator in the areas of marketing, public relations, and publishing. Indeed, its voluntaristic structure provided a model commonly followed by the age's corporate and industrial concerns. Clearly, neither the American Bible Society nor American Protestantism declined in the face of growing secularization over the course of the nineteenth century. Rather, American religion changed its institutional form. Its structure became much more elaborated, its inner spirit and content very elusive and difficult to define. Even a modern man such as Isaac Bliss would eventually find certain aspects of this transformation troubling.[38]

37. Minutes of Meetings of the Committee on Agencies, June 30, December 4, 1884; Joint Committee to Chester A. Arthur, November 1884, Corresponding Secretary's Papers, ABS Archives.

38. For an interesting analysis of the way Gilded Age corporate culture borrowed its organizational structures from antebellum evangelicals, see Gregory Singleton, "Protestant Voluntary Organizations and the Shaping of Victorian America," in Daniel Walker Howe, ed., *Victorian America* (Philadelphia: University of Pennsylvania Press, 1976).

E P I L O G U E

From "Missionary Basis" to "Business Basis"? Isaac Bliss's Strange Lament

Isaac Bliss's long career with the American Bible Society ended in controversy. In 1883, Bliss suffered a series of personal reverses. The expenses involved in raising and educating several children, as well as the high cost of living in Constantinople, had strained his financial resources for years. Now, declining health forced the sixty-two-year-old agent to borrow large sums against Bible Society funds and incur significant debts with Armenian merchants in Constantinople. Bliss's son and assistant agent, Edwin, also accumulated large medical bills during the early 1880s in an attempt to restore his ailing wife to good health. Isaac Bliss clearly needed help in this time of trouble, and he turned to his benevolent employer for assistance. The response surprised him. Money was the immediate issue, but the Bible agent's final conflict with the home office provides important insight into some unresolved issues at a time when both the American Bible Society and American society generally struggled to reconcile the reality of Gilded Age capitalism with the rhetoric of Christian benevolence.

Bliss asked the Society's committee on agencies to consider his case, cancel his debt with the Society, grant him additional money to satisfy Armenian creditors, provide his son with a paid leave of absence to return to America and resolve his wife's health problems, and pay for his own mounting medical expenses. A special three-member board subcommittee, consisting of businessman and manager William E. Dodge, career Bible Society administrator Edward Gilman, and Assistant Treasurer Andrew L. Taylor, reviewed the request and essentially agreed to Bliss's terms at a meeting on December 3, 1883. The managers moved beyond the immediate issue, however, and used this opportunity to consider the broader question of foreign agents' financial dealings, as well as the need to monitor overseas expenditures more closely. As a result, Corresponding Secretary Gilman informed Bliss, "some new measures" had been promulgated, based on "what is understood to be the established methods of our best business houses." Gilman forwarded these "printed regulations" and instructed the Society's Levant representative to bring the agency into compliance with them immediately.[1]

The "new measures" contained three stipulations. First, the board sought to regularize financial arrangements and salary disbursements by directing the assistant treasurer to remit compensation "monthly, or quarterly, in advance" as the agent preferred. Through this measure, the ABS sought to eliminate the widespread practice of granting large salary advances and "contingency" expenses to overseas agents. Second, the managers instructed agents "to keep the funds of the Society entirely distinct from their own, to avoid all intermingling of personal and business accounts, and to decline invariably to receive deposits of funds in trust for outside parties." Gilman informed Bliss that "defalcations and disasters" resulted when agents violated this rule and warned him, in the future, to "distinguish between the individual and the agent of the American Bible Society" in his dealings with Armenian businessmen. Finally, the managers provided for a semiannual outside audit of each agent's accounts. A committee of two or three individuals would now examine all receipts and expenditures, "comparing them with the vouchers and other evidences of correctness," and certify the results in writing.[2]

1. Minutes of Meeting of the Committee on Agencies, December 3, 1883, ABS Archives; Edward Gilman to Isaac Bliss, December 6, 7, 1883; Gilman to William E. Dodge, December 7, 1883, Letter Book, Corresponding Secretary's Papers, ABS Archives.

2. Minutes of Meeting of the Committee on Agencies, December 3, 1883, ABS Archives; Edward Gilman to Isaac Bliss, December 7, 1883, Letter Book, Corresponding Secretary's Papers, ABS Archives.

Isaac Bliss and his son correctly interpreted these regulations as personal rebukes and evidence of the managers' dissatisfaction with their financial conduct. Each felt he had faithfully and honestly served the Society. Isaac Bliss especially had brought business principles, regularity, and order to an agency previously conducted under a much more informal, haphazard managerial style. Yet his efforts no longer seemed sufficient. The managers wanted something different. Somehow, in ways Bliss professed not to understand, the rules had changed. Shortly after learning of the "new measures," Bliss and his son both penned angry responses to the Bible House. Isaac Bliss expressed his displeasure from Constantinople to both Gilman and Dodge; Edwin composed a twelve-page position paper while nursing his wife at a Christian seaside resort hotel in Asbury Park. Each believed that the critical problem seemed straightforward and clear: the American Bible Society had abandoned its traditional benevolent standards and had begun applying false business principles to its agents and employees.[3]

"Twenty six years ago when I was invited to become the Society's Agent for the Levant," Isaac Bliss ruminated, "all my relations to the society & the work to be done partook of a missionary character." Compensation proceeded according to a "missionary basis." The American Bible Society agreed to provide a "fair support," but the managers recognized that certain contingencies would require additional disbursements. The stated salary, according to Bliss, was never intended to provide "for expenses incident to prolonged sickness, or a vacation demanding rest or change of scene, the education of children, an impaired constitution, or the inabilities of old age." When hard times came, agents expected the Society to evidence "all the consideration & kindness which the benevolent or missionary principle required." Bliss acknowledged, however, that in the quarter-century since he began work at Constantinople, "great changes have taken place."[4]

By 1884, "new men" and "new measures" produced a new definition of Bible labor. Bliss claimed that he had seen the Society's missionary commitments decline, whereas the managers based

3. Isaac Bliss to William E. Dodge, February 5, 1884; Bliss to Edward Gilman, February 5, July 31, 1884, Corresponding Secretary's Papers, ABS Archives.
4. Isaac Bliss to Edward Gilman, February 5, 1884; Bliss to William E. Dodge, February 5, 1884, Corresponding Secretary's Papers, ABS Archives.

their decisions "more on the business idea." This shift in emphasis, he contended, was a serious mistake. American business "has little or no benevolence in it but demands absolute rigidity of principle & of course cannot be conformed to the missionary idea." Bliss somewhat lamely concluded his letter by requesting a substantial salary increase. If all other Bible Society operations proceeded according to strict business principles, he claimed, the agent's recompense should approximate the amount received by a comparable administrator in a strictly financial concern. The managers took no action concerning this complaint. Gilman's response (if any) was unrecorded, and Bliss lived out his last five years at the same salary.[5]

An obvious irony pervades this seemingly trivial salary controversy. Bliss, of course, brought a shrewd business sense and keen administrative skills to his conduct of the Levant agency. His commitment to careerism, technological improvements, novel fundraising techniques, bureaucratic business principles, and grandiose building programs placed him squarely within the tradition of successful secular Gilded Age administrators. Like many late nineteenth-century middle-class Americans, Bliss never questioned these values and techniques when they adequately advanced his own interests. The Levant agent proudly and aggressively played a critical role in bringing new managerial principles to Bible labor and helped the managers effect a great transformation in their manner of doing business. Bliss's administrative acumen and commitment to modern bureaucratic notions helped produce the very transformation that eventually threatened his personal security.

During "hard times," however, even businesslike middle-class Victorians expected large corporate organizations to behave in a different fashion. The sound, practical business principles which Bliss embraced offered little comfort and provided no protection against sickness, old age, mental weariness, depression, and personal misfortune. Late nineteenth-century Americans could no longer rely solely on their families, intimate social relations, and

5. Isaac Bliss to Edward Gilman, February 5, 1884, Bliss to William E. Dodge, February 5, 1884, Corresponding Secretary's Papers, ABS Archives. Edwin Bliss terminated his connection with the ABS upon Isaac's death. He returned to the United States to edit the *Encyclopedia of Missions* between 1889 and 1891, subsequently served as associate editor of the *Independent* for several years, published numerous books on the Near East, and became a field agent for the American Tract Society between 1901 and 1904.

local communities for protection against broad socioeconomic forces, an international economy they barely understood, and the random tragedies that might destroy a lifetime of prudence and thrift in one horrifying instant. Increasingly, Americans linked their fortunes and their futures to large for-profit and nonprofit corporations. They expected national, highly capitalized institutional bureaucracies to provide the social foundation for general prosperity and to operate according to ruthlessly impersonal economic precepts. Yet these same Americans also expected such structures to provide intimacy, warmth, caring, and protection against the harsher aspects of these same supposedly immutable laws. Within a generation of Bliss's complaints, private corporations would invent personnel departments and fringe benefits to protect and enrich loyal and responsible employees. As Americans would discover in 1929, however, corporate community and corporate benevolence contained important limitations.

Isaac Bliss misread American Bible Society history when he described its transformation as a simple progression from "missionary basis" to "business basis." Both the missionary impulse and the business impulse had been central to the Society since its founding. The meanings of those terms and the social context within which they operated, however, had changed dramatically. In 1816, ministers and merchants played out their lives within a well-defined local context. Pastors derived their social authority from demonstrations of character based on personal acquaintance with congregations. Business was governed by familial networks and social contacts, and general merchants played important public roles in their communities. The United States was a society of particularistic local cultures, largely governed by local elites who relied on traditional notions of hierarchy, deference, and noblesse oblige.

The Federalists who established the ABS accepted these traditional notions, but they believed that the nation needed reforming. Disturbed by the spirit of "party" and "faction" that permeated early national democracy, they turned to the Bible for the underlying values that would hold American civilization together and solidify the virtuous republic. The founders hoped to build a national culture, based on the Book, and thereby check the pressures of diversity, uncontrolled mobility, and special interests that threatened their own cultural, political, and economic authority. Inculcated with sound evangelical virtues and marching to a common Christian theme, nineteenth-century Americans might yet create their "city on a hill."

Ironically, the very institutions these men created ultimately helped undermine this vision. National philanthropies, headquartered in urban centers, eventually helped remove important moral, religious, and educational matters from the local milieu. They relied on salaried, career-oriented administrators and agents, not constrained by the boundaries of local communities or responsible to local congregations, to execute their policies. Successful philanthropies were sensitive to the revolutions in transportation and communication, the new methods of mass production and mass distribution, and the structural innovations that produced a new managerial capitalism by the end of the nineteenth century. Philanthropic governing boards contained the nation's most successful Christian businessmen, but by the middle of the nineteenth century these businessmen appeared less interested in preserving local civic cultures than in perfecting the smooth operations of their own increasingly national corporate concerns. Americans reconfigured their notions of community, public culture, benevolence, and capitalism over the course of the nineteenth century, and in the process they reformed the American Bible Society.

Victorian Protestants continued to believe in the unity of the missionary impulse and the business impulse, but something important had changed. As the religious historian Robert T. Handy has observed, "much of the real focus had shifted to the civilization itself, with Christianity and the churches finding their significance in relation to it."[6] Business had become the American mission. By the late nineteenth century, the ABS had forfeited its role as social critic, abdicated its responsibilities as part of an international Christianizing force, and subordinated its missionary impulse in the interest of managing a successful business concern. Its managers shrewdly effected the institutional adjustments they believed necessary for survival in a corporate capitalist environment. Many members of the "new middle classes" proved receptive to the new religion. They attended church, filled the collection plates, intensified their efforts to export the nation's business and culture to foreign lands, and remained secure in their belief that God still favored America and that the social order would not be challenged.

6. Robert T. Handy, *A Christian America: Protestant Hopes and Historical Realities* (New York: Oxford University Press, 1971), p. 110, and subsequent discussion.

I N D E X